Standing on the Shoulders

Also by Dan Walker and available from Headline

Remarkable People: Extraordinary Stories of Everyday Lives

DAN WALKER

Standing on the Shoulders

Incredible heroes and how they inspire us

HEADLINE

First published in 2022
by HEADLINE PUBLISHING GROUP

1

Cataloguing in Publication Data is available from the British Library

Hardback ISBN: 978 1 4722 9127 1

Typeset by CC Book Production

Printed and bound in Great Britain by Clays Ltd, Elcograf S.p.A.

HEADLINE PUBLISHING GROUP
An Hachette UK Company
Carmelite House
50 Victoria Embankment
London EC4Y 0DZ

www.headline.co.uk
www.hachette.co.uk

CONTENTS

FOREWORD
By Rose Ayling-Ellis

I first met Dan back in 2021 when *Strictly Come Dancing* started and we gathered to do our very first dance, the group dance. We were put in a room full of celebrities, and we were all extremely nervy. I was the most nervous I had ever been. I didn't see myself as a 'celebrity' as I had only been on *EastEnders* for a year and no one knew me, and yet here I was surrounded by these famous personalities. I couldn't believe I was in the same room as all of them!

Dan was one of the people that I recognised from his years of regular appearances on my morning TV screen. He was chatting away to someone else and, after a bit of hesitation, I finally picked up the courage to approach him and introduce myself. I immediately felt the warmness and kindness radiate from him. Our very first conversation stood out and made a huge impression on me. We talked about me being deaf, appearing on the biggest show ever and how terrified we both were; we even joked about our terrible dance moves! He told me about his dad being deaf, some of the frustration he had experienced and about what he learned from his dad. As I got to know Dan better, I came to realise that was one of his standout qualities: it was always about other people's experiences, never about him.

This is what the book is all about. It's never about Dan, it's about the people Dan meets in his life. It's an important lesson for all of us. It is what we can learn from other people's experiences that shapes us into who we are and how we could do better for others. It is what makes us all so beautiful: the imperfect, ugly, unimaginable experience that life throws at us, and finding a way to come out on the brighter side. However, one important thing that I noticed throughout the book is that all these people never did it alone. They always had someone reaching out or wanting to reach out. No one can do it alone. In the chapter that Dan wrote about me, it was my mother who stayed by my side, she was that person to me, and I am honoured that she is a part of this book.

In these crazy times, especially with what's going on around the world, we all need that someone by our side. Whether it is our friends, family, a stranger or even our pets. The act of kindness, no matter how small, can change everything for others. Sometimes we forget that. But most importantly, sometimes we forget to reach out for help when we need to. I love the fact that Dan has called this *Standing on the Shoulders*. It is all about what is important in life: that we are who we are because of the people around us. The title perfectly encapsulates the book and I have really enjoyed reading about the people in it. I hope you do too.

INTRODUCTION

It's never a good idea to make assumptions, so I am just going to remind you that the book you are about to read is a sort of follow-up to one that I wrote a few years ago called *Remarkable People*.

It was lovely that so many people read and enjoyed the last one but, if you know nothing about it, fear not . . . you don't have to have read a single page of that to enjoy this one. The themes are the same but you don't need to have any previous knowledge of the characters involved and you can always read it later. I suppose the one benefit of reading *Remarkable People* before *Standing on the Shoulders* is that you probably have an expectation of what you are going to get.

In music, they talk about a 'tricky second album'; in football it's 'second season syndrome'. After the success of *Remarkable People*, I was really keen to write about a fresh bunch of humble heroes and follow the same simple pattern as before. Here are some amazing people I have had the privilege of meeting: let's see what makes them tick and try and learn something along the way.

The last book came out in the middle of a global pandemic and things have changed a lot in the world since then. The cost-of-living crisis is biting hard at millions of people across the UK, and the conflict in Ukraine dominated the international headlines in the first half of 2022. In my own little world, I finally gave in and agreed to go on *Strictly Come Dancing* and, to my great surprise, it will go down as one of my best ever experiences on TV – as you will find out when you get to the chapter about my 'professional partner'.

Over the last few years, particularly since I started presenting *BBC Breakfast* and definitely since I went on *Strictly*, I have noticed that people are taking more of an interest in my opinion on certain issues. I did a lot of interviews about my recent move from the breakfast sofa to Channel 5 and I had to spend quite a bit of my time gently dodging questions about my thoughts on big topics of the day. Of course I have opinions, but my broadcasting has never been centred or dependent on them. I love to bring the best out of those around me.

When I interview a politician, I don't want you to watch that interview and think 'Well, I now know what Dan thinks about that'. I want you to be able to listen to them and make your mind up about whether they are someone you can trust, believe in and vote for. I firmly believe you can still do that and ask the tough, pertinent and thoughtful questions.

As a journalist, I am far more interested in what other people feel than what I think. I love talking to others and finding out what motivates them, what drives them on, what inspires them, how they respond to the highs and lows of life and how those varying emotions translate into action.

In a world where you are often told what to think or, perhaps more truthfully, what you are not allowed to think, I am not laying out an ideology in this book. I really hope that it never comes across as preachy or unnecessarily argumentative. The whole plan here is to simply show you some people who have incredible stories to tell.

You will hopefully find a huge range of voices. I conducted hours of interviews with the people in here and, in some cases, have spent large portions of my life with them. Some you will have heard of, some you will know quite well and others will be new to you. Some I met first on the *BBC Breakfast* sofa and others have wandered into my life in different ways, but one thing unites them all . . . they are all eye-openers. What I mean by that is they all allow us to see a little further than we would on our own.

Our middle daughter is disappointed by the book title. After *Remarkable People*, she told me this book should have been called *Remark at the Remarkable People* and she thought I had missed a trick. Jessica was not particularly impressed when I told her the title of this one. *Standing on the Shoulders* is half a quote from a letter written by Isaac Newton in 1675. The great physician and mathematician wrote that 'If I have seen further it is by standing on the shoulders of giants' and that's what I feel I have been able to do by speaking to the people in this book.

You will find doctors in here, three normal dads, a communications officer, a Hollywood superstar, a convicted murderer, a bomb survivor, a knight of the realm, bereaved parents, heroic friends, migrants, a couple of musical geniuses, a two-time world champion, a double amputee, a *Strictly* winner and many many more.

There is tragedy and triumph, there are heroes and villains and themes like forgiveness, rehabilitation, loss, love, grief, pain, trust, truth, faith and friendship regularly rise to the surface. We often talk about post-traumatic stress but, as one of our contributors comments, there is such a thing as post-traumatic growth and you'll hopefully see much of that too.

It is lovely that so many people have been waiting patiently for the publication of this book and I look forward to conversations about it on social media, in the street, on train platforms, in the frozen-food aisle of the supermarket, or maybe even at a book-signing somewhere. I couldn't do any of them last time because of Covid. I still receive so many beautiful messages about *Remarkable People* and I really hope this book has a similar impact. When I first mentioned that I was writing again, I received the most beautiful message from someone who wishes to remain anonymous but was happy for me to put it in the introduction.

> *Dear Dan*
> *The fact that you are writing a new book is the best news I've heard in a while. I read your last one in the middle of the global pandemic and, I have to say, the people in there got me through. They taught me so much from their experiences and, through the tears and the laughter of each chapter, I continue to learn. It was exactly the book I needed at exactly the right time. I was inspired and encouraged in equal measure and I hope the next one does the same.*

INTRODUCTION

My ultimate aim for this book is that you are inspired and encouraged by the people in these pages, as I have been. I hope through their testimony, they are able to challenge your preconceptions and your way of thinking as they did mine. Researching and writing *Standing on the Shoulders* has enabled me to understand a lot more about the world around me, and I trust it does the same for you.

'EVERY DAY I CLIMB A MOUNTAIN'

Monday 22 May 2017 was a dad-and-daughter date night for Martin and Eve Hibbert. Growing up in Bolton, music had always been a huge part of Martin's life. His mum loved The Beatles, The Carpenters and Motown, which was always on in the house somewhere. Martin was desperate to make sure his own children shared that same love of music, so he used to love taking Eve to concerts.

Martin was a dutiful dad. 'Eve was always going on about Ariana Grande, so I got all her CDs and started listening to them in the car to get into her music too. I've always been able to pick up the words pretty quickly. For Christmas that year (2016) I got Eve tickets for us to go and see her in concert in Manchester the following May. She was so excited when she opened the present. I was wearing this T-shirt which said 'Ariana Grande Is My Wife' which I think she saw the funny side of. The whole first part of 2017 was basically a build-up to that night at the MEN Arena.'

Finally, the day came. It was a Monday night and Eve had her mock exams starting in just a few weeks so Martin had promised Eve's mum that he wouldn't let her stay up too late. They had their tickets for the show and, even before they arrived at the arena, the plan was to leave during the encore to make sure they avoided the legendary arena traffic jams.

'It's impossible to get away if you all leave at the same time as everyone else', says Martin with a smile on his face that tells you he's been stuck in that traffic before. 'It can take ninety minutes to get out and I didn't want to be sat in a queue for ages fielding calls from her mum telling me she needed to be in bed.'

The night had gone perfectly. They had been to one of their favourite Manchester restaurants – San Carlo – and arrived at the venue in good time.

'The one thing that really sticks in my mind', remembers Martin, 'was the scream when Ariana Grande came out on stage. I've been to the biggest nights at Old Trafford, but it was nothing compared to the noise at the MEN that night. She put on an amazing show and Eve was so happy. Our cut-off was 10.30 and when the time came, I told Eve we had to go, but she was desperate to stay. I knew that would be the case, but I dragged her away and we started the walk back to our car.'

Martin and Eve walked down from their seats to the ground floor level and then, like many of the other early leavers, made their way out into the vestibule of the arena. Eve was just in front of Martin as they were heading towards the main doors. They walked past the terrorist but never saw him.

'I had my head down and I was running, or at least the fastest walk that I could do', remembers Martin. 'There were loads of people there either trying to get out or waiting to pick up children who were coming out of the concert.' Martin pauses as he thinks over the night in his head. 'It's hard to say for certain, but I reckon there must have been a couple of hundred people around us.'

When the bomb was detonated, it's estimated that Martin and Eve were somewhere between five and seven metres from the terrorist. Everyone around them died instantly. Pieces of shrapnel were travelling at speeds of around 100 mph. Some people died forty metres away from the centre of the explosion having been hit by a single piece of metal. Martin's body was covered in it and his daughter had been hit in the head.

'I remember it as an almighty bang,' says Martin, clearly taking his time to recall the events clearly. 'There was a really high-pitched noise. I've never been hit by a ten-tonne truck but I imagine that is what it felt like. This might sound a bit stupid, but I wasn't worried or scared at the time. I remember feeling very tranquil and surreal. I was just concerned about Eve.'

What Martin didn't know was that one of the bolts from the blast had completely severed his spinal cord. Eve had been knocked unconscious instantly by the blow to her head.

'I don't know how long it was after the explosion but the first thing I saw was an arm on the floor and I thought it was mine. I checked and thankfully I still had both of them. There was this strange, eerie silence for a couple seconds before people started screaming in pain.'

The situation was incredibly serious for many of the people in the arena that night and Martin was one of them. One of the bolts had struck him in the neck and severed two of his main arteries. The blood was pouring out of his body. A security guard called Chris was one of the first to come and see if he was ok.

'I could feel my body was shutting down,' recalls Martin. 'I knew it wasn't good and at that moment it was hard to have any hope of leaving the arena alive. I looked up at Chris and asked him to tell my wife that I loved her, but I wasn't giving up. I knew that if I closed my eyes that would be it. I could feel the strength going out of me, but I also knew that I was the only one who could make a difference for Eve. I had to try and stay awake, stay active for her sake. She needed just as much help as me.'

The 'help' that Martin and many others needed that night wasn't fast in coming. The subsequent inquiry into the emergency response highlighted a number of failings in communication and leadership which led to Martin, and many other people, being left untreated for far too long. Martin was determined that he was going to stay awake until the paramedics arrived.

'I remember that, in all the chaos and the screaming, I had a little laugh to myself. I had so many plans about what I wanted to do with my life and yet, here I was, about to die on a freezing cold concrete floor. The only thing driving me on was the knowledge that Eve needed me. Chris, the security guard, kept asking me my name and my address and I just kept saying it back to him over and over again. All the time my body was closing down, but I managed to fight it for an hour.'

Eve was lying unconscious next to her dad. The fourteen-year-old was going blue. She desperately needed help and Martin was doing everything he could.

'At one point they put a cover over her face to say that she had died. I begged them to take it off because I could still see her lips quivering. I could see she was still there. I could see she was gasping for air. That drove me on and gave me the strength I needed to stay awake. I knew that if I went under, they'd cover Eve's face again and we'd both be goners. I just had to keep going until the help arrived.'

Paul Harvey was on shift that night. He and his colleague were waiting in an ambulance outside Manchester Royal Infirmary. 'The first thing we heard was that there was a potential fire at the arena,' remembers Paul. His account tallies with the official inquiry which showed how information was both confused and inaccurate. 'Initially we got told to stand by, and then we were told to head to the arena as quickly as possible. We were the second or third vehicle to arrive, but one of the things we were told was that there might be an active gunman still inside, so all the emergency help was held back from the venue.'

When Paul and his colleague were eventually given the all-clear to enter the site, their job was initially to assess the walking wounded. That thirty-minute job continues to have a profound impact on Paul. 'I'd been doing the job for twenty years, but that was the first major incident I'd been involved in. We all take part in training exercises, but nothing prepares you for the real thing. I went into autopilot. We were dealing with a constant stream of people,' says Paul. 'I remember there were a couple who couldn't find their daughter and a young girl with burst eardrums. She couldn't hear a thing. People were just wandering around with empty heads. They were all in a daze and, it might sound silly, but that affected me so much.'

When I spoke to Paul, his wife Louise was sat next to him at the kitchen table. You could instantly tell the bond between the two of them when they started speaking. Paul has been through a lot and his wife has been there every step of the way.

'I could tell it was serious when our daughter called me to tell me I had to come home straightaway,' says Louise. 'She said that Paul was at the bottom of the garden crying.'

This was the night after the bomb at the arena. Paul was trying to get through a shift like normal, but it just wasn't happening. The shock and trauma of the previous evening was beginning to kick in. Louise remembers it well.

'He was silently struggling. He was there but he wasn't there, if you know what I mean? I could tell he wasn't sleeping. He was wide awake, and he was absolutely shattered at the same time. For weeks it was hard to see a way out of things. Every time the bomb was on the news, every time there was an Ariana Grande song on the radio, he was in pieces. It's still hard for him to listen to "One Last Time" even now. That was the last song she played at the concert that night. It was hard for me to see him crying, but I was so proud of him for being able to accept that he needed help.'

Counselling has really helped Paul to deal with what he saw that night. He has also taken great strength from his friendship with Martin. The first time they met, Paul was lifting him into the back of his ambulance on a 'stretcher' made from a security hoarding.

'We had been dealing with the walking wounded for about half an hour,' says Paul, 'when we were asked to move a patient.' That patient was Martin Hibbert.

Martin had stayed awake long enough to be seen by the trained medical staff. Eve was still unconscious, but alive, and had been taken to Manchester Children's Hospital.

'The last thing I remember from the night,' says a tearful Martin, 'was Eve being taken away on a security hoarding. I was thankful that she was being looked after and I just felt that at least I had done my job as a dad. I don't mean for this to sound morbid because I still wanted to live, but I thought, I can close my eyes now . . . I can die now. I had seen the way that people were looking at me and I had accepted that death was the most likely outcome.'

While Eve was on her way to the specialist children's hospital, Paul was told to take Martin to Wythenshawe Hospital, a thirty-minute drive from the arena. Paul quickly assessed his new patient and decided that there was no way he would survive that journey. He defied the order and went instead to the major trauma unit at the Salford Royal. That decision saved Martin's life.

Paul has clear memories of that journey and recalls it with classic medical understatement. 'You could tell Martin was poorly. He was going in and out of consciousness and I was constantly trying to rouse him. The neck injury was obvious, and we knew he was bad internally because he kept bringing up blood and his observations were all over the place. I talked to him about his family and his work. He told me about his daughter, but I think he thought that trip in the back of my ambulance was going to be the final journey of his life. Over the years I have seen lots of people deteriorate on me, but I was determined we weren't going to lose him. I assured him that he was going to be ok and, in my head, I said, "You're not going anywhere, mate. I am going to get you to the hospital alive.'"

The first time I met Martin was on the *BBC Breakfast* sofa – four years after the blast. Martin had come in to talk about his work with the Spinal Injuries Association and his desire to raise money for others in the same situation by attempting to climb Mount Kilimanjaro.

You get to meet all sorts on that sofa, and I'm fascinated by how people respond to trials in their lives. You get to see the full spectrum of human reaction. Some people struggle to talk about it, some break down as soon as they sit down, some worry about whether they are doing the right thing, and there are also some who carry that sense of responsibility to others. Martin was one of those.

'Hello, Dan! Hi, Louise!' he shouted as he wheeled himself across the studio floor and up the ramp to the raised area before shuffling across to the far side of the sofa. There was something about him from minute one. There was a huge smile across his face but also a sense of pride and just the right amount of nervousness about being on live television. As per usual, we had read all about Martin's story before he arrived on *BBC Breakfast*, but it was only when he started talking that what he had been through really hit home.

Martin had a real gift. He was able to explain what the night was like without being too graphic, explain how he felt without a trace of self-pity and describe his hopes for the future without allowing one iota of doubt to enter into the conversation. He told us all about his desire to raise funds and awareness for those with spinal injuries. He spoke passionately about disabled rights and also declared his plan to raise £1 million by becoming the first person in history with a complete spinal cord injury to climb Mount Kilimanjaro.

His enthusiasm for helping others and lust for life was infectious. As he left the sofa after the interview, I thanked him for being so honest and for lifting the spirits of everyone watching. 'When you've been as close to death as I have, Dan, every single day is a blessing,' he said as he wheeled himself back towards the green room. I knew, from that moment, that I wanted to include Martin in this book. I knew it had been a real privilege to meet him.

One of the people climbing Kilimanjaro with Martin is Stuart Wildman, a consultant nurse at Salford Royal. On the night of the blast, Stuart wasn't on shift. He was in bed but, like many people, he got a call at 4 a.m. to come in.

'You just get told there is a "major incident" and that you are needed in the hospital. I've been working for twenty-two years, seventeen of those as a nurse, and like an awful lot of people that night I had never been called to a major incident. I remember that everyone was focused.'

On the night Martin was admitted, no one thought he was going to survive. The neurosurgeon, Mr Saxena, had just finished a twelve-hour shift when he heard about the bomb and returned to Salford Royal. He operated on Martin for fourteen hours.

Martin has very little memory of the next few weeks of his life. He kept asking questions about how he was and how Eve was but was struggling to get to the truth about how serious things were.

'I knew why they were doing it,' he says. 'My wife Gabby was telling me what the doctors told her to tell me about my legs because no one wants to talk about stuff like that. The medical team had advised her not to mention my injuries in those early days. My first clear memory is of my wife and my mum standing next to a bunch of doctors in white coats. Eventually, we got to the brutal truth: they told me I had a complete spinal injury and that I would never walk again.'

The first thing that went through Martin's head was that he wouldn't be able to walk the family dog – Alfie – ever again. 'I know it sounds daft,' says Martin with a little smile, 'but Alfie was suffering from separation anxiety. He had stopped eating for weeks because I wasn't around. Then I thought I would never be able to kick a football again. I think the doctors expected me to erupt; for the air to be filled with expletives and for me to start throwing things around. But, for some reason, I stayed calm.'

'How did you manage to stay so controlled in those circumstances?' I asked.

'I thought about where I had been, Dan,' says Martin. You can almost see the determination in his face as he engages. 'I genuinely thought I was dead, and the game was over. I was lying on the floor, choking on my own blood, thinking "this is it." I had the overwhelming joy of knowing that I was alive. I knew that Eve was in a bad way, but I also knew she was alive. I was so thankful that I still had a life to live.'

Martin spent just over two weeks in intensive care before being moved to the major trauma ward. That's where he came under the care of Stuart Wildman. 'I knew about Martin before I met him. We were all amazed he had survived and, you can imagine, there was huge media interest in all the survivors, so Martin was put in a side room off the main ward for his own protection. I remember him being so incredibly calm. He was processing a lot of information and was quiet. In those early days he wasn't bright or joyful. I often think that, at times like that, it's best to talk about things that aren't clinical. It's so important to do something normal, something that feels like an everyday thing that you'd do if you were at home. I offered to give him a shave.'

I asked Martin if he can remember that offer from Stuart. 'It was amazing,' says Martin, rubbing his chin, as if he can remember the straggly beard that had grown during his weeks in intensive care. 'It was just a simple thing but it meant so much at the time to me. It's strange how something so normal can turn into something so emotional, and how one tiny act of kindness can make such a difference.'

Stuart's overwhelming memory of that time spent with Martin was his desire to see his daughter, Eve. In the same way that keeping her alive on the night of the blast had kept him alive, now it was the thought of seeing her again that was driving his recovery.

'He was so early on in coming to terms with what had

happened to him. He had gone from being busy, active and able bodied to paralysed in a heartbeat. He had hardly any upper body strength and it takes time for your core to adjust to be able to hold yourself up. You can't rush these things but I knew how much Martin wanted to see his daughter and I knew it would be important for his recovery. It was a logistical nightmare. We didn't really know how his body would cope with being sat down for a long time after being on his back for weeks, and there were also all sorts of blood pressure issues and pain medication concerns which had to be really carefully managed. But, despite all that, we managed to make it happen and I know how much that meant to Martin. It was a real privilege to be there with him on the day.'

Seeing Eve had become everything to Martin because he was well aware how close he had come to losing her. He gathers himself before telling me about the day he saw her again for the first time since the bomb went off. It was 11 July 2017, his birthday.

'The coroner had been ringing the ward she was on every day at the start because they were convinced she was going to be victim number twenty-three,' explains Martin. 'In total, Eve was in intensive care for nearly four months but I simply had to see her. I knew she was alive and I just wanted to be with her.'

Just before Martin went into the room where Eve was being looked after, the senior doctor took him to one side and let him know what he was about to see. It was all about managing expectation and it was a body-blow to an already battered dad.

'He was as kind as it's possible to be for someone in that situation. He explained to me that, what I was about to see, wasn't really Eve. She'd been hit by a bolt in the temple and it had passed into her brain and taken out the vast majority of her frontal lobe. I remember watching his lips as he told me that he didn't know if she would ever wake up and, even if she did, whether she would ever regain any memory or have the ability to communicate. He told me there was a good chance she would remain in a permanently vegetative state.'

Understandably, Martin stops as he remembers how hard those words hit him at the time. 'Are you ok to carry on?' I ask tentatively. 'It helps to talk about it,' says Martin. 'Every time it gets easier.'

'How do you respond when someone tells you that about your daughter?' I ask.

'I completely broke down at that moment,' he says with tears in his eyes. 'I was opposite this doctor and I just couldn't stop crying. I thought to myself that if she's not here then I don't want to be here either. I was glad that he told me. I needed to know the truth. I needed to know how bad things were. Eve was, and is, the whole reason that I do everything in life. She was the biggest and best part of my life. The heart-breaking thing for me, being stood outside that door, was that I had always promised her that I would keep her safe and I felt like I had failed. I still give myself a hard time about it. I used to tell her a lot that, as long as she was with me, nothing would ever happen to her. She used to smile when I told her that I would protect her from anything bad and yet, there she was, unable to breathe on her own after a night out with me. My superhero cape had been ripped off and we were both fighting to rebuild our lives.'

Martin is incredibly strong. He rarely talks about Eve because it hurts too much and yet it's clear that she is a big driving force behind his relentless positivity and desire to make a difference to others. When the dark clouds gather over him, he slots back to what he calls 'The Hibbert Mindset'. 'Crack on' is one of his favourite go-to sayings.

Martin's dad was a police officer in Bolton and his mum was a pharmacy dispenser. Growing up he spent a lot of time with his grandad who had a big influence on his outlook. He always used to tell Martin that life was littered with lumps in the road but the secret was just to keep on running.

'My mum would always say that she was waiting for her ship to come in – something that would change everything – and that used to really annoy my grandad. He would always challenge her on it and, when I was six years old, he told me something that I still think about now. He took me to one side and said, "Martin, never wait for your ship to come in. Row out there and meet it." I have always had that thought in my mind. When everything is going wrong, when the world is falling down around you, I look for the opportunity. I think it's a Bolton thing, a northern thing. I refuse to let things drag me down.'

Martin has always been a grafter. He had a paper round from the age of eleven and got up at 6 a.m. every morning until he was eighteen. He would clean dishes in the evenings to make extra money.

That day he went to see Eve for the first time, his birthday, he knew that coming out the other side would require the most 'graft' he had put into anything his entire life.

'She comes into my head quite a lot,' says Martin. 'The picture of her lying in her bed that day. She was covered in pipes, pipes that were keeping her alive. I say "keeping her alive", but she didn't look "alive" at all. She was still and lifeless. There was nothing there. I asked if I could hug her, which you can imagine was quite difficult with a bloke paralysed from the waist down and a girl in a vegetative state. It took four staff to help to get us in position but, even though it was awkward, it was beautiful. I can't explain to you why or how, but I knew in my heart that she would survive. That hug was so special.'

Weeks became months, but slowly Eve was making progress. The big turning point came the second time they tried to take her off the ventilator . . . she could breathe on her own for the first time! Martin constantly has to remind himself of what the consultant told him, that his daughter may never be able to walk, talk or eat on her own again.

'She just keeps getting better and better,' says her dad with a giant smile across his face. 'I've got a video that I look at sometimes of Eve putting triangles through holes. I never thought she would have the mental capacity to do that. She was mute for two years because of all the trauma and then, I was in Australia, getting some treatment and I remember we were on FaceTime and she just started talking to me and eating on her own. It was incredible. She said, "Hello Daddy" Her speech was broken and you could tell the PTSD was hitting her hard but it was her . . . it was Eve. The medics threw out the book when it came to her a long time ago. She keeps on proving them wrong. She keeps on breaking boundaries. She's amazing.'

Stuart Wildman, the consultant nurse, had witnessed Martin's meeting with Eve on his birthday. Like everyone who works on a major trauma ward, Stuart has seen his fair share of grief and heartache. There are some things that stick with you, some people you never forget. Martin is one of those patients.

'I see a lot of sad things in my job, but that day, Martin's birthday, when he saw Eve for the first time, I went home and cried that day. It was all just so real. I have a daughter who is two years younger than Eve. I just kept thinking about her and what I would be like in that situation. I've been to the MEN with my daughter. My friends have been there. This is my city. For any of us Manchester dads, we all know that that could have been us. We could have been there like Martin, struggling to hug his daughter. I remember his determination to give her a kiss. There was no way he wasn't going to do it. It was almost physically impossible, but you could tell from his face that he wouldn't be taking no for an answer. That was the first time I saw the determination. That was the first insight into what drives him on. If there is even a 1 per cent chance of something happening, Martin is one of those people who will do absolutely everything in his power to make it work, to bring it to life.'

After seeing Eve, Stuart took Martin to St Ann's Square in the centre of the city so that Martin could light a candle for the victims of the Manchester bomb. From that day forward, Stuart saw a new motivation in his patient.

'He had down days but he never turned down a therapy or a care session. You get some people in Martin's situation who just can't see a way out. They get lost in the grief or the pain and they just start to waste away. You can see the depression ruling them and it just keeps getting darker and darker. Some people don't want to get out of bed. They don't want therapy, they don't want help, they can't see a way out. Martin was the complete opposite. He couldn't wait to get out of hospital. He quickly became one of the reasons I love my job. I have always thought it is a real honour to give someone personal care, for them to allow you into their personal space. That is a rare privilege and, once you're in there, you form a special relationship. Sometimes dressing his wounds would take up to two hours. You get to talk, you share stories, you see what makes someone tick. I was helping him, but caring for Martin gave me so much reward and reaffirmed why this is the job I was born to do.'

When Martin finally left Stuart's care, Stuart didn't think the friendship would continue, they rarely do. But, every time Martin returned to the hospital to visit the Spinal Injuries Unit, he would go back to Stuart's ward and make sure everyone was ok.

'He would always ask us all how we were,' remembers Stuart fondly. 'Despite what he'd been through, he never made it about him. He was always more interested in us, in other people.'

The second time that Martin came into the *BBC Breakfast* studio, he brought Stuart with him. They spoke about their friendship, the shaving incident and Martin said something that I still think about all the time. I ask Stuart if he remembers what it was because I remember looking at Stuart's face as Martin said it and I felt it had a similar impact on him that it had on me.

'The thing about feeling disabled?' Stuart said.

That was precisely it. Towards the end of the interview, Martin was talking about his new life in a wheelchair and why he felt so passionately about campaigning for others to have access to the spinal care that he had.

'It's not my injuries that make me feel disabled, it's people's attitudes that make me feel disabled.'

'I think about that a lot,' says Stuart. 'He's right, isn't he? It's so easy to get stuck in that mindset where you concentrate on what people can't do rather than what they can. Do you know what, Dan?' says Stuart as he shuffles in his chair. Stuart is always smiling, but now there is also excitement in his voice. 'I talk about Martin a lot to other patients. I can't tell stories like Martin can, but I can tell other people about Martin. He is the example I use to so many.'

Martin has also had a profound effect on Paul, the paramedic who took him to Salford Royal that night and saved his life. Paul picks up the story. 'I'd checked in on him that night and the following morning to make sure he was still alive but, after that, it was difficult to find out what had happened to him. Then, one day, my wife (Louise) saw him being interviewed on Channel 5!'

Louise jumps in. 'That's right. I messaged Paul straightaway. I took a picture off the telly and said, "Is this him? You know, the guy from the arena?" and then Paul came back with . . .'

'That's him!' says Paul. 'I did a bit of Facebook stalking and then I thought I would send him a message and see if he wanted to get in touch. We've been friends ever since.'

'Do you remember that ball we went to?' says Louise.

'Yes, that was the first time we actually met him,' remembers Paul. 'Martin was doing this black tie charity do at the Midland Hotel in Manchester. Ron Atkinson was there! We met Martin and we just got on straightaway. He sat us on the top table and then, when he made his speech, he introduced me to the crowd and said, "This is Paul, the paramedic who saved my life."'

The other thing that Paul and Martin share is a love of Manchester. One thing that has always struck me about this city is the way people come together in grief. Where terrorists try and sow discord and pain, Manchester gives birth to strength and togetherness. The Manchester bomb made those bonds stronger than ever.

'We've both got bee tattoos,' says Paul proudly. 'Me and Martin, we both have them.' The bee became an even more powerful symbol for Manchester in the aftermath of the bomb. The worker bee has long been a symbol of the city's hard-working past. In the 1800s Manchester was full of textile mills and they were often described as 'hives of activity' and the workers inside them compared to bees. The bee symbol was a part of Manchester's coat of arms which was given to the city in 1842. After the bomb, it was associated with unity and defiance; it represented Manchester's indomitable spirit. People added it to their social media profiles as an act of solidarity and many, like Martin and Paul, got tattoos. If you ever visit the city and go to the Koffee Pot building in the Northern Quarter, you find an image of twenty-two bees on the side of it. Each bee is swarming around a honey pot and each one represents a victim of the attack.

'I've got bees painted on my garden fence too. Just to remind me.' Paul, like many Mancunians, was moved when he heard the words of the local poet Tony Walsh and his 'This Is The Place' poem which he read at the memorial service in St Ann's Square.

'I've got those final words on the inside of my left forearm,' says Paul. *Always remember, never forget, forever Manchester.*

Paul has another reason to use Martin for inspiration. In July of 2021 he had an accident on his road bike. He hit some debris on a road near Wigan and ended up with fractured vertebrae, broken ribs, a brain injury and underwent spinal surgery in the Salford Royal. Guess who has been his great encourager during recovery? Martin Hibbert.

'Watching Martin has helped me come out the other side of all this,' says Paul. 'We all know people who work hard to support a charity but Martin just takes things to another level. He's superhuman. I am determined to show my family, to show everyone, that I can be just as positive as him going forward. Martin is a permanent reminder to me to make sure that I don't accept average. I want to push the boundaries just like him.'

As I write this, Paul is back in the office just seven months after being in a drug-induced coma. He says that Martin's example pushes him every day but, because of his injuries, he wasn't able to take part in Martin's greatest challenge: climbing Kilimanjaro in a wheelchair.

'I was talking to him about the trip the week before my accident,' says Paul. 'He was like a little kid. Once he gets something in his head there is no stopping him. As soon as I came round after the accident he contacted me and told me not to worry and that, even if I couldn't be there, I'd be part of the team. I know some people laugh at him and think he's mad. I've seen the way some people look at him when he talks about climbing Kilimanjaro, but if there is one thing I've learned in the last few years . . . never doubt Martin Hibbert.'

'Where did the idea of Kilimanjaro come about?' I ask Martin. 'That sounds like one of yours.'

'It was,' says Martin, 'but it wasn't all my fault. I was asked to speak at an event in London for the Spinal Injuries Association. I was addressing a load of multi-millionaires. We were pitching to them to see if they would take us on as their charity of the year. Anyway, we had a dinner and it raised just short of a million quid. One of the guys from the charity jokingly said, "That's amazing, what are you doing next year to raise a million quid?" My brain started ticking straightaway and I thought, if this is going to work, you've got to do something that is an actual risk to your life. Otherwise what's the point? My first suggestion was to climb Everest but then I discovered that I'd have to be carried about 90 per cent of the way, which didn't really seem fair. I looked into things and Kilimanjaro was actually possible. I would only need help 10 per cent of the way and it was tough enough to be worth it. Only 6 per cent of able-bodied people make it to the top, only two other people have done it in a wheelchair. I look at it this way, Dan, every day I have to climb a mountain so I might as well actually climb one.'

Martin has assembled an impressive team around him for the climb. Paul is unable to go because of his injuries, but Stuart will be there alongside him on the trip. The phone call from Martin came through one Saturday morning.

'I was lying in bed and I saw this WhatsApp message arrive,' recalls Stuart. He is laughing as he remembers the story, but he tells me that's because it still all feels a bit bonkers. The messages between the two of them went like this:

Martin: 'Hi, Stuart. Hope you're ok. I've got a challenge I want you to be part of.'

Stuart: 'What is it?'

Martin: 'You might need some time to think about it? I want you to climb Kilimanjaro with me.'

Stuart said 'yes' immediately.

'I turned around to my wife and said, "What on earth have I just volunteered myself for?" There was a mixture of excitement but also apprehension, but I know all about Martin's drive and determination and I know that, at the heart of it, he just wants other people to have the same access to the best care that he had. Having a spinal injury turns your entire life upside down. It's not just the practical things like bladders and bowels, it's everything. The Spinal Injuries Association are amazing but they need money to make a difference and help people to live a fulfilled life.'

Martin Hibbert is a pretty amazing man. You don't have to spend much time in his company to realise that his passion and enthusiasm can convince anyone to do virtually anything. I haven't often seen him without a smile on his face but, as you would expect, there are dark days. There are flashbacks to that night at the Manchester Arena and the time spent in hospital. There is the lingering spectre of PTSD. He has visions of seeing Eve for the first time after the incident and it can hit him at any time and anywhere. Sometimes it keeps him up all night. He has to keep busy. He always wants something to look forward to so that he doesn't have to look back.

I don't know about you, but Martin is one of those people who makes me think about how I would act if I was in the situation he has found himself in. I wonder if I would be able to think as quickly as he did on the night itself. I wonder how I would react to being told I would never be able to walk again. I wonder what it would have been like for me to see one of my daughters under the same circumstances that Martin saw Eve, and I wonder whether I would devote myself to helping others when life remains an uphill struggle every single day.

Martin isn't religious but does enjoy talking to friends about what he describes as 'life, the universe and everything'. He doesn't have an answer to why that night happened to him and his family but, within a few minutes of meeting him, you realise he is a deep thinker. So what does he see as his reason for being here?

'There has to be a reason I survived,' he says, more earnest than at any other point in the interview. 'The bolt went through my neck. It was travelling at about 100 mph but somehow I swallowed it. No one can understand either why, or how, that happened and believe me, I've asked everyone. My story has given me a voice that I never dreamed of having and that is what I use as my motivation, my reason for still being around.'

When Martin tells his story at events, the whole room falls silent. His tale is solemn, painful, but also inspirational. He talks about the fact that he has never wanted revenge for what happened to him that night.

'Forgive me if I don't use his name, Dan,' says Martin carefully, 'but I don't hate him, you know, the bomber. I use him. On the bad days, I use his face to get me out of bed. Sometimes I want nothing more than to stay under the covers. I know that's what he would have wanted and, if I stay in bed, hiding, even for one day, then he wins. I'll happily admit that sometimes I cry in the shower, but I always come out and think . . . right, crack on. I was at the re-opening of the arena in September 2017,' says Martin proudly. 'I wanted them to see that they couldn't stop me. I virtually broke out of the spinal unit to be there but it was important to me. Yes, I got in trouble for it when I got back, but every little win for me is a little defeat for the people who wanted to detonate a bomb at a concert. When I climb Kilimanjaro, they fail. When I get my message around the world, they fail. They nearly took my life away; they did take my legs away but they've actually made me stronger than ever.'

Martin often thinks about the people who didn't make it that night, particularly Saffie Roussos, the youngest victim, who was just eight years old. He has survivors' guilt over why he made it and she didn't. He wants to know why a forty-year-old man who had 'lived a great life' made it home and she didn't. But that has also driven him on to make a difference for others.

'I had no idea about disability before it happened to me. You very rarely see disabled people out and there are many reasons for that. It's because of parking, it's because of a lack of lifts, it's because there are no ramps where they need to go or there just simply isn't enough space. When I'm out and I see another disabled person, I always wave at them because it's so rare. I went to Bond Street in London and I couldn't get in the shops. You go in and ask where the men's stuff is and they tell you it's on the first floor. "Where is the lift?" you ask. "We don't have a lift." It doesn't have to be like this. I go to Australia for treatment sometimes and, when I'm there, I hardly feel disabled at all. Facilities are incredible and so far ahead of what we are doing here. We have the equality act in this country,' says Martin passionately, 'imagine if someone from the BAME or LGBT community was told they couldn't use a shop, or a service, because they didn't have the facilities? This is what I'm trying to change for disabled people and I will use the rest of the time I have on this planet to sing and shout about it. We have to change the mindset. When we look at disabled people we only ever see either a Paralympian or a benefit scrounger. I am neither of those and nor are the vast majority of disabled people. They want to work, but they can't get there. When they do get there, it can be a struggle to get in and, if they do get into the office, they can't get their wheelchair under the desk. I'm sorry, but that's just not good enough.'

Martin's real gift is that he is a campaigner. He doesn't make you feel guilty for not doing or supporting something but he convinces you that things need to change by the sheer weight of reason and enthusiasm. It's hard to disagree with that, particularly when you consider the path he has taken to get to where he is. Martin doesn't wear slogan T-shirts but, if he did, it would read 'Don't Write Me Off Because I'm In A Wheelchair'. I don't think there is any danger of that happening.

Martin wants Eve to be able to live her life to the full too.

They now talk about what happened that night in Manchester. It has helped Eve to deal with the trauma and eased her PTSD. Martin has reminded her that, throughout that night, while she was unconscious on the floor, he was never more than a few feet away from her. That reassurance is as much a help to Martin as it is to Eve. Neither of them like the idea of being alone.

They haven't been back to a concert at the arena yet, but that is the plan. At the moment, loud noises and bangs are too triggering but, eventually, Martin is confident they'll get there. He knows it will be a hard day, but also a hugely important one.

Eve is always making progress. At the moment she is in a wheelchair. At the time of writing this, she is twenty years old and currently doing work for a nine to ten-year-old. 'I know life will be tough for her,' says Martin. 'She probably won't be able to hold down a relationship, but she's here, and that's the important thing. All the time there might be chances of seizures and strokes. There will be constant trips to hospital but, listen, I often laugh when I think about where she was five years ago and where she is now. I have my daughter back and, for a long time, I never thought that would be possible. Ever since that night, she has been defying the doctors' predictions. Look at her now, back at sixth form, kicking ass. She will inspire the world when she's ready to do it.'

I love talking to Martin. He makes you look at things in differing ways. He allows, and occasionally has to persuade you, to see things from a new perspective and his motive always seems to be to improve the lives of those around him. I have no doubt in my mind that he will go on to achieve great things in life and, if Eve is anything like him, she will too. He may well spend the rest of his life in a wheelchair, but standing on his shoulders gives me one of the clearest views possible of what it is to cling on to the positive in the bleakest of situations. That's what I told him at the end of our long conversation. I thanked him for his time and thanked him for coming out from under the covers every day and inspiring me and many others. He answered in typical fashion.

'We could all sit in a corner and cry. It's much easier to mope around and feel sorry for yourself and blame others, but I want to use that as my drive, my motivation, to live life to the full.'

And that's exactly what Martin was trying to do when he set himself the enormous task of climbing Kilimanjaro in June of 2022. If you followed any of his journey on TV, or in the press, you'll know that he managed to make it, but when we caught up a few days after he made the summit, he was in typically down-to-earth mode.

'I don't think it has sunk in yet, I have just come back from having my catheter taken out, so it's been back to normal with a bump. I've had messages from all over the world,' says the proud Mancunian. 'America, Pakistan, India, Australia . . . so many messages from so many different people who all seem to know that we managed to do what most people thought would be impossible.'

Martin made it to the top on 9 June but the last few hours of the climb produced so many doubts. 'Walking through sand is hard enough, but imagine trying to shift a wheelchair through it. I have never done anything like that before. We were spending ten minutes going up and then slipping back to where we started. I told the porters who were helping us that I just didn't have anything left in the tank. One of them just kept saying, "Twenty minutes, twenty minutes," but it was the longest twenty minutes I have ever experienced.'

Martin and his team had already seen the mountain bare its teeth. His best friend, Steve Lloyd, had to pull out on day two with altitude sickness, and the team lost their medic, Chris Paton, on day four in similar fashion. 'Chris was the man looking after my skin sores but also checking on my bowel and bladder movements. They were my wingmen so once they had gone I felt totally alone. I had to sleep with the light on. I felt so incredibly vulnerable, which is strange for me. I hardly slept at all and then we set off at 5 a.m. the next morning. I remember what you told me though, Dan, and I did it.'

When Martin first informed me about his attempt to climb Kilimanjaro he asked me if I had any advice from the time I went up there for Comic Relief. I told him to make sure he had plenty of snacks and, even though it was easy to get distracted by the seemingly endless final morning, I said don't forget to turn your back on Kilimanjaro and enjoy one of the greatest sunrises you will ever see crack across the horizon.

'I remember that picture you showed me,' says Martin, 'and, when the sun rose, I got really emotional. It was the sort of thing you only ever see from a plane. I thought about our talks quite a bit that morning, Dan. I took a photo with the team (which you can see in the picture section) and I had a little cry. There is something amazing about being that free, that silent, that in touch with your surroundings. It was magical.'

Martin also got to keep his promise to his mum. He sprinkled some of her ashes at the top and played their favourite song on his phone. 'I know I was raising money for the Spinal Injuries Association and raising awareness but, from a personal perspective, it was all about my mum. I wanted to have a picture at the top with my Manchester United flag but I knew my mum was with me all the way. It was a really emotional moment when I played "For All We Know" by The Carpenters on my phone. I cry every time I think about it. She knew all about the climb and knew how much I wanted to do it before she died back in October 2021. I had a good sob and sent my two brothers the video from the top and that was pretty special.'

Martin is rightly proud of becoming only the second paraplegic to climb Kilimanjaro and has been staggered by the reaction to his successful summit. 'A guy came up to me on the way down and said, "Martin, you don't know me, but my name is Paul. I was up there a few days ago but I stayed on at base camp for another two days because I wanted to see you." I was really touched by that but also by the porters. Lots of them kept telling me that they had never seen a wheelchair on the mountain. They nicknamed me "Lion" because of the tattoo on my arm. At the end, one of the guys took me to one side and said, "You have inspired me. I have never seen anyone like you before. I am not going to live my life like this anymore, I am going to live like you, live like Martin." I will never forget those experiences.'

On the day that we speak, Martin tells me the total raised has gone up £100,000 in the last forty-eight hours. The million-pound dream is within reach and there is no sign of him taking his foot off the fundraising gas.

'I want to do base camp at Everest,' says Martin, giggling at how crazy it sounds. 'It has never been done in a wheelchair and, since I've come back, I've been contacted by two Royal Marines and two Gurkhas who have told me it's possible and they'd like to help. I know I still need to do a lot of checking but I'll keep going until ministers listen and we get those changes to social care and everyone gets access to the care that is available. Seven people a day get a spinal cord injury and only one in three get help and support. That means four of those seven go home without any rehab, any help or any education. How is that possible? How can they be expected to get on with their lives? During the pandemic I was constantly hearing stories of people in a wheelchair being left in a bed, in their own mess, for two days, or left waiting at the bottom of a flight of stairs for the same amount of time. While that is still happening, I'll keep going.'

I ask Martin if he has taken the time to reflect that it's only just over five years ago that he was lying on the concrete floor in the Manchester Arena on the night his life changed forever. 'I have thought about that, Dan,' says the forty-five-year-old. 'I have thought about the fact that I was told I would never walk again. I thought about that at the top quite a bit. I was lying in a bed in hospital back in 2017 and the only thing I could move was my head and here I am at the top of Kilimanjaro. What a message that is to disabled people everywhere. I've had wheel-chair users contact me this week and tell me they've watched what I did and have left the house for the first time in ten years. I am so humbled that I have inspired anyone by what I have done. It's not just a message to disabled people but it's a message to the people who tried to blow me up. They wanted me dead, and if they couldn't have that, they wanted me terrified and silent in a corner somewhere. We'll, I'm very much alive and, I might spend most of my life sitting down, but I won't be in a corner and I won't be quiet. There is too much to do.'

A ROSE IN BLOOM

'My mum always made me feel like I could do anything,' says Rose. 'She would always tell me that there was no job that was beyond me.'

'Maybe not a telephonist,' interrupts Donna. 'But anything else, Rose. Anything.'

Rose Ayling-Ellis was the undisputed star of *Strictly Come Dancing* in 2021. She will probably go down as the greatest contestant in the history of the show. She is also the only celebrity ever to take to the dance floor who hasn't been able to hear any of the music. If you didn't know, Rose is deaf. What she did over those thirteen weeks was truly incredible. Giovanni Pernice was with her every step of the way on the floor, and her mum was just as supportive off it – as she has been for the whole of Rose's life.

'I've always had people telling me there are things I can't do. I always think that's the wrong way round,' says Rose with that permanent smile on her face. 'Mum was always fighting my corner, weren't you?'

'I was, but that's because I was always getting told what was the best thing I could do for you,' says Donna. 'Most parents get that, but it happens even more when you have a deaf child. "Teach her this", "Make sure she doesn't do that", "Don't teach her sign language", "She's never going to be able to speak". I know you're the deaf one, but I learned very early not to listen! Every deaf person is different and, when I watched Rose, the way she was with people, from a very early age, I just knew there would be no boundaries for her. I knew, I was convinced she could do anything, and I just kept telling her that.'

I first met Rose on week one of *Strictly* when we were all saying 'hello' to each other. My dad is deaf. He has no hearing in one ear and has a cochlea implant for the other. He hates rooms with lots of people in them. The background 'fuzz' drowns everything out and he normally just switches off the box on the side of his head and keeps himself to himself. Rose was nervous – as we all were – but she was also positive and confident. She stood out.

'She's always been like that,' says Donna as I recount to her my first meeting with her daughter. 'When she was young, you know, at school, everywhere she went, she used to blow people away. Everyone would be taken aback by her. She has always had that effect on people. She would get the "poor little deaf girl" reaction, but she was the complete opposite. People would always expect her to be the quiet kid who would hide in the corner, but Rose has always been full of life.'

'You used to send me to everything, didn't you, Mum?' chirps Rose.

'Exactly,' replied Donna. 'She didn't care. I would send her to every club going. I never wanted her to think that a door would be closed to her because she was deaf. She was at Brownies, swimming clubs, after-school stuff. If it was on, Rose was there.'

Rose and Donna have this endearing way of talking when they are together. They have a gorgeous habit of teeing each other up.

'You used to like surprising people, didn't you, Rose?' says Donna, encouraging Rose to share.

'They would always be surprised if I could write a sentence, weren't they, Mum? I felt like saying, "I'm deaf, I'm not stupid."'

Donna jumps back in. 'If she ever had a bad day or had a knock-back, I would always remind her that she could do more than people expect, that she could be more. The great thing about Rose is that she was always so enthusiastic. Do you remember the doctors, Rose?' asks Donna. Rose nods.

'When we used to go to the doctors, or somewhere like that, they would always talk to me and not her.'

'I used to hate that,' says Rose with a smile.

'Do you remember, Rose? I would deliberately turn my head away. They would be talking to her but looking at me. "I'm so sorry" was another one. "Why are you sorry?" Don't be sorry. She's happy and she's fine. I know almost all of it comes through ignorance. It's just because people don't know.'

Rose lifts her hand to jump in. 'And that's what we are trying to change, Mum!'

'That's what you're changing,' says a proud Donna. 'There wasn't a Rose Ayling-Ellis to look up to when she was growing up.' She turns to me and points at Rose. 'Now there is, and that's my daughter.'

That is exactly what Rose did during her time on *Strictly* and is continuing to do. The week after I spoke to her for this book, British Sign Language became an official language – a huge step forward for the deaf community and directly linked to the awareness associated with Rose's time on the biggest show on telly. Everywhere she goes she makes practical suggestions, things that make you feel daft for not thinking of yourself. In the first week of our *Strictly* experience, Rose put a message on the group WhatsApp.

'Hi guys. I would love to be able to follow all the training on your Instagram stories but it's really hard without captions.' She then sent through a how-to video link which explained how simple it was. We all apologised for not thinking of it but thanked her for the heads-up and most of us will keep doing it forever. She wasn't judgey, she wasn't angry, she wasn't frustrated, she just calmly explained why it was important and it all just made perfect sense. She opens up the doors to her world and lets you in. She does that a lot. She's very good at it.

'When I was a child, I thought I was the only deaf person in the town,' explains Rose. 'I went to a deaf club once a week. There were a lot of older people there and occasionally we would go on camping weekends together. My mum is right, I never really had a role model'. She giggles. 'Do you remember, Mum? My nan used to give me books about Helen Keller, that American author who went deaf and blind when she was about 19, but I couldn't relate to her. She would tell me about Dame Evelyn Glennie, who is a deaf percussionist, or the film called *Children of a Lesser God*. I do remember, from a very early age, I wanted to be an artist. I found that I could communicate through drawing, and I loved it. It wasn't until I was older that I realised acting could be art.'

Donna jumps in. 'She was so creative, Dan. She was really gifted.'

'Stop it, Mum. You'll be getting my old pictures out next. She's kept them all, Dan. It's so embarrassing: fabric, textiles, arts and crafts. She's got everything.'

Donna is laughing into her cup of tea. 'There is nothing wrong with being a proud mum, Rose. Tell Dan about that weekend you went on, the acting one.'

Rose picks up the story. 'I didn't really have any interest in acting at all at the start. I saw it as something for the popular kids. How old was I, Mum, when I went to the weekend?'

'Fourteen or fifteen?' offers Donna tentatively.

'That sounds about right. I went for a weekend. I was convinced that all the kids would be younger than me and I was worried because I had never done it at school. It was like a deaf children's acting weekend, wasn't it?'

Donna nods. Rose continues. By this point they are just telling the story together, one sentence at a time.

'It was run by a charity.'

'You made a short film, didn't you?'

'Yes, I thought maybe filming could be something to do but I didn't enjoy it.'

'And the director, he asked you if you wanted to act.'

'That's right, and I remember that I wasn't intimidated for the first time.'

'Later on, Dan, I got there to pick her up and she was this star and she'd had a lovely time. I honestly thought she would hate it.'

'And,' says Rose, 'that director asked me to be in his short film and that was really the start of it all.'

Rose explained that throughout her early childhood she knew she was different to most other children, so she was determined to make sure she had no other reason to stand out. She didn't mind going under the radar.

Donna is listening carefully and asks a question. 'Do you think that's why you didn't want to be on stage at the start, Rose? Maybe it was because you wanted to hide that from people?'

Rose thinks about her answer. 'I was always confident, but I didn't want to be front and centre. I was blurred into the background. It wasn't until year 10 or 11 that I grew in confidence, and I became more of myself.'

Rose's first job was at a dog school. She was a gardener for two summers and then she got a gig at Sainsburys. 'I was stacking shelves,' she says proudly. 'I specialised in the fridge section.'

'She was so amazed when she got that job,' says Donna. 'I think she convinced herself that, because she was deaf, she had no chance.'

That supermarket job also gave Rose a first taste of discrimination. 'I loved that job and sometimes, during an emergency, when there were loads of people in and it was really busy, you had to jump on the tills to help. They would train people up to do it, but I was the only person who was never trained to work on the till! That's the problem with discrimination. It's hard to prove. You're never told that you don't get the opportunity because you are deaf, but you also never get the chance to prove that being deaf isn't a problem.'

Rose was destined for much bigger things than a life on the tills. The short film after the acting weekend led to wider recognition which eventually brought the offer of a job on *Casualty*. There was no agency which represented deaf actors, so Rose was getting her opportunities through Facebook.

'What about *Summer of Rockets*, Rose?' says Donna. *Summer of Rockets* was a cold-war drama series directed by Stephen Poliakov for BBC Two. 'I remember the night before the audition for that,' continues Rose's mum. 'I remember she went to bed early, and I thought she was so professional. I tried to manage expectation and told her it didn't matter if she didn't get it, but I was excited. Most of her jobs just came from impressing people when they met her for the first time.'

'I enjoyed that one,' says Rose, managing to get a word in. Donna is on a roll.

'*EastEnders* was massive, Dan. We used to watch it together, didn't we, Rose, when she was a little girl. I know *EastEnders* is mad and completely over the top, but you can use it sometimes in a way to explain situations. That's why we used to watch it. When she got that job, I couldn't believe it. It was all so surreal. We sat and watched that episode, do you remember, Rose?' Donna pauses and the pair of them laugh and then she pretends to take a picture with her phone.

'I paused it and I took a picture of you there, with you in the background on the telly.'

As Donna is talking, you can see it all coming back to her. All the battles she had along the way. All the times she was told 'no'. All the times she had to fight for Rose to be included. All the times she was the only one who believed in her daughter.

'I always knew she could fly this high,' says Donna, staring at Rose as only a mum can. 'I have always seen her work so hard to get to the same level as other people. I knew she was unstoppable. That's why, when *Strictly* came calling, I had no doubt she'd be brilliant. I know some people just couldn't understand how a deaf girl could dance on the telly like that, but I was like, that's my Rose. She can do anything.'

Donna works in a local hospital in the outpatient's department in cardiology. She was at work when Rose gave her the call about *Strictly*.

'I answered the phone and she just said, "Mum, guess what, *Strictly Come Dancing* want me." I couldn't tell anyone. I was so excited.'

Rose was invited in for a trial with Executive Producer, Sarah James. She would be dancing with Giovanni Pernice. 'I was terrified,' remembers Rose. 'He made it so easy, and we got on really well, but it was so difficult. I had never danced before. If I was a bad dancer, people would think that it was because I was deaf. I didn't want to let down the deaf community. We did some jive, and I was quite bad at it, and we did some ballroom and I left. I thought that might have been it.'

Her future professional partner had other ideas. 'Quite a few of the celebrities are asked to dance before they go on *Strictly* and I was told the next one would be a deaf girl called Rose,' recalls Giovanni. 'We got on straightaway. I tried to make her feel comfortable and I was really careful in the way I explained things to her. I could tell she was nervous, but she was great. As soon as she left the room, I went up to Sarah James and said, "She has to do the show! I am not asking for much, but please, I want Rose. I would love to dance with her."'

Sarah James remembers the conversation well. 'He was desperate to have her as a partner after that session. I couldn't tell Rose at that point because we were seeing other people, but I knew we already wanted her on the show. We had met her on Zoom, and we were blown away by how much she had thought through everything. In our first meeting she talked about interpreters, about music and subtitles. She explained to us all that she hadn't really watched the show before because it wasn't accessible to the deaf community. I remember being ashamed as she told me that the live subtitles were totally unreliable and that all she was able to do was watch catch-up clips of the dancing. She was already improving the show and making it more accessible before she'd even started! The dance session was more for her than for us. We just wanted to see how it would work and Giovanni was amazing with her straightaway. She could lip read him really easily and she'd already told us that Italians were easy to lip read because they were so expressive. He didn't patronise her at all and they were already taking the mickey out of each other. We knew it could be a special partnership.'

'There was a connection straightaway,' says Giovanni. '*Strictly* lasts a long time and I wanted to be with someone

I could get on with. She didn't feel worried and she was very comfortable with me. I was hopeful that we'd be paired together but there were some nervy weeks ahead.'

Three days later, Rose had a call from her agent to confirm her place on the show. She had just done a night shift filming *EastEnders* and was told she could only tell her mum and her then boyfriend, Sam. It had to remain a secret.

'I'd not even been in *EastEnders* for a year, had I, Mum?' says Rose, laughing.

'I know,' replies Donna, 'but no one turns you down after they've met you, do they? I knew she'd get it,' says Donna confidently. 'As soon as Rose told me she was going to meet the team at *Strictly*, I knew she'd be dancing.'

'Stop it, Mum,' complains Rose, rolling her eyes.

'No, I won't,' replies Donna giggling. 'I'm your mum and I'm meant to be your biggest supporter. At least I was able to keep a secret!' Donna widens her eyes and flicks an accusatory glance at Rose.

It was all coming out now. The pair of them were chuckling away. Donna told no one, not even Rose's brother. Her daughter's lips were a little looser.

'I told Danny Dyer the next day on the set of *EastEnders*!' confesses Rose with her head in her hands. 'I kept having a big mouth. I am so bad at keeping a secret. They always ask someone from *EastEnders* to do *Strictly*, and everyone kept asking who it was. I told Danny and he was great. He cried and was so proud of me. I told him it was a secret and that he couldn't tell anyone.'

'Didn't someone find out though, Rose?' says Donna, laughing.

'That's right,' says Rose. 'The next week someone from *EastEnders* asked me if I had talked to anyone on the show about doing *Strictly*. I just panicked.' At this point Rose is laughing her head off. 'Guess what, Dan? I was so embarrassed that I just told them I hadn't said anything to anyone. I was becoming really stressed holding on to the secret. That's why I was so happy when it finally came out.'

The *Strictly* announcements are incredibly carefully choreographed. They are meticulously planned by the team with everyone having a certain slot on a certain show. I was announced alongside Katie McGlynn on BBC *Breakfast* and there are various other segments on shows like *The One Show*, Zoe Ball's Radio 2 *Breakfast Show* and so on.

'I remember being on BBC News,' says Rose. 'It was really positive. I hadn't even started dancing and everyone was talking about it already. I started on *EastEnders* during Covid so I think I managed to be under the radar a little, but this was big news and there was no going back.'

The memories are all coming flooding back for Donna. 'I was so excited. I didn't really sleep well at all the night before. Loads of my friends were messaging me. I was also a little worried about Rose, to be honest. Would she be able to cope with being in the public eye? I worried about the press, you know, how they would portray her. I never worried that people wouldn't like her, but I was worried that she would be put out there in the wrong way, but it was ok, wasn't it, Rose?'

'Yes, it was great, Mum,' replies Rose. 'I worried about being the first deaf one. Do I need to behave in a certain way? The day before I went for my first interview I spoke to Danny Dyer. "Do I need to put on a personality, Danny? Maybe I should pretend to be someone." Danny just said, "The best advice I can give you is, be yourself and just own who you are." He told me that I would feel like it wasn't real, and he reminded me that people will always see if you're faking it. He reminded me that was the only thing I could control. It was just what I needed to hear.'

Donna is giving her daughter the proud-mum look again. 'She was just being herself, Dan. That was her. Quirky, geeky, funny. As her mum, you watch that and think, "There she is. YES!"' She turns to Rose. 'Don't you think, if you hadn't stayed yourself, you wouldn't have been able to do it? No one can keep an act up that long.'

'Yes,' says Rose, 'but it's also hard, because being yourself is much more vulnerable. I think that's why some people put on an act, because if people don't like it, you can always say, "It's not really me." I also think Gio helped a lot with that. He just let me be me from day one.'

'Day one' for Rose and Gio was actually their 'meeting VT' at a pie and mash shop in the square that provided the inspiration for *EastEnders*.

'It's a bit strange really,' says Gio laughing, 'because I don't eat that sort of stuff and Rose is a vegetarian.'

'It took a lot for him to eat that,' admits Rose. 'I'm not even sure if he'd ever watched *EastEnders* before.'

I ask Gio if that's true. 'I'm a busy man, Dan,' he laughs. 'I was hoping I was going to get Rose, so I'd done my research, like I always do. I was so happy when it was her that I even forgot how bad the pie and mash tasted. I don't watch *EastEnders*, but I know we always have someone from the cast on the show. I knew that Rose was special from when we danced together at her first session, and I was looking forward to a brilliant season on *Strictly*. Like all good partnerships, it wasn't always smooth, but I will never forget it.'

Things were always going to be different with Rose. *Strictly's* first deaf contestant was going to open the eyes of her profession, her professional dancer, the production team and the watching public to the deaf community.

'We can't train in here. It's just too echoey.' That was day one. Gio had taken Rose to one of his favourite studios, but she couldn't hear a thing with all the sound bouncing off the walls.

Gio realised he had to completely change the way he had done *Strictly* in the past. 'When you dance with someone who hears, you don't think about sound. You don't think about the size of the room. Rose was lovely about it, but she just said, "I can't hear you. I can't be in here. I can't learn in here." We looked around for a new studio for a few hours and eventually we settled on the rehearsal room at Elstree which was much better for Rose. That was my first big lesson. The second one was a reminder that, when someone has never danced before, jive is a tough one to start with.'

'I think Gio was really worried that first week,' remembers

Rose. 'The room was bad, we'd had to move and I was really struggling with jive. I get asked a lot about what I can hear during the dance and it's hard for me to explain because I don't know what you hear. I have nothing to compare it to. I don't hear the music. Sometimes, I can feel it. There is like a hum in the background, but that's it. What Gio did really well was never letting go of me. I followed him really well and that's how we survived those first few weeks. That and a lot of ice-packs!'

Rose isn't joking about the ice-packs. I remember seeing her in the studio on the Friday before her opening dance and her ankles were the size of melons. 'I haven't told many people this, Dan,' says Gio, 'but I didn't know if Rose was going to make it through those first few weeks. I pushed her too hard for someone who had never danced before and for someone who didn't do that much exercise. It got to the point that I was going to ask the bosses if we could have a week off because Rose could hardly walk. I thought I might lose her. I told her it would be ok, and I changed the choreography for our jive to make it less intense and less jumpy and I did the same for the salsa in week two. I think that helped.'

'There was no way I was going to stop,' says Rose. 'I had to prove to myself that I could do it. No one was going to stop me getting on that dance floor. My ankles were massive, but I couldn't let people down. I couldn't bear the thought of someone saying, "It was probably too much for her" or "The poor deaf girl couldn't do it". I didn't want it to be an excuse.'

'I was really worried,' says Donna. 'I knew mentally she was so strong, but her body was stopping her. You were on those painkillers, weren't you, Rose?'

'I took painkillers but it still hurt. I would wake up my boyfriend in the middle of the night and ask him to carry me to the toilet so that I didn't have to walk. The team at *Strictly* were so supportive too. Ugo (Monye) got me this ice machine and the production team took care of everything. Gio just carried me around everywhere. The only thing I had to do was dance, so by the time we got to our first ballroom dance in week three, things were much better. I really like ballroom.'

I don't mind telling you that I voted for Rose from week one. I told Donna that too. I told her how amazing her daughter was and explained that, as the son of a deaf dad, it was blowing my mind how she was doing it. I found dancing hard enough and I can hear everything. Everywhere I went people were saying the same thing. 'Dan, we love you and Nadiya on *Strictly* but . . . how amazing is Rose?' She had captured the attention and the hearts of the nation and the fella who got to dance with her every week was equally enraptured.

'She is different to everyone else,' says Giovanni with a huge smile. 'I love *Strictly* but every year it can be the same for me as a professional. It depends on your partner a little, but you teach each dance the same way. Not with Rose. She made me change the way I choreograph. She made me think in a different, deeper way. She helped me to grow as a dancer, as a teacher and as a performer. Rose reinvigorated my love of *Strictly*. Dan, you saw how it works with Nadiya. It's a waltz . . . we teach you how to waltz. I have always taught waltz the same way, but with Rose, everything is different. Everything is better. She made me fall in love with the show and fall in love with teaching again. I will always be thankful to her for that.'

I'm about to ask Giovanni a question about when he thought Rose could go all the way and, before I was even halfway through, he says, 'Week three. Movie week was a big one. Ask Rose about movie week.'

When you talk to Rose about dancing, she doesn't talk about it like anyone else. Maybe it's the natural performer in her. Maybe it's the fact that she doesn't need the music but, while the rest of us could easily get bogged down in the fog of technique, concerns about hand position and whether it was a heal-lead, Rose was all about finding the character. The breakthrough was when Rose found Rose. When Rose from *EastEnders* found Rose from *Titanic*. I did exactly what Giovanni told me to do; I asked Rose about movie week.

'I didn't really listen to the music at all, Dan, to be honest. In my head, there wasn't any. It all became about muscle memory. During the week I would learn the technique and just religiously follow Gio. On a Saturday night all I could hear was a little bit of noise, the rest was all about the character.'

I ask her to explain how it works. 'Dancing for deaf people is just totally different. It's still beautiful but it has nothing to do with the music. All I'm trying to do is tell a story. I love telling stories. With *Titanic*, I watched the film, I learned as much as I could about that character, their personality, I read the subtitles and then, that's who I would become on the Saturday night. It was the same when we did the dance from *Frozen*, and

I was Anna. I don't know any of the songs from *Frozen*, but I can understand who she is and what makes her tick. She's a bit clumsy, lots of fun and a bit daft. She's a lot like me.' Rose laughs before declaring, 'I would love to play a Disney princess.'

I ask her what she does if there is no character and it's just a song? 'I would study the lyrics and find a character in the lyrics. You should see my Spotify playlist,' says Rose proudly. 'I went through all the lyrics carefully every week and then, when the time came, I gave it 100 per cent every single time. On Saturday night, you saw it, I was a different person. During the show, with the costume, the hair and the make-up, I wasn't Rose anymore, and I loved it.'

It's incredible, isn't it? It's easy to see why most of the professionals watching Rose dance every week were open-mouthed at what she was able to do. Giovanni had to keep his mouth closed on the dance floor.

'I still don't know how she did it,' he says. 'When you dance with her you can't understand that she doesn't hear the music. You get reminded every now and again. I have been a dancer for 23 years and Rose made me realise that music is not as important as I thought it was. She made me look at dancing in a different way . . . and I thought I knew everything. Her connection to the dance was stronger than anyone I have ever met and, because she doesn't hear the music like I hear it, that meant our connection was so important. She had to connect to me. She needed me to touch her to help her, to guide her and that meant we were so finely tuned to each other which, in dance, means everything. Sometimes your partner gets distracted by the audience, the band, the music, the noise, the occasion, but never with Rose. It was just me and her.'

It was just the two of them on the dance floor, but it was the rest of the country falling in love with them every week. Rose was changing opinions, starting conversations and also breaking records. In week six, their tango produced the earliest ever perfect score in *Strictly* history. Four 10s from four jubilant judges.

'I felt the pressure that week,' says Giovanni. '*Strictly* always makes this big thing of me being the "King of Halloween" because I'm always top of the leader board each season. Rose and I were doing a tango. It was a good tango, but it was not a 40-point tango all week. Something happened when the music started in the studio. I felt like I was dancing with a professional. We had made a mistake in the dress rehearsal, and I think Rose used to like doing that because she only wanted one routine to be perfect. I can't describe how good she was that night. She was incredible. She came to life. I could see the public were falling in love with her. That tango, for me, will go down as one of my best ever dances on *Strictly*.'

Rose had become the overwhelming favourite to win the show in a year when the standard of dancing was the highest it has ever been (with the occasional exception). It was all getting a little tense for Donna.

'I went to five shows in total. I would spend the whole week talking to her. She would be the same every week. Monday and Tuesday were the "I can't do it" days and then, by about Thursday, she would start to say she had it and then I would spend the whole of Saturday a nervous wreck.'

'Did it get easier to watch me as I went further, Mum?' asks Rose.

'I think it was easier after week three – when you did *Titanic*. I think that was your breakthrough week. My favourite week was your Couple's Choice one. I think that was everyone's favourite. People still talk to me about that one all the time.'

Rose and Giovanni's dance to 'Symphony' by Clean Bandit was the standout moment of the 19th series of *Strictly Come Dancing*. I don't think it's going too far to say it was the standout moment of TV in 2021. The dance has picked up award after award, including a BAFTA for TV's 'Must-See Moment'. It was such a privilege to be sitting there on the night and witness the magic from just a few metres away.

At the point when Rose put her hands over Giovanni's ears and the music stopped, everyone in the studio, and I imagine everyone at home, held their breath. I was sitting next to Nadiya at one of the tables and I remember she reached out and grabbed my hand. When the music kicked back in, she just burst into tears and after the show she went up to Rose, still in tears, and thanked her for letting us all into her world. It was an epic bit of TV; an epic bit of TV that took an awful lot of planning and an epic bit of TV that almost went horribly wrong.

'We spoke to Giovanni about the idea really early on in the series,' says Sarah James, Executive Producer. 'The whole idea was that we wanted to try and give people an idea of what Rose's world was like, but at the start we didn't really know how to do it. We had so many meetings about whether we cut the music completely, whether there was complete silence, or should we have some background noise? Giovanni was totally invested in it and wanted it to be perfect. We all did.'

'I remember that Giovanni told me what he was planning,' says Rose. 'He said, in week eight we are going to dance in a silent moment. The music would stop and then come back on. I told him that I loved the idea but that I didn't want it to be sad. I don't want people to watch it and think, "Oh, look at the poor deaf girl". I've had enough of that in my life. I love being deaf. I wanted to show people that, if they came into my world, we'd be having a party.'

Lead choreographer Jason Gilkison, who works with all the couples and is a genuine genius, came up with the music and Giovanni was determined that Rose had to be happy with the dance.

Sarah James knew it was going to be a big moment. 'Some things happen for a reason, don't they? Jason had been wanting to use that song for a while. We had actually offered it to a different celeb the year before, but it didn't work. We wanted it to be emotional but also uplifting. Whenever you do a Couple's Choice on *Strictly*, the professional dancers are always assisted by our choreographers. Rose was really clear on what she wanted.'

'When I first saw the choreography, I didn't think it was right for me,' remembers Rose. 'The choreographers who worked with Jason, Ash-Leigh (Hunter) and Arduino (Bertoncello), had got to know me really well so we worked on it together with Giovanni. They both knew that I was so positive about being deaf and they poured all of that into the dance. Gio kept saying, "Is there any bit in it you don't like?" and we kept changing things right up until the Thursday morning. The thing I love most about it was, if you watch it closely, up until the silent moment we were dancing little bits from our routines in the previous weeks then I put my hands on his ears and open the door into how I dance.'

'I had so many meetings with production about that moment,' recalls Giovanni. 'At the start we were going to have the silence at the beginning, then we thought about doing it at the end but, eventually, we got it just right. Sarah James was amazing. At one point I think we were going to do the whole dance in silence, but I'm so glad we did it the way we did. It was perfect.'

One of the big concerns about the moment of silence was how Rose and Giovanni would get back into the dance. Rose couldn't hear anything but, for the first time, neither could Giovanni. They settled on a loose spin to get themselves back in time. Giovanni could control that but there were still worries over following the beat in the music when there was no beat. *Strictly* provided Giovanni with a belt that would pulse with the music. He could wear it underneath his clothes and that would keep him in time.

'We tried the belt in rehearsals a few times,' says Giovanni. 'It worked but it didn't feel right. Those ten seconds of silence were going to be the most powerful thing I had done in my life. It was all about the message and it had to be authentic. It had to be real. I called Sarah James and told her I couldn't wear the belt. I told her it was about Rose. The whole point of the dance was that I was experiencing what Rose feels, we all were. The belt defeated it. I would have been cheating. I needed to feel what she feels. When I told Rose I was getting rid of the belt she was so thankful. She knew that I understood her. She said, "Welcome to my world." It was beautiful.'

Strictly Saturdays are busy. Everyone arrives at some point in the morning, depending on how much time you need in hair and make-up. To give you an idea, when Nadiya was dressed up like Sleeping Beauty in week three, just her hair (crafted by the brilliant Anna Winterburn) took about five hours. All the couples have the chance to go through their dance twice with the band playing the music live. It always sounds very different to the track you rehearse with during the week so it's invaluable. That gives you the chance to iron out any issues and make a few tweaks. The rest of the day is filled with interviews, lunch, filming for social media, meetings about music, physio and then, at about 2.30, there is a full dress rehearsal.

Rose and Giovanni's dress rehearsal did not go well. I have to say that the band and singers on *Strictly* are the most phenomenally talented bunch of musicians I have ever seen but, during the 'moment of silence', there was quite a lot of noise. Giovanni had a word.

'I told Dave Arch that this was the most important thing I had ever done. I wanted it to be perfect. Dave is so good, and he promised me they would get it right when it mattered, but the pressure was on. I could tell everyone was nervous. We only had one opportunity to do it. They were amazing. Rose was amazing. The whole thing was amazing.'

'I was confident it would work,' says Sarah James, 'and it was wonderful. I was glad that we had achieved what we wanted. I was glad that Rose was happy. I had no idea just how huge it was going to become.'

'When we finished the dance,' says Gio, 'I could feel it. It was different to every other dance. I looked at Rose and she could feel it too. You don't get many moments like that in your life.'

When I speak to Rose about it, her partner at the time, Sam, is working on the table behind her.

'Sam was there that night, Dan. With his mum,' says Rose.

'What did he think of it, Rose? Can you ask him?' I said.

'Hold on. He's deaf. I'll have to tap him on the shoulder.' She reaches over the back of the chair and gets Sam's attention. 'Dan wants to know what you thought of the Couple's Choice.'

Sam turns round. 'It was wonderful,' he says with a smile. 'When I watched it, I knew it was a huge moment for the deaf community, but also for society. It was beautiful and I was just really proud of what Rose had done and I was so happy to be there.'

He turns to Rose. 'It was only you and me in the whole studio who were deaf that day, wasn't it?'

Rose nods. Her former partner continues. 'When you're deaf, we are really careful about how we share what our world is like. It's hard to explain to a hearing audience who have such a small knowledge and can never understand. We have our own culture, and we talk a lot about how positive it is to be deaf. What Rose did that night was invite the whole of the UK to experience what she sees, and what she hears every day. That is a game changer for the deaf community.'

Rose extends her hand and holds Sam's. Donna joins back into the conversation.

'She showed everyone that she was happy, Dan. The whole story was one of happiness. She showed the audience that too.'

'She showed that there was nothing wrong with me,' says Sam. 'I can't tell you how powerful that is for me and every deaf person out there. It's society that makes me feel different.'

This is why *Strictly* was so important for Rose. She wasn't just dancing. She was on a mission.

'*Strictly* gave me that access,' she says. 'We don't give disabled people a chance. Ask anyone. They will tell you the same thing. Every day is a battle sometimes because, as a society, we put all these obstacles and barriers in the way. The world is designed for hearing people. We are so proud of being deaf and we are very good at adapting to things.'

'People started to learn about our culture,' says Sam. 'Rose made the deaf community step forward years. She didn't do it by shouting or screaming or slashing tyres. All she did was open the door.'

'Lots of people just didn't know,' says Donna. 'What Rose did was educate a whole nation in the comfort of their living rooms, as part of Saturday-night telly. I told you she was amazing.'

'I didn't want to shout at anyone,' says Rose. 'I always try and teach with humour. It's so easy to be angry about it, because it hurts so much when you are discriminated against. Some days

I want to scream but all you get is, "Oh, she's a bit angry" or "She's too aggressive". I wanted to be positive.'

'That's who you are, Rose,' says a proud mum. 'You are such a positive person.'

On the day I spoke to Giovanni, British Sign Language had just been recognised as an official language: a campaign supported and inspired by Rose. The Italian still can't quite get his head around the impact that his partner has had on wider society.

'I knew we were going to do something so special for the deaf community and I knew it was going to be a big statement for Rose, but since then things have gone crazy. She has changed the world. Rose has opened everyone's eyes. After years of waiting, who would have thought that just ten seconds of silence on BBC One would make such a big difference?'

If you talk to Rose about the impact she has made, both during and since *Strictly*, she is quick to point out the support she received from the whole team on the show and particularly Sarah James and Stef Aleksander, the talent executive.

'They listened to everything I said from the start,' says the *Strictly* champion. 'I talked to them a lot about the interpreter. I didn't want all the attention and the camera to be on them all the time like it normally is. They are not here to help me, they are here to help hearing people to communicate with me. I had a responsibility to every other deaf person in the country. I wanted it to be about the deaf person and not about the interpreter. I didn't watch *Strictly* before I was on it, because the live subtitles are so slow, and you don't feel part of the show. Even twenty-four hours later, it's still live subtitles. Even a year later, it was still the live subtitles. Sarah James changed all that. We now have subtitles which will be on time within twenty-four hours and an interpreter on iPlayer and they have also added audio description for blind people.'

Donna has been listening carefully to her daughter. 'She won't say it herself, Dan, but she's changed TV forever. That's what everyone keeps saying. Everyone on the show had deaf awareness training too, didn't they, Rose?'

Rose nods and smiles. 'It was amazing. They couldn't have done more for me.'

'You know,' says Donna, 'I started following you all on Instagram and I watched you all putting these captions on for Rose. I was so proud. My little daughter changing the world. There is not a word that is big enough to say what it means to me as her mum. I've always been proud, since she got that first job in Sainsburys.'

Rose laughs. 'It's a bit bigger than Sainsburys, Mum.'

'I know. I know,' says Donna. 'It's also just a bit surreal. I always knew you'd do something like this.'

'She has always said that, Dan,' says Rose, giggling again but looking lovingly at Donna.

'I did. Maybe every mum thinks that. I didn't know she was going to be famous; I just knew she was special. She always had an impact on everyone, wherever she goes, and she has always worked so hard and . . .'

'Tell Dan about the World Cup,' interrupts Rose. 'You know, the score.'

'No, he'll think I'm daft,' says Donna, throwing her head back.

'Tell him, Mum, he'll love it.'

'Ok,' Donna admits defeat. 'I've always been a bit of a dreamer. I don't watch football at all, but once, England had a big game in the World Cup and, the day before, I dreamt the exact scoreline and then it came true.'

'She should have gone to the betting shop,' howls Rose.

Being in the studio for Rose and Giovanni's Couple's Choice was amazing. That weekend I gave Rose all three of my online votes. She normally got two and then I'd give the other one to either my favourite dance of the week or whoever had been in the dance-off the week before and survived. Channels will keep showing that dance for years to come. I watched it four times the next day with my kids, I'm sure lots of people did. What they did the following week in their paso doble was even more impressive. For much of the competition Rose would be in close contact with Giovanni to help her keep time with the music. For the paso, Rose started on her own on the stage and Giovanni was completely out of shot behind the camera. There is no footage of what he did anywhere, but it was incredible to witness.

'She was getting better every week,' recalls Giovanni, 'but I wanted her to be able to dance on her own. Sometimes when I was dancing with her, she was so good, I forgot she was deaf, and I wanted people to see that.'

'I remember that week,' says Rose. 'I was having a bit of a panic because I didn't want to look stupid. Gio was dancing behind the camera and I just had to follow him. It was really complicated, but it worked.'

'We tried it in rehearsals,' explains Gio, 'but she was always a little behind. I had to count her in and then dance one beat ahead of the music. If she copied me straightaway, we found out she was on time. I'll be honest with you, Dan, it felt completely wrong for me as a professional. Every time I did it I was like "WHAT ARE YOU DOING?" but she was amazing and it was perfect.'

That perfection, or as close to it as possible, continued right the way to an emotional final. AJ was out injured, so she and Kai had to watch from the sidelines. John and Johannes were equally sensational, but it was impossible to stop Rose and Giovanni from lifting the glitterball trophy.

'I was exhausted that week,' remembers Rose. 'My body started to shut down. That Monday after the semi-final was one of the worst days. Gio wasn't happy. "What is wrong with you? Why are you giving up?" he said. "This is one last week. You've got to go for it." He was quite military about it all, but it did help me get my head together. I just told myself that this was my last ever week on *Strictly* and I was going to enjoy it, every second of it. The one thing that caught me out was the emotion of the final. It just hit me on the day that it was going to be the last day that we would dance together, and I was overcome by the sadness of that. I cried all day.'

'I have never cried before over *Strictly*,' says Giovanni, 'but that final day with Rose was ridiculous. Every time I heard her name, it would set me off.' He starts running through some of the things Rose had to do to prepare for the final and then making the sound of someone sobbing.

'Rose needs to go to make-up.' [tears]

'Rose needs to get her hair done.' [tears]

'We need Rose for an interview.' [tears]

'Rose is in the toilet.' [tears]

'I know,' says Giovanni, gesticulating wildly as only an Italian can. 'I even cried when she went to the toilet! I didn't want it to finish. I was a complete mess. I am addicted to her. She wasn't just a great dancer. She was wonderful to be around and just so funny. When we went up to see Claudia, I had no idea what she was going to say. I have got to tell you; she completely ruined my reputation. She killed off the "Italian Stallion",' he says laughing.

'People keep telling me I have changed, but I think the truth is that Rose brought out a different side of me. On *Strictly*, you get used to people saying you are sexy or attractive, but with Rose it was completely different. After our amazing Couple's Choice, the whole nation is in tears, and Rose tells Claudia that I have horrible feet, like Gollum! She said she didn't like being so close to me in the Argentine tango because I had "smelly breath". She would always talk about me being too sweaty and I used to tell her that people would pay a lot of money for that. She didn't care. That's Rose. I have never had a partner like her before and I loved it. I wasn't nervous when we were in the final like I have been in the past, because I knew that what Rose had done was bigger than all of that. In one sense, we had already won.' He stops and has a little giggle to himself. 'But, it was still nice to lift the trophy.'

'I reacted when Gio reacted,' says Rose. 'I didn't hear my name, but I knew from his scream that it was us and I just went completely blank. I was out of my body. I couldn't feel anything. It was like my eyeballs were coming out of my head. Everything closed in. I felt like . . . that's it. We've done it.'

Donna was even more of a mess at the side of the dance floor. 'I remember thinking, "It's going to be Rose", "It might not be Rose", "She's going to win" . . . "It's going to be John and Johannes". It went on for ages. I was trying to take everything in and enjoy the moment, but I also just wanted Tess (Daly) to get on with it. And then, before I knew it, it was all over. I remember crying because I was sad that I wasn't going to watch her dance again.'

'I felt the same,' says Rose. 'If you'd have said to me that night that it was possible for me to dance for another ten weeks, I'd have done it in a heartbeat. We spoke to Claudia and then Gio and I just burst into tears. We knew that was the end.'

It was an emotional night for Giovanni. 'Donna came up to me and thanked me for what I had done for Rose,' he says, 'and that set me off again. She told me that I had made her feel more confident and that I had changed her life forever. I am just a dance teacher but that was so special. I went off to thank everybody and Rose and Donna had some time on their own.'

I took a photo of Rose and Donna having that 'time on their own' and the following morning, I posted it on social media. You can find it in the photo section. The caption said this:

Of all the photos from last night ... this might be my favourite. Rose's mum knows how hard she has worked, how many barriers she has had to run through, how many times she has been told 'no' and how much all this means. That's why I voted for her from day one.

Donna remembers the moment well. 'The lights went off and the sparkle just sort of disappeared. I was watching as everyone was looking at my daughter and I needed some "mum-time" with her. I think I just said, "Well done." I think that was enough. I couldn't really speak.'

'I was still in shock until Mum came and gave me a hug,' remembers Rose. 'She sort of snapped me out of it. Do you remember, Mum? I was surprised that it affected you so much.'

'I know,' says Donna. 'I wasn't sad. I was so happy for you. I didn't need to say anything because you knew it already. You had worked so hard for so long, doing everything in the public eye with everyone talking about you. I had bottled all of that up and it just all came out ... It was just little Rose up there.'

They look at each other for some time. Remembering the moment before Rose breaks the silence. 'The only person who knew me before all this was my mum. She is the one who understood why it was important. I didn't want to get a pity vote, and I think we won because I became a good dancer and that was all because of Gio. He always wanted more from me. He wanted quality in my movement. He kept teaching me to finish and to shape things and to use my body. He was never happy to just do well. "You can always give me more," he used to say ... and he was right. He believed in me more than I believed in myself. He was exactly the person I needed him to be.'

I loved my time on *Strictly*. I don't think I will ever have as much fun as I did in those three months of dancing and learning alongside Nadiya, but a huge part of the enjoyment came from being a small part of a very special series. Each Saturday, I was mesmerised by Rose and, sitting on the *BBC Breakfast* sofa every week, I got to see that the rest of the country felt exactly the same. Every couple would get letters sent to them each week which would arrive at Elstree on a Saturday morning. Most of us could carry them in one hand; Rose and Giovanni needed a bag for life! I was desperate to include them in this book because they are the epitome of what it is to lift others up. Donna never allowed Rose to think she was anything other than special. At times it was a fight, but she dug in, time and time again, and made sure that her daughter had the same opportunities as everyone else. Giovanni lifted Rose up – literally – to allow her to shine on that dance floor. He worked hard to make sure her deafness was never an obstacle. He turned it into a superpower! And then there is Rose. The 'deaf girl' who fine-tuned all our senses, and gave us a much-needed kick up the backside at the same time.

She inspired and highlighted the deaf community.

She made the biggest show on the box far more inclusive and turned Saturday-night television into a force for societal change.

While changing others, I asked Rose, Donna and Giovanni how the experience has changed them. 'I woke up on a Monday morning after *Strictly*, says Giovanni, 'and I think I was talking to you on the TV and it hit me . . . I am not going to see Rose today. It was horrible. I don't mind telling you, I am addicted to Rose! You cannot stay away from her. She is contagious. I have to talk to her every day

'But seriously,' he says, composing himself, 'I have done the show for seven years and I have never thought about deaf people. I learned from her that all things are possible, and I think I have a responsibility now to make other people aware. At my solo tour now, we have a section where we do the sign for clapping instead of clapping, like we did on *Strictly*. I do a little bit of sign language myself in the show. We can all do that – just a little bit. I have deaf people coming to the show for the first time. I have an interpreter for the first time. We had the same thing on the live *Strictly* tour. It's better than a standing ovation and it's all because of Rose. She should be a dame. She has changed the world. She has made me think about so much. What do I do as a dancer? What can I achieve? I can do a good dance. I can win a competition but, what she did, what we did together, is so much bigger than any of that. If she was here now, I would say . . . I would say thank you "Rose," he says, as if speaking to her, "you made me a better person, you made me more kind, you made me more aware, you made me less selfish and you taught me to enjoy what I have and to remember to not be in a rush. You showed me the importance of joy and happiness." We all forget that sometimes. Rose can do anything she wants in life. A deaf person can win *Strictly*.' He says it again and shouts it at me. 'A DEAF PERSON CAN

WIN *STRICTLY*! I know you don't swear, Dan, but write this down . . . If Rose can do that, if you have the right mindset, you can do whatever the $%££ you want. I'm dreaming big for Rose. I look forward to her inviting me to do the opening dance at the Oscars one day when she picks up the top prize. There is no stopping her.'

Rose and Donna are sitting having a chat, like they do most days. This time, they are reflecting on that *Strictly* win and what it means to the pair of them going forward.

'I learned that I can be confident in myself,' says Rose after much thought. 'I can be myself. I learned most of all about how, even at your lowest, you can still keep going even if your body is crashing. I didn't think I had that in me. I was always comfortable when I did exercise. I did swimming or yoga. I never understood why people pushed their body to the limit, but that is where you learn so much about yourself. You go into survival mode, and you realise what and who you really are. I was confident in private before *Strictly*, but I am now that way in public. I used to have to be so careful but, during the show, I would just go up to Claudia and whatever came out was fine. I don't need to plan what I say anymore. I can just be me.'

'What about what you showed people about the deaf community, Rose?' asks her mum.

'I think people saw that sign language is beautiful,' says a reflective *Strictly* champion. 'They learned how different deaf people could be. When I talk to deaf people now, they say, "You started the conversation". People aren't frightened anymore. Anyone can do anything.'

'For me,' says Donna, 'people have learned that it's ok to ask questions. They will ask me all sorts of stuff and, for the first time, they are interested in the answers. That's a big change. Rose won't like this, but she taught me to be brave. Rose was so courageous to go on a show that was about dancing and music. I know she did it to make people more aware and that makes me feel even more emotional. She showed me that I could be brave. I'm more confident now. I'm quite a shy person. Everyone wanted to talk to me, and I have become more confident and don't worry so much. That's all because of Rose.'

'It does get a bit scary sometimes,' admits Rose. 'I went on the tour and there were posters of me, books with me on them, T-shirts and everything. Before *Strictly*, I could do anything, and people didn't care. I was wondering if this is what my life is going to be like forever, but thankfully it has relaxed a bit now.'

'You can go back to Sainsburys now, can't you, Rose?' laughs Donna.

Rose rolls her eyes and brings things back to the big issues. 'I'm glad we've managed to use the awareness to make a difference and get British Sign Language to be recognised as a language. The government can't just sweep it under the carpet. They can't do that anymore. It has to go further. I want to make a documentary about that, and I still want to do what I love. I feel responsible, I'll keep fighting, but I also want to enjoy life. I know we used to say, "Keep dancing", Dan, but it's "Keep acting" for me now.'

'I would love to see her play an evil character in a movie!' says Donna. 'I want her to be in a film which really pushes her . . . a baddy! Something to really test her. I know she can do it. She can do anything.'

'Mum!' says Rose.

'What?' says a proud Donna. 'I watched you at the BSL [British Sign Language] rally in Trafalgar Square. Tell Dan about it.'

'It was amazing, Dan,' says Rose, full of enthusiasm. 'It's the first time I have seen such big a group of deaf people and they were so kind. They said I had changed their lives and one said that she had been discriminated against at work for so long and had taken them to court. She said she saw me on *Strictly* and thought, "I will never give up." Soon after that she won her case because, she said, attitudes were changing. Isn't that amazing? It's a bit overwhelming sometimes. I only danced on a show!'

'It was brilliant to watch her that day,' says Donna. 'It was a big moment for me, as her mum. She got on the stage, and she signed a speech. She presented it really well. It blew me away. She signed a poem. It was like watching someone from the UN. I cried!'

'Oh, Mum,' says Rose, in a mixture of embarrassment but obvious love.

'I have to remind myself,' says Donna, 'my daughter won *Strictly Come Dancing*!'

They both laugh.

'You're never going to stop going on about it, are you, Mum?'

'No, and why should I? A deaf girl, my daughter, won *Strictly*, and millions of people watched you do it. You showed me, you showed everyone, that nothing is impossible.'

THREE DADS, THREE DAUGHTERS

I want to tell you about Sophie, Beth and Emily – three young women with so much to give.

Sophie was bold and brash. She was very loud, always entering a room with a raucous 'hiya'. She was just a fun person to be with. She had always been incredibly sociable. For much of her life, Sophie lived in Kendal in the Lake District and used to love walking the fells with her dad.

Everyone always said how considerate she was. She always thought about other people and was really well liked. She was deputy head girl at senior school but she also discovered alcohol and boys before going to Newcastle University to study history. She hated it and by Christmas had dropped out. She made a pact with her parents that she wouldn't just lounge about and she learned to drive, had her tonsils taken out and ended up going to Kenya for four months where she worked in an orphanage. Sophie came back from that trip and announced she was going to be a nurse. Her caring and empathetic nature made her a brilliant nurse. Sophie met a lad called Sam. They fell in love, moved to Edinburgh – where she worked at the Western General Hospital – and got married.

Beth was a wonderful person. She was tactile, loving, happy, always the centre of attention. She was born later in the year so was always the youngest in her class, but was incredibly popular at school – always the centre of attention. She loved going out and was a huge fan of Harry Potter and Johnny Depp.

During her time at secondary school, Beth developed a talent for singing. She was a natural dancer and was always right at the front of any performance. Her mum was a professional dancer and Beth had clearly inherited that talent. All her friends saw her as loving and loyal.

She went to a performing arts college after school and was brilliant. She started gigging around Manchester. It was her dream to be on the stage.

Emily was a brilliant artist. She was also the life and soul of every party, but the public perception was very different to what was happening in private. She was struggling through life. At 16, she was diagnosed with autism. That private diagnosis was a huge breakthrough. It helped Emily know why she was different and her family all noticed a big change. She wanted to keep the autism quiet though, and only her family and a few close friends knew about what she was going through.

Disguising the autism took a lot of effort – effort that would leave her completely wiped out. After her GCSEs, Emily went on to art college, did a personal training course and she learned to drive. That was so important to her because it gave her the freedom she was lacking. She worked in the village pub which had been bought by the local community. It was never her plan for that to be her forever job, but it was really good for her. The job, combined with the freedom of being able to drive and the ability to regularly go to the gym, kept Emily going.

Sophie, Beth and Emily: a nurse, a performer and an artist.

Three young women adored by their families.

Three young women with so much going for them.

Three young women who all took their own lives.

Three young women who all left behind three broken dads.

Three dads who it has been my privilege to meet and interview on several occasions.

Three dads on a mission to make a difference.

Andy is Sophie's father. Sophie was a daughter from his first marriage to George. Andy is now married to Fiona but everyone had a great relationship with Sophie. Andy and Fiona have a son, Gregor, who is nine years younger than Sophie.

'When I look back now,' says Andy, 'I can see that she struggled to get her head around who she was. There was a period, when she was at university, where I think she had that feeling of not knowing what she was going to do with her life. There was a weight of uncertainty. She was very much like me.' He pauses and looks upwards. 'She was always internalising. You convince yourself that you don't need help and you are sure that the best thing to do is just deal with it yourself.'

Sophie was in her late twenties and living in Edinburgh with her husband, Sam. 'I was in contact with her all the time,' says Andy with a huge smile on his face. 'We saw her regularly and, every time we did, she seemed fine. Her and Sam were living what looked like a great life. We talked about stuff. If I was worried about her, she would listen to me and would always answer questions.

'In September 2018, they came and stayed with us in Kendal on a Saturday night. During the day, Fi and I had taken Gregor to university in Liverpool. We expected Sophie and Sam to be there when we got back but, as we were driving back down the road, we got a tearful call from Soph to say she'd left Sam and she was struggling. She said she didn't love him anymore. Both Fi and I were stumped. Where had this come from? We went to Edinburgh the next day and brought her back home with us. I had never seen her that low . . . it felt like she was self-destructing.'

Andy knew that relationships changed and that people split up all the time. Sophie was sad, but there was nothing that suggested what she was going through was life-threatening.

Andy continues, 'For the next couple months she tried to sort herself out. She got herself a new flat a little nearer to the hospital. She had a new job to look forward to which started just after Christmas, and it looked like she was pulling her life back together. Sophie was down every now and again, but there was nothing that I looked at that made me worry. Things were looking up.'

Sophie turned twenty-nine on 12 December 2018. She took her own life seven days later, just before Christmas. Andy will never forget that day.

'I remember we were in Boots in Carlisle on the afternoon of the 19th. It sounds crazy now, but we had booked in to get our yellow fever injections because we were planning on going to visit Fi's brother who lived in Gambia. Like a typical dad, I had somehow managed to bum-dial Sophie while this was happening. She was in the car at the time.' Andy pauses and smiles as he remembers Sophie's response to a typically embarrassing dad. 'She was telling me how stupid I was and we were laughing together. I apologised for being daft and we said goodbye and I put the phone back in my pocket.' Andy later found out that at that precise moment, Sophie was on her way to take her own life.

I cannot imagine what it must be like to lose a daughter or a son like that. I know you're probably reading this at the moment and thinking . . . where is the light in all of this? Where is the way out? Where is the hope? Believe me, it's coming and, strangely, Andy is one of those who provides the hope with a little bit of help from two other dads called Tim and Mike.

Tim is Emily's dad. I'm sure everyone reading this will have very strong memories of what it was like when we went into coronavirus lockdown in March 2020. Tim has a particularly vivid memory because that was the week that things started to unravel for nineteen-year-old Emily.

'It was the week when everything was changing. Gyms were closed, the pub was closing and then on 16 March some people in the family started to cough. The next day Emily started to cough. There were three things she really needed in her life to keep things ticking over: the gym for the physical release, working in the pub for money and being able to drive around in the car for freedom. All of those were taken away in the space of a few days. Things changed very quickly with Emily. We were locked down in the house and had a lovely Monday and Tuesday watching Disney films but she woke the next day incredibly agitated. She was desperate to take the car to the coast and take our dog for a walk but we said "no" because she had symptoms and we were one of those families who were carefully following the rules.'

By the end of that day Emily had tried to take her own life. The family have understandably asked that I don't go into details of what Emily did, but she was in a bad way. Her own dad tried to resuscitate her after finding her at the family home. After twenty minutes of CPR, he'd managed to find a heartbeat but then came the hospital experience that so many people found during the middle of the pandemic.

'Because of her symptoms, Emily went into a Covid ward and we couldn't see her for two days,' says Tim. 'She tested negative and we finally got to see her on that Friday in a normal intensive care ward. Things weren't looking good. She'd signed up to be an organ donor when she was younger and by Friday evening, we were having that discussion with the team at the hospital. The Saturday was a long day as the transplant team tried to line up recipients. You can imagine that the pandemic was causing all sorts of issues for the people involved. On Sunday, just after midday, Emily's life support was turned off. The fact that her organs were donated was the only light in a sea of darkness. Thinking about that is what gets me through some days. It was the following day that the Prime Minister appeared on television to announce the nationwide lockdown.'

Tim is married to Sue. Annabel, Tom and Evie are Emily's surviving siblings. Tom, who was fourteen at the time, was the one who called 999 that day. Both Tom and Evie, who was only nine, saw their dad performing CPR on their sister. Those are scars which don't heal easily and the whole family had the gruesome experience of a lockdown funeral and the brutal brevity of saying goodbye to someone you love.

'We couldn't see her at the undertakers,' explains a tearful Tim. 'We were all so terrified of getting Covid and not being able to go to her funeral that we just kept ourselves to ourselves. People dropped off food at the house but we didn't spend time with anyone in the build-up to her funeral. There was only a twenty-five-minute service at the crematorium. That was it. Just six of us went to the funeral – the five of us and our eldest daughter's boyfriend. It was all over in a flash, and we were back home by 10.30 in the morning with the rest of our lives – without Emily – ahead of us. I've never seen someone in as many pieces as my wife was that day. She was totally broken. I remember that after the funeral, Sue said, "She's gone and no one will remember her in a year's time." That is one of the hardest things to get your head around, but it was also one of the things that convinced me that I had to find a way out of the pain and the misery. I had to try and find something to cling on to.'

One of those things which Tim found was companionship.

Strength came from talking to people who had been through the same heartache as him. Eventually it would be Andy, but it started with Beth's dad, Mike.

Mike lives in Manchester with his wife Helen. He has a daughter, Charley, from his first marriage, and Emily, who was Beth's sister, with Helen.

Beth was seventeen when she took her own life. It was just five days after Tim's Emily had died in Norfolk. Mike, like everyone who has lost a family member or friend to suicide, has spent hours, sometimes days, mulling over things she did and said before she died.

'Looking back,' says Mike, 'I can see she was losing hope. She was great at the singing, but I think her music was becoming slower, maudlin. I can see now that she had lost the bounce and the power. In the months before she left us, she had become quite moody and dark with the music. I remember all the conversations.'

He pauses. It looks like he is going back over things in his head. Suddenly, he jumps back into the conversation. 'It was at that time that only one person was allowed to go shopping. I remember that week I'd worked hard in the garden so we could spend time in there during lockdown. Beth had been going for a few runs with her sister, but she wasn't really herself. The day before it happened, she hadn't got out of bed, so I went into her room at midday and told her to get up. She told me she was having a bad day. I told her to stop being ridiculous, to get things together and to come downstairs. She did come down and played with the dog. The next day I remember her coming down from her room. I had loads of phone calls that day and in the evening I had to go to work.' Mike is a firefighter at Manchester airport.

'I was doing a bit of a workout just outside the house and I looked inside to see that Beth was chatting to her mum. She went down into our cellar which is where she used to go to practise her signing. I heard her voice in there. I used to love listening to her. She had such a beautiful voice. I'd finished my workout and I was getting ready for work. I went down to the cellar to get my coat, but I remember that I decided not to go in because I didn't want to interrupt her recording. I went to work and came home early in the morning and me and Helen went out for a dog walk. We talked about getting the girls out a bit more, so they didn't feel so cooped up. We got back to the house and had breakfast. The girls weren't down yet but there was nothing unusual about that.'

Mike, as he usually did after a nightshift, went for a snooze on the sofa. 'I was woken up at about 12. I heard screaming. Helen had gone into Beth's bedroom and found her body. I ran upstairs . . . my legs were like lead . . . I knew she was dead as I sprinted to her room. Emily was up and I raced into Beth's room and slammed the door on the rest of the family. I wouldn't let them in. I didn't want them to see her. I am a first responder. I'd used defibs many times and I knew she wasn't coming back. It wasn't long before the paramedics arrived, and they confirmed what we already knew. She was gone

'That is the worst day of your life. A nightmare that never finishes. Tears wouldn't come at first. It just didn't happen. It was just absolute horror and shock. The police turned up, a friend across the road turned up. That day will never leave me. I go through it every day . . . every day.'

The words are just pouring out of Mike at this point. 'The guilt comes from missing behaviour that is unusual. Beth had maybe started to become a little eccentric and annoying at mealtimes and that wasn't her. She was pushing the boundaries of going out, but she was seventeen and she was at music college. "Dad, you don't understand," she would say. "I'm having a bad day." I just wish I'd opened my eyes a bit more,' says Mike. 'Why couldn't I see that she was going from a high to a low so often? I remember talking to her about getting some new equipment for her singing and she just wasn't interested. Now I look at that like a red flag. I wish I'd had the knowledge then that I have now.'

In my last book I wrote about the death of Gary Speed. That was over ten years ago, and I still think all the time about the final day I spent with him before he took his own life. There are many questions I ask myself about things I could or should have seen, things I could have asked about and whether he'd still be here if I'd done something differently that day. I have gone over the day in minute detail. Gary was a good friend of mine, but I imagine when the person you lose is a daughter the pain is magnified, and the questions never stop. That is certainly how Mike feels.

'The opportunity arose to talk to Beth the day before and I

missed it, he says. 'My wife Helen feels the same and she, just like me, is wracked with grief and remorse. Helen couldn't be a better mother. She doted on Beth and couldn't have done more for her, but here we both are without a daughter, wondering if we could have done more to help her.'

Mike himself needed help. He was spiralling into a dark place. That help would come from an unusual source. In Norfolk, Annabel, Tim's eldest, sent a message to Mike's daughter, Emily. She'd seen what the family were going through and decided to reach out. Emily showed the message to Mike, who ended up talking to Annabel on the phone.

'She suggested that I talk to her dad, to Tim,' remembers Mike. 'I was desperate. I had tried a support group, but I just didn't get it. I didn't know what to say or how to say it, but for some reason, I thought I could talk to Tim. It was the best thing I ever did.'

I have had the privilege of meeting hundreds of people over many years of interviews who have been through incredibly low moments in their lives. It may be illness, trauma, loss, fear, so many things which have the ability to bruise or crush us. I have always been fascinated by the way people pull themselves out of the mire. So many of those stories involve talking to someone who has fallen into the same hole as you; someone who carries the same scars, who has had the same thoughts and carries the same burdens. Tim, Mike and Andy are a classic example of gathering strength and finding a reason in a shared experience, however grim that experience continues to be.

So how was it for Tim to find out that his twenty-one-year-old daughter, Annabel, was talking to a dad in Manchester? I ask the pair of them that question together and they both laugh. Mike turns to Tim with a look on his face that suggests he is quite interested in the answer.

'It was so odd at first. Forgive me, Mike,' Tim says with a big grin on his face, 'but it is a little weird to discover that your daughter is speaking to a strange bloke hundreds of miles away. This was just three weeks after the deaths of our daughters. It was a strange way to start a friendship, but we quickly found common ground. Mike is a firefighter and I used to fly Tornados. Both our daughters were very artistic and brilliant singers. We were both in a very similar place and we both had other children. I remember being really frank about where we were. We just held each other's hands all the way through the inquests. We were just speaking to each other and going through what we could learn from each other. Everything we had planned and built for our families had gone. It's a strange foundation for a relationship but it worked.'

Mike jumps in. 'You've got to remember, Dan, I had no one. I was desperate. I'd tried grief counselling, but it just wasn't working. I was in a place where I didn't even know how to talk to anyone about it. What do you say when you've lost a daughter like that? How do you even begin to see your way out of that? My way out of that started with Tim.'

Tim has an incredible memory for dates and names. Out of the three dads, he is the one who writes everything down: when things happened, who was there, who said what. Several times during our conversations he asks me to wait a moment while he flicks through his notes to check the name of someone or the exact time that something took place. Unsurprisingly, he has a clear memory of that first conversation with Mike.

'I remember we had so much in common. We both had a link through aviation. I was in the RAF and Mike worked at Manchester airport. We both had families; families who were struggling. Most painfully, we'd both given CPR to our daughters. We spoke graphically about those final moments; things you wouldn't think you could say to anyone, but with that openness and honesty you find a validation for how you are feeling and how someone else feels. I needed Mike and he needed me. I just instantly knew that this was a man who knew what I was going through. I didn't have to explain to him the depths of my feelings because he was there too.' Mike nods in agreement and adds that Tim was always there in the dark times for him.

'The best thing about it,' explains Tim, 'is that I could call him at any time. Professional help really works for some people but it's always at an allotted time. We could call each other whenever we needed it.'

'The most important thing for me,' adds Mike, 'is that I felt no shame talking to Tim. There were no areas that I felt I needed to conceal from him. Sometimes the tears just flowed. Sometimes you couldn't find the words and you just listened. We just discussed everything brutally and openly and with no shame, which was so important for me.'

Grief is such a complex issue. It affects people in all sorts of ways. One thing that all three of the dads said to me when they spoke to me in the studio, on the phone or in person was that they felt I understood what they were going through. All three of them referenced the death of Gary Speed and how they had seen how that had affected me deeply. I am well aware there is a big difference between losing a friend and losing a daughter, but there is common ground. There are the complicated feelings of guilt mixed with sadness and anger. There is an overwhelming sense of loss combined with a helplessness and a nagging – sometimes crippling – feeling that you should and could have done more to help. That 'why didn't I see it?' scream that wakes you up in the middle of the night or lingers for hours in the back of your mind.

All three of the dads have been through all those emotions time and time again. What Tim and Mike felt they both needed was to know that there was a way through it all. Tim has always been incredibly practical about navigating the grief of suicide, it's the way his brain works. He saw things quite clearly quite quickly. If he and Mike were going to come through this, to find a way of living without their daughters, they needed the support of someone who had walked the path they were tentatively stepping out on. They needed Andy.

At this point, I need to mention Papyrus. Papyrus is a charity which is dedicated to the prevention of suicide, particularly in young people. Their vision is all about encouraging society to talk openly about suicide and equipping young people with the tools to deal with thoughts that could lead to them thinking about taking their own lives.

The three dads have all benefited from the work of the charity and are all passionate advocates. We'll talk about that more a little later. Papyrus was also responsible for bringing Andy into the equation.

'Our son, Gregor, was at university in Liverpool,' explains Andy, 'and the head offices of Papyrus are in Warrington. We dropped in and Gregor registered on one of their courses. He was always keen to learn and to help others. You'll never guess who he sat next to on one of his courses?'

'Gregor told me all about his rough Cumbrian dad,' giggles Mike. 'I'd already heard a little bit about him because I knew he liked walking and I'd had this silly idea about doing some sort of charity walk. I'd watched some of Andy's films online and that had got me thinking. Now, here I was sat next to his son. I thought to myself, "I'm no good at map reading, I could do with finding someone who is." Gregor said that his dad might be interested. That's where it all began.'

Andy and Mike met for a walk. It was an incredible, emotionally charged occasion. They were open and they were honest. Andy laughs as he remembers Mike producing a 2010 AA Road Map with some lines on it. Penrith was marked on there, so was Mike's house in Sale in Manchester. There was a dot at Derby and another one at King's Lynn, Tim's hometown. Mike told Andy all about Tim, and the idea of a walk between their three homes to raise awareness of suicide prevention was born.

Each of the dads was leaning on the others. The walk provided a focal point for all of them; something to concentrate on. They all speak powerfully about those dark days when death comes calling on the family home.

'I was desperate,' recalls Mike. 'I was surrounded by so many people, but I was totally alone even when I was stood next to my wife. The world completely changed. I had to go out very early in the morning to walk the dog. It was like I was walking in a parallel universe. It's quite hard to describe it to you . . . I could recognise things but nothing felt right.'

Mike composes himself for a moment and addresses the heart of the issue. 'The thing is, I couldn't have loved anything more than Beth and to lose her like that, it's overwhelming. If I'm honest, at times, I struggle with still wanting to be here myself. I even got to the point of planning it, but every day something would happen to put me off: the phone would ring, I'd have to do something for one of my daughters, or they'd say, "Dad, I'll call you tomorrow." My sister was great. I would call Lindsey in the middle of the night, just like I would call Tim. The pair of them were massive for me and there were other people like the chaplain from Manchester airport, Chaplain George. I'm not really a man of faith but he listened to me. He didn't say much but he just listened. One of the things you think about is, what happens when you die? Is that the end? It was wonderful to talk those things through with George. I started to read a lot of stuff about the afterlife.'

Mike pauses again before returning to thoughts of his own future: 'I'm not proud of it, Dan, you know, planning it. I've dealt with a lot of death through my job. I always work absolutely to my limit to save people. I was good at it. This was totally different. She had taken her own life. What went wrong? What had I done? Sometimes the knock-on effect of suicide is suicide. Every day I have to look at my wife, my daughters and the rest of the family and see the pain that they still go through.'

Sometimes anger grips Mike hard. 'It's still very much there, if I'm honest. I see what it has done to the people she loved. I think a lot about the whole issue of forgiveness. Is it a case of us forgiving Beth for what she did, or is it about us forgiving ourselves for not seeing her pain? It feels like life is a fight. A fight with your mind and for positive mental health. There are so many questions I will never be able to answer. Was it a teenage thing? Was she cross with us? The police took her laptop and her phone and there was nothing on there to indicate she was thinking about it. The thing is she's gone . . . I can't talk to her but there are two things that drive me on: trying to better understand why Beth might have taken her own life and trying to stop others from doing the same. That is a huge part of the healing process for me. I was a dad. I was Beth's dad, and I didn't see this coming. I just want other dads, other parents out there, to be able to see things more clearly than I did and to talk to their children before it's too late.'

Tim asks himself the same questions that rattle around Mike's head. 'I often wonder why she felt she couldn't tell us how she was feeling,' says Tim. You can tell by his delivery that it's a question which weighs heavily on his mind. 'Why didn't we let her go out driving that day? If only we had let her. We all think that if we'd let her go to the coast that day then she'd have been fine. She'd still be here. We have a nephew who lives in Northern Italy, and he was telling us how bad it was there, and we all felt that we were just a couple of weeks behind. I think that concern about the future just got on top of Emily. She couldn't see a way out.'

Tim pauses and gathers his thoughts for a moment. 'What could I have said to her? I think about that a lot. We were doing the right thing by society by not letting her go out, but not the right thing by our family.'

When I first spoke to Tim for this book it was right in the middle of the revelations about parties at Downing Street during lockdown. I asked him if he found that hard to process given that he and his family tried so hard to stick to the rules during that period and they still feel that Emily might be here now, if the government had been willing to relax them slightly. He takes his time to respond. A smile comes across his face, and he looks at me. I can see there is great wisdom behind his eyes. 'I think I need to be very careful about what I say here, Dan.' Safe to say that Tim and his wife share the view of many people who lost loved ones during the pandemic. 'We felt we were doing our bit to save lives, to help others. We listened to the politicians. We followed what they said. We did what they asked and because we did that, we lost Emily that day. The idea that the rule-makers weren't following their own regulations leaves us with a bitter taste in the mouth.'

Emily's ashes were scattered down in Cornwall. The family are trying hard to move on. Emily's brother and sister started to go back to school in the September after they lost her, but every little step has been hard. Tim couldn't handle the memories of their old house. He couldn't bear to be there. 'We'd spent our whole lives dreaming of this house. I built it. It was overlooking fields and it was beautiful, but it was also the place our daughter died and it will always be stained by those memories. All our life plans were completely blown out of the water.'

There were two incidents which had a huge impact on Tim. They were two crucial steps on his way out of the grief. The first is something we've already mentioned. It was his wife, Sue, saying after Emily's funeral that no one would remember her. That forced Tim to think about doing something to make sure that never happened. The second was a bizarre situation which came about after his mother-in-law fell down the stairs of her home in Coventry.

'About four weeks after Emily died, Sue's mum hurt herself. She broke her ankle falling down those stairs, so we all decided that the best thing for her to do was to come and stay with us. We didn't have a spare room so that meant our only option was to clear Emily's room for her to stay in. Up to that point we hadn't touched a thing in there. The police had gone through all her stuff, but it was exactly how she had left it. We started clearing it out and I took a cloth bag out of her wardrobe. As I picked it up a piece of folded paper fell out of it. It was a suicide note.' Tim stops for a moment, recalling the emotion of that day.

'The police must have missed it because it was so thin and easy to gloss over. I opened it up and collapsed as I read it. I'm so glad she wrote it, but I can't tell you how hard it was to read. She said she felt she was a burden and that she couldn't cope.

She wrote that she could see no other option and she asked us not to worry about anything.'

I am struggling to hold in the tears as I think about Tim finding the precious note from his daughter. He is taking regular pauses as he recalls perhaps the most important thing he has ever read.

'Two sentences really got me. There were two things in there which changed my life. Emily had written "don't be ashamed of what I've done" and also, and even more importantly, she said "if others can learn from what I'd done, please let them". I knew I had to do something. I knew that Mike had rowed the Atlantic before, so he was intrepid. I knew he was planning some sort of walk but what we needed to make it all happen was someone like Andy. Not only was he an expert adventurer but he became the man who showed me what the next chapter of my life could look like. I kept thinking, how do I get out of bed in the morning? How do I get beyond today? Andy was the man with the answers.'

'Do you remember that day when I called Sophie in Boots from my pocket?' says Andy. 'Well, that night we came home, Gregor was back from university and he was working in a pub up the road. He'd done it since he was fifteen. I remember there was a ping on the family group chat: a message from Soph. "I love you all so much," it said. The words just didn't seem right. They didn't ring true. That wasn't Sophie. The house phone went, it was her mum, George, in a right state. She had been called by

Sophie's husband, Sam, who had just had a long text from Soph saying "sorry" and telling him that she was going to kill herself. She told him where to find the car and said please don't bury me. He'd called the police.'

When Andy told me this I was rooted to the spot. I was meant to be taking notes on the interview, but it's one of those times when your mind races and you think about what you would do in the same situation. How would any parent react if they are told that their daughter, who is about 130 miles and three hours away in a car, has probably taken her own life? The shock and despair kick in straightaway. It's not a scenario that ever crosses your mind. Andy did the only thing that he felt he could do. He got in a car and drove to Edinburgh. That was the worst journey of his life. Sophie's mum, George, and her uncle, Bill, also made their way to Scotland. They were all as lost as each other.

'It's amazing how so many things bring it all back to you,' explains Andy. 'I was watching TV recently and that show *Anne* was on; the one where Anne Williams (played by Maxine Peake) loses her son at the Hillsborough Disaster. Her son has gone missing, and she and her husband face that awful drive from Liverpool across to Sheffield. That's what we felt on the drive up to Edinburgh that day. What were we heading into? What would we find?'

They got to Sam's flat. Sophie's friends and the police were there. All the family could do was to sit and wait. The police found the car but there was no sign of Sophie. No one was able to sleep. Andy was still awake in the early hours of the morning.

What were they meant to do? They went and checked into the Premier Inn down the road feeling desperately lost and alone.

'We phoned as many people as we could,' remembers Andy. 'I was just trying to get the message out there. I put an appeal out on social media just trying to get people to help us find our beautiful daughter. I'd had some dealings with Alison Freeman who worked for the BBC in Newcastle. She was presenting the regional news programme that night and she mentioned the appeal. We were helpless. We sat there for a couple of days and eventually decided there was simply nothing we could do. We came back home and just sat and waited. We got a phone call on that Saturday morning to say that they'd found Soph's body. That was it. Confirmation of what we had known. She had gone. Our daughter had gone.'

Suicide leaves a mess. There is so much wreckage to try and sift through both physically and emotionally. Sophie had signed up to run a half-marathon which finished in Bamburgh. Andy knew he needed something to fill the void, so he tried to sign up to do it himself. There were no places left so he had to call the organisers and explain that his daughter had died, and that he would love to take her place in the race. That was the start of #RunForSophie. Andy started a video diary of his training. The physical effort gave him something to occupy his mind. It was essential to his well-being in those first few months after Sophie's death.

'I didn't really realise what I was doing,' says Andy, who used to run mountain marathons in what he describes as his 'more active' days. 'It gave me this laser focus going forwards.

My only concern was what was going to happen to me after the run. Thankfully, what actually happened was, over the space of a few months, I became heavily involved in Papyrus. It was a real help to me. In a relatively short space of time, I became some sort of suicide prevention guru. It wasn't long after that that I met these two fellas called Tim and Mike.'

Andy saw quite a bit of himself in the other dads when they all met up together. Mike was the one who carried the heaviest weight of guilt. He often finds himself in a trough of despair. He finds himself getting stuck in the anger and the guilt. It's lovely that they are able to help each other through the darkness. Mike reminded Andy of himself in those early days. 'He was in the desperate place,' recalls Andy. 'You try and live your life, but you just can't help yourself falling into it. Mike was going there regularly. I just saw the pain and the anguish. Tim and I have a very similar attitude to it all and we've been able to bring Mike with us. I think we can see where we want to start and where we want to get to.'

What really strikes you when you speak to Mike, Tim and Andy is their determination to try and find a way out of the wreckage. They all came to the realisation that the best way to help themselves and their families was to help others. 'I would sometimes sit there and say, "we can't let this knacker our lives forever,"' remembers Andy. 'None of the girls would have wanted the situation to strangle us and that's why the walk became such an important focal point.'

The idea of walking between their houses seemed like a simple one. No one ever expected it to turn into the epic journey it became. In September of 2021 they set a tentative target of raising £3,000 each. The premise was a pretty simple one: three dads, three homes, 300 miles raising £3,000. 'Do you remember how guilty we all felt when we made it £10,000 each guys?' asks Tim. Mike and Andy drop their heads in mock shame with big smiles on their faces. 'We felt bad because we didn't want to ask so much of our friends and families,' says Tim, 'but, for whatever reason, it just felt like it was the right thing to do.'

The plan was to walk for fifteen days, starting on 9 October at Andy's house in Morland, and finishing on 23 October in Shouldham with Tim and his family. The whole route with timings was posted on the 3 Dads Walking website so that people could come and support them or join them on the way.

It was at this point that I met the 3 Dads for the first time. I got to meet so many guests on the *BBC Breakfast* sofa but there are always some individuals who really stick with you. Mike came on the sofa with Ged Flynn, the CEO of Papyrus, and was captivating. I could see the sadness in his eyes but also the hope that the walk had given him. He talked with such love about Beth, and the heartache was just as real as his obvious desire to try and see if they could do something to help anyone who found themselves in the same position as his daughter.

The *BBC Breakfast* audience is loyal and generous, and when they get behind a story it is something quite special. Mike came on the sofa on 28 September with the total hovering around £10,000. By the end of the day, it was five times that.

In the weeks before the walk started, we spoke to all three of them on the sofa and their story was gathering pace and some high-profile supporters, as Tim can explain.

'I was at Wigan station catching the train to see Andy when I heard that Daniel Craig was going to donate £10,000,' he recalls. 'The actual James Bond! I read the WhatsApp message from the charity, and I just sat on the floor and started crying straightaway. I must have looked like a complete idiot.'

'What about the letter from Prince William?' chirps Mike. 'It was so touching. It doesn't matter where you are in society, it affects all sorts of people.' I told the dads that I made a documentary about mental health with Prince William a few years before. It was all about addressing the stigma that surrounds men and how they feel. We sat in a dressing room at Cambridge United and William (he said we could call him that) was alongside the England coach Gareth Southgate, French World Cup winner Thierry Henry, England international Danny Rose, pundit and presenter Jermaine Jenas and former footballer Peter Crouch. They all spoke about some of the struggles they had faced in their careers. It was incredible to watch how, as each one of them opened up, it encouraged the others to follow. William was so engaged that day. I think he wanted to lead from the front and show that if he was willing to speak honestly it might encourage and help others. The 3 Dads were following in the same footsteps.

James Bond was followed by another £10,000 donation from Nicole Kidman, who had seen the interview on *BBC Breakfast*. 'I was over in the UK filming *Aquaman 2*,' says the Hollywood superstar. 'I was getting ready to leave for filming that day when I caught the item on *BBC Breakfast* about the 3 Dads. I had a huge mix of emotions. It was utterly devastating to think about what they had been through and what they were doing in memory of their daughters. Despite that, they were so strong, and determined to make a difference for every child. You couldn't help but be truly inspired by them and the journey they were on.'

I asked her about that leap from being moved by a story to wanting to help. 'Who wouldn't?' says Nicole. 'Their story inspired not just me, but people around the world. What they did, what they started, and why they did it, mattered then, and continues to resonate. I honestly think it would be impossible not to be deeply moved by theirs and their daughters' stories. As a parent, we all do everything we can to protect our children, and so the loss of a child hits hard, and I can feel nothing but huge empathy for them.'

Nicole doesn't want to go into any details about personal loss but, like many people who watched and supported Tim, Mike and Andy, she was touched by the beautiful bond between father and daughter, between fathers and daughters. 'As a daughter to the sweetest father,' she says, 'I really connected with them. The care and the love they showed really reminded me of my own dad.'

Nicole's testimony says a lot about her but also a lot about the power of story and the impact the 3 Dads were able to have on so many people. She's right, it was impossible to watch them and not be moved, to not be touched by their love and their loss and their desire to try and protect others from the pain that had ripped their lives apart. Nicole, like thousands of others, has continued to follow their stories since watching them for the first time that morning.

'I keep an eye on them on social media and it's incredible to see their continued work, and the difference they are also making to Papyrus, who they were fundraising for. If I could pass on a message to them it would be this: I would send them love, I would send them strength and I would want them to know about the huge admiration I have for them, both now and always.'

The donations just kept coming. There was £10,001 from former Manchester United footballer Lou Macari, who said he didn't want to be outdone by Daniel Craig. Despite the stardust, it was Macari's donation that really put a smile on Andy's face.

'Nicole Kidman and Daniel Craig were amazing; especially with the timing of the new Bond film, it couldn't have been any better, but meeting Lou Macari was a real highlight for me,' beamed Andy. 'I am a Manchester City fan, but when we were in Manchester, going to Old Trafford, meeting Lou was amazing. What a lovely bloke he was. He lost his son to suicide all the way back in 1999 so he knew about the importance of what we were doing. The extra pound was just a bit of fun. Like everyone else, he just wanted to help.'

The dads were live on *BBC Breakfast* again on the morning they set off. By lunchtime on that first day, Tim decided to turn off the JustGiving notifications on his phone because there were 2,708 of them! The money was great, but more important to all of them was what they wanted to happen along the way. They wanted to engage, they wanted to start conversations, they wanted people to come and find them and see a safe space where they could talk about loss and grief and share that burden with people who had been through it themselves. They were all blown away by what happened during those fifteen days. I asked each one of them to pick one or two people who had the biggest impact on them.

Tim has lost friends during his time in the military, and he'd had to train to deal with that loss. After losing Emily, he was self-aware enough to understand that he didn't have the toolbox to deal with the grief that was tearing into his family. He knew he needed help. He was brought up in a Baptist church but had grown cynical about what happens to religion when humans get involved. After Emily died, the local padre from RAF Marham used to come around and talk to Tim at a social distance in his back garden. They talked about everything and that helped Tim to see the importance of discussing what he was going through.

'There were so many people on that walk who, just like me, needed someone to listen,' remembers Tim. 'We met Angela and her daughter Tash who set up a charity called Bags for Strife. Angela had lost her husband and daughter to suicide, and they were both struck by the lack of practical support that is available for people when they are at their most vulnerable. They wanted to change that by allowing people who were suffering to get simple things like a water bottle, tissues – the stuff you don't think about. There were moments of laughter followed quite quickly by a huge emotional switch. I remember one day we were all eating ice-creams and started talking to a dad who had lost his wife just a couple of weeks before. He was there with his two children who just looked completely lost; like their world had imploded. We spent some time with them and then, as we left them and wandered out of the town, we all just wept as we walked.'

There were also tears when the 3 Dads were sent a poem by a lady called Helen Taylor. Mike started to read it and 'we were all blubbing,' says Tim. 'I'll send it to you, Dan, maybe you could put it in the book.'

Each day on the walk was just as emotional as it was inspirational. Each day they would set off and find various people waiting for them along the route. 'Nothing was ever forced,' says Tim. 'Most people would just say "Can I join you for a bit?" and then, after a while, we'd ask why they had come, and they'd just share their story. You learn to see grief. You can tell from people's faces what they have been through. A couple had lost their son just three weeks before they came to see us. All they wanted to do was tell us about him. They weren't ready for anything else. What really struck me was the number of people who had never spoken to anyone. A guy near Buxton had never told anyone about what happened to his son seven years ago. A lady came and told us about her dad who had taken his own life seventy years before. She finally felt able to tell someone how she felt about it. It really helped as people unburdened themselves on us.'

When I ask Mike if anyone stands out to him from the walk, he launches into a story without a breath. 'Right at the beginning, day one, there was a couple who came to see us maybe a mile from the start. They had come from Lancaster.

I could see the mum was desperate to talk. She had that pain in her eyes and she told me about their daughter. Suicide had taken her in August, and they only just had the funeral a few weeks before. She showed me the order of service from that funeral. I told her I would carry it with me for the whole walk. I kept it in a plastic bag. It meant a lot to her, and it certainly did to me. A few days later, I met a man in a Mazda sports car. He was there with his wife, and I stopped, and spoke to them. I remember he simply said, "I've joined the same club." He told me about their daughter-in-law who had died a few weeks before. A little later we came into the town of Kirkby Lonsdale. We met the dad who Tim told you about, with the two kids. We talked to him about his wife who had taken her own life. It was just so sad. Once the walk had finished, I had taken the details of the mum I spoke to on day one about the funeral, so I gave her a call to make sure she was alright. We talked about some of the other people I had met on the walk and, incredibly, it turned out that the couple in the Mazda car were talking about her daughter! They were the mother- and father-in-law of the girl whose mother I spoke to on day one and . . .' Mike continued, still amazed by what happened, '. . . the dad who we met in Kirkby Lonsdale, that was her daughter's husband, and those two children were her grandchildren! I had no idea who they were at the time, and they had no idea that I was carrying the order of service of the funeral of the gorgeous daughter-in-law, wife and mum they had so sadly lost. I will never forget that.'

Wherever they went there were people who needed them.

There was a lady waiting for them on the sea wall in Lincolnshire. She was standing on her own, getting battered by the wind. 'I've been waiting for you,' she simply said as they approached, before telling them all about her son.

'Some would spend a day with us and some just a few minutes,' said Mike. 'Suicide is a powerful word. It's a horrible word. It's hard to say, particularly if you've been affected by it. Other people really find it hard to talk about. All three of us have seen that in our own lives. You lose friends, people you've known for a long time find it impossible to mention and almost run away from you. If you can't find the right words to say, then some people find it easier not to say anything at all. I think because we'd been so open, it gave them the strength to talk about it.'

That has certainly been my experience, to a much lesser extent, since writing about Gary Speed's death. So many people have felt able to reach out since my first book *Remarkable People* came out. I still think about Gary a lot and, for the tenth anniversary of his death in November 2021, I was asked to film a piece for BBC Sport to remember him. You can read a little bit more about that in the chapter about Nadiya and our time on *Strictly Come Dancing*.

Initially, I'd said 'no' but the family said that they would like me to do it, so I did. It went out on the Saturday afternoon, and it also went on social media where it quickly picked up millions of views. I think his death still touches an awful lot of people. I still regularly get stopped in the street by people who want to talk about Gary and, after the tribute was shown on telly that weekend, I received hundreds of emails, letters and messages from people who had also been touched by suicide.

There were people who, like me, felt that if they'd said something on the final day before they lost someone it could have made a difference. There were people who opened up about their own suicidal thoughts, depression, abuse, bullying or wanted to talk about the person or people who had helped them at their lowest point. There were some who wanted to talk about how much they loved Gary, how they were still scarred by his death and how the film had helped someone in their life. One loving mum sent me an email describing the joy at how her daughter had watched it and finally found the courage to tell her friends about the attempt she'd made on her own life five years before. She had shared links to the film on Facebook and spoken to her friends in the hope that it might help others to see a way out.

There was one email which I keep coming back to. On the day I received it, I sent it on to the then editor of *Football Focus*, Helen Brown, who was the one who persuaded me to do the piece about Gary. I didn't want it to be about me. I wanted it to be about the need to talk, and the importance of looking out for your friends. This was the email.

Dear Dan,

I've had a really, really, rotten year. I know lots of people have and unlike them, a lot of my woes are self-inflicted but on top of all the travails involved with Covid (which I also had a rotten time catching) I have lost my job, run up huge debt, had major health issues and now my wife has rightly left me so I am barely seeing my kids. I really was at rock bottom, then, as a huge football fan I watched your Gary Speed tribute.

It saved my life.

Particularly after watching the part about his sons, I have begun talking about my issues and whilst I have a long way to go I am miles away from the darkest of places I was in not so long ago and I will hopefully now be able to play even a tiny part in watching my daughters grow up.

So, thank you.

Thank you, a million times. You have no idea what an absolutely wonderful human being you are.

Keep doing what you are doing. You are an inspiration.

Thanks again.

I remember reading that for the first time in my *Strictly Come Dancing* dressing room and having a gentle sob for about ten minutes. I am so glad it made a difference. Gary's family were keen for me to do the piece because they wanted people to be reminded of the importance of communicating with each other before it's too late. I think that really resonates with the message at the heart of what the 3 Dads are all about.

Their big push now is all about teaching suicide prevention in schools. In February 2022, Mike, Andy and Tim all met with the Health Minister, Gillian Keegan, to start the conversation about adding suicide prevention to the Personal, Social, Health and Economic (PSHE) curriculum in schools. For Tim, it seems like a no-brainer. 'It's so simple. Our children learn about drugs and knife crime. They learn about county lines gangs and pregnancy. Statistically, the biggest risk to their safety is actually suicide. Why don't we teach our children about that? If you're at school and your mate is really struggling, what are you going to do? If that kid takes their own life, you've got to live with that for the rest of your life. Knives, road safety and drugs are all huge issues, and we rightly make all this effort with those subjects, but the numbers affected by suicide are just so much higher.'

It's a subject I often think about with my own children. How do we best arm our kids to deal with the toxic landscape they sometimes have to live in? We need to teach our children to be resilient, to realise that it's ok to feel stressed and anxious, that it's normal to feel worried about an exam, a boyfriend or girlfriend or what someone has said about you on social media. There is no break for this generation of children. Issues like bullying don't stop at the school gates. It can be a non-stop, twenty-four hours a day drip, drip build-up of pressure. There can be no release and no let-up. Tim is convinced through his own experience, and through spending time working with Papyrus, that there is such a better way of doing things. 'If we train them young,' he says, 'if we give them the tools, they can use them. If we just simply talk about these things, then maybe we can save some lives.'

At the time of writing, the 3 Dads are not far off raising £1 million and they haven't stopped there. They will keeping walking, but they are also keen to put the money they have already raised to good use. 'Awareness is the key,' says Mike, sitting up in his chair. 'Suicide is the biggest killer of under-thirty-fives in the UK. Parents have lost children and only then found out that the most dangerous thing in the kids' lives were the kids themselves! We want to use the money to encourage suicide prevention and get the kids to talk to their families. Everyone we spoke to and met along the way on our walk said they were very grateful that we have encouraged people to have conversations. I know that is already making a difference, but there is so much more we can do.'

When I ask Andy if someone he has met really stands out, he tells me about Sandy. Whenever you talk to anyone who has been touched by suicide, you instantly realise that it affects so many people. The ripples spread far and wide. Sandy was one of those caught in the ripples.

When the police found Sophie's body, they didn't tell her dad much other than that a man had called them with the information and that he'd stayed with her body until they had arrived. Understandably, that meant an awful lot to Andy at the time. Sandy was the man who found Sophie's body.

'We live right by the side of the water,' says Sandy in his beautifully soft Scottish accent. From the moment he picked up the phone, I knew he was kind. I could tell in the lilt of his voice and the way he asked if I was ok. 'I'm so glad you're writing about Andy,' he says. 'He's an amazing man and it's been a pleasure to get to know him.'

Sandy and his partner, Anna, live in South Queensferry on the banks of the Firth of Forth. Sandy is an architect who works in Edinburgh, and he has a painful memory of looking out of his living-room window that December morning.

'It was 8.30 a.m. I looked out to the beach and my first thought was disbelief. I instantly knew what it was I looking at and I knew I didn't want Anna to see it. She had been at a Christmas party the night before and is far more sensitive than me. I ran to close the curtains as quickly as I could. I went outside and I called the police and waited for them to arrive. If I'm totally honest with you, when I first saw the body, I went into shock. It seems a bit of a blur. My heart just completely went out to her. I remember feeling angry that no one had been looking after her. I waited next to her and presumed she'd had a hard life and I was upset that it had come to this for her. I passed on my details to the police and said I would happily talk to the family. For whatever reason, the police never passed on my details, but I couldn't stop thinking about her.'

Sandy did his own research and found Andy on social media. He saw when and where Sophie's funeral was going to be held and decided that he had to go to try and learn a bit more about the woman he had found. He drove for hours.

'I knew her name,' he says. 'I knew where she was from, but I was compelled to go to the funeral. I thought I would be one of just a handful of people there and I wanted to pay my respects. I just sat in the car outside and watched people go in. I was so relieved to see so many people there. I knew she was loved. Don't ask me to explain why, but that just meant an awful lot to me. In that moment all the anger, the questioning and the concern subsided.'

Sandy went to the wake afterwards. He stood in the corner: shaking, waiting, thinking what he should do. 'Do I talk to someone?' he thought. 'I didn't want to make their life more difficult. I was standing at the bar deliberating. One of the gentlemen who had been talking to the family came to the bar to get a drink and I managed to pluck up the courage to tell him who I was. His name was Nigel and I told him why I was there, explained that I didn't want to get in the way and asked him if he knew the family well enough to know if I should tell them that I was the one who had found their daughter's body.'

Nigel immediately introduced Sandy to Fi, Andy's wife, and, fighting back the tears, Sandy explained why he had driven three hours to attend Sophie's funeral.

'Fi is never normally rude,' says Andy, 'but she was that day. I was standing at the wake talking to some of Soph's university friends when she came over and said, "Come and meet this bloke." I could tell that she wouldn't take no for an answer, so I walked over, and she introduced me by saying, "This is Sandy. The man who found Sophie's body."'

I ask Sandy about that moment of meeting Andy for the first time and there is a long, pregnant pause. 'I'm sorry,' says Sandy, quietly. 'Just . . . give me a moment . . . this is the bit that I always struggle with. I have hardly told anyone about Sophie other than close family members, and meeting Andy for the first time and telling him about his daughter, is still the hardest part.' I tell Sandy to take his time and only tell me what he feels is right. He thanks me, takes a deep breath and continues.

'He was so lovely and gave me a hug and thanked me.' Sandy has to stop again and compose himself. 'I know this probably sounds a bit silly. Here I am talking to the father of a girl I had never met and I'm grieving her loss. I was grieving someone I knew nothing about. It is a very strange experience. I am a bit jealous that I never got to meet her, but I also feel the shock that she is no longer here.'

On the first anniversary of Sophie's death, Andy, Fi and her mum, George, all went to Sandy's house and stood on the water's edge where Sophie's body was found. 'I knew he felt better knowing that I had stayed with her body at the end, even for a short time,' recalls Sandy. The connection these two men have is as strange as it is captivating. The most unusual and awful circumstances have produced an incredibly strong bond.

In the months after Sophie's death, Sandy wasn't in a good place. He still sometimes walks the paths around his house and wonders if he could have done something to save Sophie. 'Did I walk past her on the day she took her own life? Could I have stopped her? Could I have helped her? It's so strange to have that guilt when I never met her. I just wish there is something that someone could have done, because I see that mess her death has left behind.'

Sandy spoke to an old friend who had served in Afghanistan about his feelings, and he told him about post-traumatic stress disorder (PTSD) and how it can affect people. He told Sandy he needed to try and turn whatever he could into a positive rather than let it eat away at him. When Andy ran the Northumberland half-marathon in Sophie's place, Sandy cycled for two days from Edinburgh to Bamburgh to meet him on the finish line. Sandy is a remarkable man.

When the police went to Sophie's flat on the day she died,

they found her final purchase on her kitchen table. It was a Christmas present for her dad: two tickets to the Scotch Whisky Experience on the Royal Mile in Edinburgh. She and her brother, Gregor, had bought it together.

'You can understand that, for a while, we never felt like using it,' explains an emotional Andy. 'But things change with time and this year we went and did it together. We went to see *Hairspray* too. Sophie would have loved that.' Andy and Fi also took the opportunity to meet up with Sandy and Anna. 'The whisky was very popular that night,' remembers Andy.

'I do feel like a bit of a fraud,' explains Sandy when I ask him about his continued friendship with Andy. 'I suppose you never realise the implications and the depth of the effect that these things have on you. I think I thought I was anesthetised to it, but that couldn't be further from the truth. It has had a much bigger impact on me than I ever thought possible. I wish I'd had the opportunity to meet Andy under different circumstances, but maybe this is the way it was meant to be. He's amazing and I find his strength and determination a huge source of inspiration.'

Sandy isn't the only one. Every time I speak to the 3 Dads, I am impressed by the way they carry themselves. They have all been to some dark places but are constantly searching for the light. It must be impossible to imagine what it is like to have the life you build for your family explode like that overnight. Everything that feels normal changes in an instant. There is that first awful scream of realisation that life is never going to be the same again.

Tears aren't enough. Every emotion is turned up to eleven.

You are completely overwhelmed. The shock blinds you and is only broken by the feeling of sheer horror at what has happened and the constant questions. How did they get to a place where they felt that this was their best option? What didn't I do? How could I have helped? If the noise ever dies down there is the unbearable, heart-breaking desire to turn back the clock, but you know it's impossible.

'If I could speak to Emily now,' says Tim, 'the first thing I'd do is just cuddle her. I'd tell her she was an idiot and tell her how much we love her. She genuinely thought she was helping us and unburdening us. Her little sister, Evie, will struggle with this for the next seventy years of her life. The thing that crushes me is that all three girls were so talented – a nurse, an artist and a musician – and they couldn't see it. You worry about the scores of kids who are in the same situation. We aren't a mega rich family, and we aren't destitute. We were a normal middle-class family. You think you are doing everything right and it makes it feel worthless at times. Spending time with Andy and Mike has given me something that it's hard to see at first; it's hard to see the hope.'

'That's the key word for me, Dan,' Mike jumps in. 'We are not qualified in counselling or anything like that. I have some mental health training now because of Papyrus. Did it help me? I hope it has helped both me and others. We will never be the same, but trying to do something positive was massively important for us. We are hoping that positivity has transferred to others.

'If I saw Beth now, I think the first thing I would do would be to boot her up the arse. I always used to say to her before she went out: "Don't be a d*&*head, be wise." I'd just tell her I love her. I see the anger and the pain she left behind every day, but she is still loved.'

The 3 Dads have a fascinating relationship. A deep and meaningful friendship has emerged from a situation that each one of them would have given everything to avoid. From just a few minutes in their presence, you realise that their bond is such a strong one, cemented by the love of father for a daughter and soaked in tears. They have the utmost respect for each other, and they truly do want to make a difference. They cannot understand why they've lost their girls, but the driving force behind all they do is the desire that other families would be able to avoid the paths they have had to walk down. Friendship has helped them rebuild their lives.

'I dread to think where I would be without these two,' says Mike. No one speaks for a moment. 'They are diamond geezers. I am not the person I was. I'm smiling now but I'm still a mess. I struggle to work. I have PTSD. Everything has changed and I find life so hard to deal with at times, but Tim and Andy are always there, and believe me, this journey is far from over.'

I get the feeling the 3 Dads are going nowhere. They have so much more to do.

As promised, I wanted to finish this chapter with the poem that Mike, Tim and Andy were sent by Helen Taylor during their walk. When I approached Helen to ask her if I could print her poem in this book, she said she would be delighted. 'I was prompted to write it after seeing them on *BBC Breakfast*. Their story gripped my heart and I was so pleased to meet them. The poem simply fell out of the end of my pencil.'

Helen not only wrote 'Our Girls' for the 3 Dads, but she and her husband also drove all the way from Coventry to Buxton to see them during their walk. Making an effort to help someone else goes a long way.

Our Girls

We can still hear all the giggles,
See the smiles and feel the love
For our gorgeous girls who left us
Yet have given us a shove
To step out into all weathers
As the road ahead uncurls.
We're out walking,
We're out talking,
We're out walking with our girls.

We three know the depths of sorrow.
We've lost count of all the tears
But we've found our hearts and legs again
And hope to crush the fears
Of the lonely, frightened, helpless
As their turmoil twists and swirls.
We're out walking,
We're out talking,
We're out walking with our girls.

So, we're striding down the country.
If you see us, give a wave.
Even better, find your wallet
Or look up our 'giving' page.
If we help a few and save them
As these scenes of life unfurl.
Now you're talking!
We're out walking.
We're out walking for our girls.

For Beth, Emily and Sophie.

FOUR NOTES

'And for that week, he was the biggest star on social media!'

'Who was?'

'You were, Dad!'

'Was I? What did I do?'

'You played your piece based on those four notes.'

'Well, that sounds nice.'

Paul Harvey is a brilliant musician. He has an incredible musical ear, perfect pitch and a remarkable ability to create on the spot. Paul also has dementia. His story is sad in places, but it is packed with joy, laughter and talent . . . so much talent. For much of his life he was a teacher, inspiring his students for decades, and now, in his eighties, his music is reaching millions more.

I first met Paul on social media thanks to his son Nick. Nick is also an accomplished musician and has always been amazed by his dad's party trick of being able to compose a piece from any four random notes picked for him.

In the depths of his dementia, in October 2020, Nick recorded his dad doing just that and posted it on Twitter. It was picked up by Radio 4's *Broadcasting House* programme and the host, Paddy O'Connell, helped to arrange for the song to be recorded by the BBC Philharmonic orchestra, conducted by the man who wrote it. It was the culmination of a life-long dream for Paul Harvey.

This is Paul's story.

We spoke to Paul and Nick on many occasions on *BBC Breakfast*. I used to love it because Paul was so full of life, and I enjoyed watching their beautiful relationship. You could see how much Nick loved his dad and how proud he was of him. You could see the dementia was taking its toll on Paul, but it was also clear that their coping mechanism was a gorgeous mix of care and humour. All this was happening when the world was in the grip of coronavirus and, alongside the actual vaccine, it gave us all a much-needed injection of inspiration and reminded everyone of the power of music.

One of the great things about chatting to the Harveys is that you never quite know where the conversation will go. Both Paul and Nick are gloriously unpredictable. The only thing you can be certain of is that they will never be far away from a piano.

'Hello, Dan,' says Nick, as the Zoom kicks in. 'It's Dan, Dad,' says Nick, pointing at the screen.

'Hello, Dan. How are you doing?' says Paul with that giant grin that has become so familiar. He is sitting with his regular red jumper on, next to his son, with his famous piano just slightly out of reach on his left.

When I used to speak to them on *BBC Breakfast* we'd only have about five or six minutes, so I remind them that we have loads of time and there is a lot to get through. With that in mind, I ask them to take me back to the beginning.

'It's a good job we are talking about the old stuff,' says Paul. 'I can remember the old stuff. It's the new things I struggle with sometimes.'

Paul was born into music. His parents called him Paul Ragle Harvey. His middle name is 'Elgar' spelt backwards, as the famous composer was a big favourite in the Harvey household.

'Imagine if they'd liked Shostakovich,' says Nick, laughing. He regularly punctuates the conversation with jokes and his dad loves them.

'Ha!' snorts Paul. 'That's a good one!'

'That's one of the benefits of dementia,' says Nick. 'I can tell Dad the same joke a hundred times, and he'll laugh a hundred times because he can't remember me telling it before.'

Paul's dad – John Augustus Harvey – was a working-class man who taught himself the piano in his twenties. He started up a music school in Stoke-on-Trent and Paul was always surrounded by a love of music. He took his first exams at the age of four and his progression was incredibly quick. He received the highest marks in the UK in his grade 8 exam and went on to study at the prestigious Guildhall School of Music.

'I was quite a good footballer, you know,' remembers Paul. 'I had a try-out with Port Vale as a keeper, but I was desperate to go to music college and that is what happened. I think that's what my dad wanted too.'

'Your dad was great,' says Nick. 'Our youngest son has "Augustus" as a middle name because of your dad.'

'I'd forgotten that,' says Paul. A smile breaks out across his face. 'Isn't that lovely? I'll have to write that in my book.'

More about Paul's 'book' later . . .

The talented Mr Harvey got a highly sought-after scholarship with the Russian pianist, Iso Elinson, and went on to become a concert pianist and composer. His 'Rumba Toccata' is still used in grade 6 piano exams. He used to play on the BBC Home Service in the early 1960s.

'It was just before we won the World Cup,' says Paul enthusiastically. His memory of that part of his life is still razor sharp. 'I used to play on a programme called the *Variety Playhouse*, Dan. It was the most popular show on the wireless, presented by a chap called Vic Oliver. He was a comedian but also a very good musician. Do you remember that Mozart piece, Nick?' he says, turning to his son.

'Dad found an old CD in a box, and it was some of his old performances. It was amazing, Dad, wasn't it?' says Nick, encouraging his dad to recall the story.

'I don't think I could play them now. There were fingers all over the place,' he says, laughing.

'Why did you leave all that behind?' I ask.

'I was born to teach,' says Paul. 'I just loved it. I had inspiring teachers and I wanted to do that for others. I wanted children to love and appreciate music and sounds. I wanted to bring it to life for them. It gave me so much pleasure for so many years.'

Paul puts his hand on his chin as he launches into a story. 'I used to love getting a new class from the primary school. It was always full of kids who thought that music class was going to be dull and boring. I loved that challenge. "Listen to this," I would say and I'd bring out the *Match of the Day* theme tune and I could see their ears prick up. I had got them. Nick understood that too. He's a wonderful composer too, aren't you?'

'That's what happens when you have a mum and a dad who are music mad,' says Nick. 'I was taught to play the violin, but I taught myself the piano. When Mum and Dad used to argue, I would disappear into the piano. You remember that, don't you, Dad?' he says, poking his dad, who giggles.

'Some of my favourite memories are when Dad used to say, "Nick, do you fancy having a play?" And we would just go off and improvise on the piano. Those moments will stay with me forever. Do you remember that, Dad?'

'I do now you've told me. I'm sorry.'

'Don't be sorry,' says his son.

There is a lot of that between them: Nick gently probing his dad's memory and Paul being totally honest about what he does and doesn't remember. There are a lot of gaps, there are a lot of sketchy patches, but the real magic still happens when he sits in front of a piano.

'It's just something I can do,' says Paul. 'I used to do some teaching at a jazz summer school and one day I thought, "Let's try something." Somebody picked four random notes and I started improvising.'

Nick was also there. 'I was ten at the time and it was incredible. I just remember thinking, "That's my dad . . . he's amazing". I can't tell you how beautiful it was. It's hard to put it into words how difficult it is to do what he does. If you gave me four notes, I could do something with them, but Dad's talent is outrageous.

'Maybe this is the best way of describing it,' says Nick,

gathering his thoughts. 'Lots of people play music, but Dad lets the music inhabit him. He's made of music and now he has shown the world what he's made of.'

If you ask Paul how he's feeling now, he normally makes a joke about his ears going or the hearing aids he has to wear or the fact that he's falling apart. His family first noticed something was wrong a few years ago.

'I've known for years that my memory was going a little,' says Paul.

'I think you try and ignore it for a while, don't you?' says Nick. His dad nods quietly. 'I remember that day we knew we had to do something. It was maybe four years ago when we invited Dad round for Sunday lunch, and he arrived at 6 o'clock in the morning. He started to struggle.'

Nick turns to his dad.

'Do you remember you had a fall at home, Dad?' he asks, putting his hand on Paul's arm.

'Did I?' says Paul.

'You did,' replies Nick, before turning to me to explain. 'His cognitive state reduced considerably during those weeks in hospital.'

Paul jumps in with a question. 'What does cognitive mean?'

Nick answers with his usual patience. 'It's to do with your brain, Dad.'

Paul nods, almost looking like he's been told that before.

'He was there for nearly three months, and, in all honesty,

we thought he was drifting away. The medication has been amazing but his short-term memory particularly is shot to pieces.'

I ask Paul how his dementia affects him day to day. Does he think about it a lot?

'I suppose I have to,' he says. 'Things have to be in the right place for me. I get rattled sometimes when I wouldn't have done before. Routine has become so important to me, which is frustrating, but I know that it helps.'

Once Nick had his dad back at home, he knew there was only one thing that would really get his dad's brain firing again. It was the thing he loved more than anything else. It was his music.

'There was just one day when I was at home with Dad, and he was really struggling. As I often do, I persuaded him to get on the piano and play something. He was sat there with a classical piece of music in front of him and it wasn't happening. He couldn't find the notes, he couldn't get his feet on the pedals, and you could tell he was frustrated. I remembered his old party trick and asked him if he could do it. I love watching him play so I just recorded it for posterity. It was so amazing that I decided to put it on Twitter and, well, that was the start of all this but, more importantly, it brought him back to life. I got my dad back.'

And with that, they both turn and looked at each other as only a proud father can look at his son and an adoring son can stare at his father. It's a beautiful moment to witness and that is one of the reasons why Paul's story has spread so far, and his music has been heard by so many. There is an unstructured warmth when you watch them interact with each other. You can tell that Nick loves spending time with his dad, cares for him deeply and nothing gives him more pleasure than seeing those little flashes of the father he grew up with who loved to teach him about music. The other thing I love about their relationship is the brutal British humour. Nick breaks the adoring look with a zinger.

'Before all this you were just sat watching TV all day, weren't you?'

'I just didn't want to see anyone,' says Paul.

Nick jumps in. 'The good thing about this was that it gave you the lift you needed; like a firework up your arse.'

Paul leans forward in his chair, roaring with laughter.

'Oh, that's good . . . I'll remember that one,' he says.

'No, you won't!' retorts Nick.

And that's the beauty of it. Dementia is brutal, painful, heart-breaking, but everyone deals with it differently. Paul and Nick do cry about it, but they also love to laugh.

'I took Dad out for dinner last Friday,' says Nick. 'We had fish and chips. There was half a lemon on his plate and Dad just ate it. You should have seen his face.'

Paul starts giggling. 'I'd forgotten what you're meant to do with it. Do you squeeze it on or something?'

Paul's dementia is getting worse but it's such a treat to talk to him. You get wonderful sparks of humour. You get powerful recollections from half a lifetime ago and then, every now and again, you catch a glimpse of a musical genius.

'Shall I play you something, Dan?' he says out of nowhere.

'Off the top of your head, Paul?' I ask.

'Yes! Let me get around to the piano.' He hauls himself up onto his Zimmer frame and shuffles over to the piano and collapses onto the stool.

'Now,' he says, pointing at his instrument, 'I must confess that this hasn't been tuned for a while, but we'll see what we can do.' He stretches his fingers.

'This is for you. It's a one-off because, once I've played it, I won't remember it,' he laughs.

'Are you ready? This is Dan's tune.'

For the next ninety seconds, Paul plays the most gorgeous piece of improvised music.

It's all off the top of his head and all mesmerising. I'm struggling to stop the tears from pouring down my face. As he finishes, I applaud and Nick rushes in to hug his dad, but someone is still clapping in the background. 'That was beautiful, Paul,' says a voice from the depths of the living room.

'Have you got an audience?' I ask.

'That's Louisa,' says Nick, helping his dad back to his feet. 'She is dad's home help, and she's popped in to bring him his lunch.'

'Hi, Louisa!' I shout from the other end of the Zoom call. 'Wasn't that great?' I ask her.

'I love listening to him play,' she says.

'Did you get that?' asks Paul. I explained to him that because my AirPods were plugged in, even though I was screen recording, I didn't pick up the sound. 'Let me do you another one,' he says with a skip in his step. He sits back down and produces another ninety-second improvised masterpiece. It is completely different to the first one, just as beautiful and emotional, but more haunting. It is just pouring out of him as his fingers caress the keys. Nick and Louisa are standing either side of the piano, just out of shot; I'm filming the screen back in Sheffield and we are all in total silence watching a master at work. There is a big round of applause as he finishes, Nick gives his dad another hug and Louisa puts down his lunch as Paul shuffles back to his armchair.

In the days after Paul's original video went on social media, there were various appearances on TV shows and pages of coverage across the papers. 'Four Notes: Paul's Tune' raced up the charts and things were put in place for Paul to conduct the BBC Philharmonic playing the piece he had written. Did they have a chance to stop and think about what was happening?

'No, is the simple answer,' says Nick. 'It was lovely to see the impact it had on people, and I love the fact that it came from a dark place. Dad was feeling really low, and me giving him those four notes somehow gave him a path out of that. We were all in lockdown at the time (October 2020) and we all needed an escape. The piece is beautiful, and what makes it beautiful for me is that Dad wasn't just playing the music, he was communicating with it. He wasn't really talking too much at the time, but he told all of us how he was feeling with "Four Notes". There was sorrow in there but also great uplifts of joy. If you listen to the end of it, it's almost a question mark, it's almost like it doesn't end at all. It's so clever and that is what he was going through. He told us with his piano.'

Nick is also convinced that the planets aligned to make it

special. 'It was meant to be, Dan. Twitter has a video limit of two minutes and twenty seconds. Obviously, Dad has no idea about that, but he played for just short of that, so I was able to upload the whole thing.'

I remind them both that it wasn't just the music that people fell in love with; it was their relationship, that father-and-son magic.

'That really surprised us,' says Nick before laughing, 'I have this habit of saying the most inappropriate things, but I will never tire of telling him how great he is.' Paul turns his head towards his son, and they share each other's gaze. It's another beautiful moment before Nick again breaks the silence . . .

'He is very annoying, too.'

'Who is?' says Paul in mock disgust.

'You are, Dad,' laughs Nick.

'Am I?' responds Paul before a glorious change of direction. 'I do like your car though.'

'I'm sorry you keep banging your head on it when you get in it. Every time, Dan,' says Nick.

'Do I?' says Paul. 'It's a good job I don't remember that or I'd never go anywhere with you.'

The pair of them are once again lost in laughter.

If you ask Paul how he sees himself, he answers as quick as a flash: 'I'm a composer, a pianist, a conductor and a teacher. I spent much of my life teaching and that was a real pleasure. I just wanted to show people the joy of music.'

And that is precisely what Paul Harvey has done his whole life. That is why I was so happy when he and Nick agreed to feature in this book, because Paul is exactly the sort of person I love to write about. He inspires those around him. He lifts spirits with that beautiful mixture of talent and enthusiasm, and I'm going to demonstrate that to you now by introducing you to six people. Three of them are former students of Mr Harvey, one of them is a former colleague, one is from a dementia charity and the other is a millionaire who was watching Paul's first appearance on *BBC Breakfast*.

'The most important thing a teacher can do is try and connect with a pupil and offer them options in life. That's what Mr Harvey did for me and many others.' Nick Van Eede was one of many taught by Paul at Imberhorne School in East Grinstead in the 1970s. He went on to become a musician, producer and lead singer in Cutting Crew whose single '(I Just) Died In Your Arms' was number one in nineteen different countries.

'I went to Imberhorne when it was changing from a stuffy grammar school to a comprehensive. There was a big influx of fresh young talent and Paul Harvey was part of that. We used to call him one of the 'Three Ps'.

The Three Ps were Paul Harvey, drama teacher Pete Talman (who we will meet later) and music teacher Pete Caruana. Between them they would put on big school productions. Pete Talman would write the lyrics to Paul's masterful score.

'Mr Harvey was always so generous with his advice,' remembers Nick Van Eede. 'He would come in with his keyboards and microphones and it was the first time I'd seen anything like that. I'd write some songs and he'd suggest different notes. "Try a B-sharp instead of a G, Nicky," he'd say. He always called me "Nicky". I know that most music lessons were all about "London's Burning" on the recorder or getting out the tambourines, but his lessons were never like that. He wanted you to love and appreciate music like he loved and appreciated it. He taught me to never lose that. Sometimes, it's easy to forget what makes you tick. We used to go on tour with Cutting Crew for six months. It was amazing but then you'd spend six months talking to lawyers and managers and you'd forget about the magic of making music. Then you pick up your guitar again and you're back in the right place. I don't think Mr Harvey ever lost that. I have a rehearsal in thirty minutes. My voice will be croaky, but I know I will love it.'

Nick was inspired by those epic school productions, but so too was Alix Lewer who now runs a music charity. 'Mr Harvey drove a Ford Capri, he was cool. He loved it and we loved that he loved it. The job that I'm doing now, using music to include and help people with learning difficulties, all goes back to him.'

Alix runs a charity called Include.org. She loves her job but found life at school hard. 'I was mercilessly bullied. I was academic, my mum would never buy the trendy clothes and I'd arrived from a small school, so no one knew who I was. I was a moving target every day, but music was my release and Mr Harvey was the man who opened the door. He just had the ability to bring the best out in people, no matter how hard he had to dig. If you were willing to work, he was on your side, whether you could play an instrument or not. I remember once, he asked me to play the clarinet in assembly. I was terrified and thought that everyone would go for me, but I loved it. He was the cool teacher and was so proud of me, and that gave me the confidence to be myself. Life was fun when he was around. He built teams of good people and you just wanted to be around him. He built these wonderful environments that we wanted to be a part of; places where you could be yourself. That's exactly what I try and do now in my job. I'm just trying to be like Mr Harvey.'

I ask Alix if she, and the other students, knew how talented he was, or was it all about the Ford Capri. 'This is weird,' says Alix, 'but I actually played the piano at his leaving do! I wasn't even a pianist but the guy who was meant to be playing couldn't be there, so I had to do it. I was pretty average, but Mr Harvey came over and was so complimentary about my playing and, later on, he sat at the piano and the whole room was like "Wow!" We knew he was a great teacher but that was the first time we saw he was really special.'

Dominic Glynn, a prolific composer of music for TV and film, is a third former student of Paul Harvey's. 'I always looked forward to his lessons. The school was very progressive, and Mr Harvey was at the forefront of that. He would sit there, play something on the piano and just talk to us about the music and why it was important. Over the years, he inspired me. When I was in the sixth form, we started a band and Mr Harvey was in charge of the music block. He would always encourage us to use the facilities and even trusted us with the keys. He just wanted us to experiment and find our feet. We'd play him something and he was always encouraging. You could tell he was desperate for us to do well.'

Paul kept a close eye on his students even after they had left school. I remember when we reintroduced him to some of them on *BBC Breakfast* and you could see the joy on his face. One of Dominic's most well-known arrangements was the iconic *Doctor Who* theme tune and he was so touched that Mr Harvey had followed his career.

'It was wonderful when Nick said that his dad remembered me. Nick said he used to bring me up during his lessons with other students, which is remarkable and really humbling. When I spoke to Paul, that was the first time we'd seen each other in forty-five years. He was the man who set me on my way and it was great to get the chance to thank him for all of that.'

While Nick, Alix and Dominic all studied under Paul Harvey, Pete Talman shared a staff room with him at Imberhorne. 'Paul was a born teacher,' says Pete. 'I was head of drama, and he embodied the music department and was a larger-than-life character. I didn't go in his classroom much but, when we worked on the school shows together, the enthusiasm just poured out of him. My fondest recollection is of composing with him. Paul wrote the music, and I would take care of the lyrics. I would go round to his house on a Sunday morning with a lyric in my mind and he would just sit at the piano and the magic would happen. It was like his hands were remote controlled, searching the keyboard for a melody that suited the words. It was fascinating to watch it evolve in his mind, in front of your eyes. The piano was his best friend, and he just couldn't stop himself.'

Pete and Paul lost touch for a few years, but Paul's first wife contacted Pete to let him know that Paul was ill and the pair of them got back together. 'His dementia is sad but also fascinating. When I saw him at Christmas,' says Pete, 'his recall of students he taught was remarkable. I was running through some of the children and would ask him, "Do you remember Alison? You wrote her a song," and he would say, "Yes! Alison, restricted vocal range and sometimes I had to play a little louder to cover for that." That was nearly fifty years ago and it was there at the front of his mind. His mind is still brilliant but the more immediate seems to just drift away.'

I ask Pete what it was like to watch his old friend play 'Four Notes' in his eighties and go on to conduct the orchestra. 'I was just so moved by it all,' says Pete. 'When I watched him, I just felt that he looked at home – that he belonged there. In another life, that's where he should be, that should have been Paul. He could have gone on to fulfil that dream and ambition of being a musician, but he found that fulfilment in teaching. He's not a frustrated musician because teaching was always at the very centre of his being. I know his mind is failing him, but I like to think the dementia can't get to his music because he plays with his soul. Music and Paul are indivisible.'

It wasn't just Pete Talman who was mesmerised by Paul's performance. His old students couldn't take their eyes off him. 'It is impossible to watch it without a tear in your eye,' says Dominic Glynn. 'His talent is just so visible. I'm not surprised it caused such a stir and went around the world when you think about what he is going through and how much skill it takes to do what he did. It's not just that,' adds Dominic, 'it's the fact that it's technically beautiful. The way it ends, the very last note, is perfect. You wouldn't put it there. It's not a cliché and a lesser composer wouldn't see it or hear it the way he does. With every note he's telling us a story, he's telling us how he is feeling and that is wonderful.'

Alix Lewer was equally inspired but also sad to watch her old teacher struggling. 'I'm a speech and language therapist. My musical journey began with Mr Harvey. He gave me the confidence to do what I do now. I set up the charity and we help people with dementia and there he was playing music with dementia. It was a little overwhelming. For me, he was always a brilliant teacher, but I also looked up to him and you always put him on a pedestal, so it was hard to see him so upset, with his emotions so open and near the surface, but that's what happens with dementia. The thing that encourages me is that, even though he has dementia, he's showing us all his skills. What an example to others! By playing the piano every day, he is keeping that part of him alive. It's coming from his soul, it's so much deeper than cognitive function.'

When you talk to Alix, it is obvious very early on that she is one of those wonderful people who searches for the positive. She talks with great passion about the work she does and, because of that, she focuses on the inspiration in the life of people like Paul, rather than the sadness.

'My first experience of dementia was working in a nursing home at sixteen. You got the patients up, they had lunch and then you put them to bed. There was no investment in finding the things that made them who they are. That is the problem with social care. Paul is in a position where Nick can help and encourage him to share his gifts with the world. Nick is integral to all of this, and Paul is proof that people with dementia aren't gone, they can still contribute. I know that there are so many more Paul Harvey's out there. Not all of them can play the piano like him, but they can all teach us something. That's why I loved watching him conduct the orchestra,' says Alix, once again getting emotional. 'I just sat there in tears watching him because that is where he was meant to be: not in a nursing home watching TV, but living his dream and lost in the music. He was so proud, and how often do people with dementia get to feel pride rather than shame? He was eighty, he has dementia, but he's not finished. He has so much more to teach us.'

Nick Van Eede was just as emotional when he watched his old teacher in action. 'When I was a lot younger, I played some songs at what used to be called the Horsham Mental Institution. It tells you how much things have changed that we don't call it that anymore, but I was playing some Tom Jones to the residents and one of the women there came up and sang the song with me. Afterwards, the doctor told me she hadn't spoken in three years. That's what music can do to you, that's how deep it sits in our bodies and that's why watching Paul was so wonderful. What really struck me was . . .' he pauses to find the right words . . . 'it was brilliant. I love classical music and what he captured in that piece was how he was feeling at the time, at that precise moment. It was beautifully sad but also uplifting. He couldn't tell me how he felt, but he played to me how he felt and that is the very essence of a musician. There is nothing sadder than watching your loved ones drift away. I am very thankful that my mum is eighty-seven and currently sharp as a button, but watching Paul was inspirational.'

I am about to thank Nick for his time when he jumps back in. 'There is another thing, Dan,' he says, with a degree of urgency. 'What he did will last forever. That will probably never happen again. You get moments like that, and they don't come around very often so you must treasure them. I had one a few months ago. I was at the London Palladium with Cutting Crew performing with a thirty-two-piece orchestra. I sang the first line of "(I Just) Died In Your Arms" and it was a forever moment. I knew I would never get the chance to do that again. That is what Paul created with his son. That is his hand-me-down to the rest of us. I know what it's like to sit down and write a song – a good one and a bad one. I know what great musicians look like and he is one of them. I hope he realises how special he is, because it all works through him. It's a lovely story, it's a lovely piece of music, but it's Paul who has the charm and the talent, it's Paul who can see the humour in the darkness, it's Paul who provides the magic.'

His former students and colleagues weren't the only ones who saw that 'magic'. There were millions watching Paul and his piano and one of them was sitting at home with his wife in Scotland, businessman Sir Tom Hunter. Sir Tom's tale is a book in itself – a young man borrows £5,000 from his dad which he uses to start selling trainers from the back of a van. He turns that into the retail chain Sports Division which is sold to JJB

Sports in 1998 for around £290 million. More importantly for this story though, Tom had lost both his parents to dementia.

'My wife and I were watching *BBC Breakfast*, like we always do, and on came Paul and his son. We just sat there in silence. I had never really talked about my mum and dad's dementia, but it all just came flooding back to me. It was the father-and-son element, the bond over music and the way that the music was able to reach into this man's mind. We were both sobbing.'

Tom's dad was called Campbell. He owned a small grocery in New Cumnock when 90 per cent of employment was down the coal pit. Tom worked in the shop with his dad from the age of six. When the Miner's Strike happened in 1984, the business disappeared. 'He had to sell the shop and he thought he was a failure,' explains Tom. 'He put a little bit of money in with another man selling slippers in markets. I noticed that trainers were a big part of what they were doing, and I thought I would start trying to sell them. I wrote to a shop and asked if I could start selling some trainers in their store. Remarkably they said "yes" and asked if I could start with their shops in Leeds, Sunderland and Aberdeen. I told them I would see as our shopfitting team were really busy. I didn't have a shopfitting team; I didn't even have any trainers! I told my dad what was happening, and that's when he loaned me the £5,000.'

That money enabled Tom to enter the trainer business at just the right time and he went on to have enormous commercial success. When he became Sir Tom Hunter, he was allowed to take three people to Buckingham Palace and he took his wife, Marion, his son and his very proud dad.

Tom's mum was the first to be diagnosed with dementia in the family and his dad became her full-time carer. 'That was one of the things I loved about Nick and Paul. I saw that love and that care. My mum was much worse than my dad. It was death from a thousand cuts. She was drifting away and then he started to deteriorate. It wasn't as sad with my dad. We had said all that we had wanted to say to each other. My mum was much harder to watch. She just vanished in front of my eyes. I would visit her at the nursing home and then just wept as I left. She disappeared. She couldn't talk, walk or speak and when you held her hand it was like she just wasn't there. She had always loved her music. She was Welsh and had a great voice. We would listen to Andy Williams, Matt Munro and the Mike Sammes Singers'.

I ask Tom if that was another reason why Paul Harvey made such an impact on him. 'I don't cry, Dan,' he says, 'but Marion and I were just quiet for a few minutes. I loved the way that Nick looked at his dad: a father's love for his son and a son's love for his father. That did it for me. The music was beautiful, but I don't even think you need to have had an appreciation or a love of music to be affected by it all. I was crying because of the way my mum slipped away too. I wish we had known some of what Nick and Paul had for my mum. I turned to Marion and said, "I think they are on to something. I am going to do something." My wife just said, "On you go."'

That morning I was sitting on the sofa alongside Louise Minchin. She had met Tom at a charity event, and they had swapped numbers. At the end of the show Louise said, 'I've had a message from Tom Hunter. He says he wants to support the charity.' You only have to do a quick Google search on Tom to see how wonderfully generous he is with his money. There are so many good causes he supports, and after a few phone calls and emails, it was all organised. Tom was donating £1 million to dementia charities after being inspired by Paul Harvey.

A few days later we got Paul and Nick back on *Breakfast* and made the announcement 'live on the television to Grace Meadows from one of the charities, Music For Dementia. Everyone was crying.

'I still sometimes watch it back in absolute shock and euphoria,' says Grace, laughing. 'The lift that it gave during a lockdown and a pandemic was just so memorable. It validated all the times I have stood at a conference and talked about the power of music. It reminded me that someone was listening, it was worth investing in and it was life-changing and life-affirming. You know that Tom still sends me messages, Dan?' says Grace, full of enthusiasm. 'Just little things like, "Keep up the good work." For this to be on his radar is incredible. He is so busy, but he has shown us all that recognition makes such a massive difference.'

Every penny of that donation has already been spent across thirty-one organisations in all, covering a huge number of schemes and courses: dementia discos, orchestral work, therapy, singing groups, music in care homes.

'That money has genuinely changed lives and saved a lot of those organisations from money lost in the pandemic,' says Grace. 'But it's not just the money. People come up to me and say, "You did that piece with that old guy." Paul has allowed me to go and have conversations with people because they have been emotionally moved by his music and what it does. He has opened the door for so many people living with dementia.'

Grace is a bassoonist. She plays in the World Doctor's Orchestra, and she has also been a music therapist for the past decade. In 2018, she became campaign director for Music For Dementia. I have to say that Grace is one of those wonderful people who inspires you the second she starts talking. She has so much passion for what she does, it spills into all those around her.

'I have always known about the power of music,' beams Grace. 'I will never ever forget when I was doing a session at the Chelsea and Westminster Hospital in London. Two people were getting married and one of them had terminal cancer. They had a full-on wedding but there was no music so I stopped and offered to play my keyboard for them. It was really poignant for me. I will never forget that. I just think that music enhances relationships in the same way that it has for Paul and Nick.'

I tell Grace that what really strikes many people about Paul is just how talented he is. 'That's it!' she says, beaming even more than before. 'My uncle has dementia and is a musician. He can sit and play but it's not coherent. It just sounds like random notes. Paul is quite special in terms of what he can do. He is a standout. I often think about what happens to all those amazing musicians who will get dementia in the next twenty years? How painful will it be for those who can't do what they once did? If I get dementia one day, will I know how to play?

Will I forget that I ever played? What Paul demonstrates is that there is something extraordinary about the way that music touches the brain. It's not just cognitive, it's emotional. There are some studies that suggest it's all tied in with sounds we hear as a child but, whatever the answer, music is part of Paul's fabric.'

I don't know about you but I am fascinated by music therapy and how we interact with it. Music is so intrinsically linked to so many of our memories and standout moments in our lives. As soon as I hear the first note of 'Killing Me Softly' by The Fugees, I am instantly transported back to our university corridor in 1996 where my next-door neighbour, Jason Power, started each day by playing it at full volume. All the songs we danced to on *Strictly* instantly take me back to the dance floor, and just a few strums of Chas & Dave and it's 1987 and the FA Cup final again when Coventry City beat Tottenham.

I ask Grace how she uses it in her therapy. 'You might start with a piece of music that they know,' she says. 'They may know the lyrics. You may start with the la la la's. You use anything to bring them into the session. You wait for that moment when they are there in the room and then you can build on that connection with them. You can then watch carefully as that music plays out.

'Are they grasping for something?

'Are they looking to you for guidance?

'Are they following the tune?

'Do they need help?

'Are they waiting for the next verse or the chorus?

'Are they agitated?

'You are constantly micro-analysing to see if there is any reaction to what you play. You are constantly creating a stage for them to be on beyond their diagnosis. Whatever they give you, you can work with it. With some brain injury patients, you might be working with something as small as a finger movement or an eye flicker. You are always looking for a call and response and then, suddenly, you have a conversation going with someone who can only tap a finger. With someone with dementia, they might not be able to speak, but you might mirror a sound or a motion. You do all that you can to find a means of communicating with them. There is also some powerful work you can do with families. You are creating musical memories for that family, which happens a lot in palliative care. Lots of people work with the music therapist and maybe rewrite a song to create a musical legacy.'

'What difference did Paul and Nick make to all that?' I ask.

'Dan,' says Grace, 'I cannot even begin to tell you. They took awareness to a stratospheric level with "Four Notes". Their relationship was inspirational for so many people because Nick can see his father and his dementia. He still feels and sees his dad through the music that he plays. I will never forget him playing with and then conducting the Philharmonic. It was the most thrilling thing I have ever seen; just the sheer joy of watching a man fulfil his lifelong dream. I was sobbing already before I looked across and saw Nick arm in arm with his brothers, watching their dad. The pride was pouring out of them. It was such a powerful celebration of family.'

I don't mind telling you I was in tears listening to Grace. She gets me every time. I think it is the fact that she understands and explains the subtleties of dementia so beautifully. It is scary and sad and painful and heart-breaking, but there can still be joy and fun and a celebration of talent that shouldn't be allowed to go to waste.

'Paul has allowed people to see the power of music,' says Grace. 'There are so many families who are now doing music therapy with their loved ones because of him. He has inspired people to set up their own programmes, inspired a £1 million donation and he has changed lives. Aside from the help he has given others, there is so much to admire about his music: the harmonic progression, the lyrical phrasing and the way he feeds rhythm into that. There is so much depth and richness and colour. The way he gently lifts his finger off the keys. You can see the musicality is still there; he still feels it through his body. I love that he decided to teach all that to the next generation and now he shares it with everyone. He has radically changed how many of us see people living with dementia. He is one of a kind. He has shown how music can keep connections that can keep you alive. His son thought he had lost him. Dementia can be such a painful, drawn-out process as you watch that daily decline. Anything that can give you back a sense of connection or togetherness is so powerful and gives everyone the strength to keep going. I hope Paul keeps playing for many years to come.'

'Can you still remember what the four notes were that started all this, Paul?' I ask.

'F, A, D, B.' He sings them back to me. Nick is open-mouthed next him.

'How do you remember them?' asks his amazed son.

'I don't really know,' says Paul. 'Maybe I wrote them in my book.'

I did tell you I would come back to the book. Paul keeps it by the side of his piano.

'I write things down in here,' he says. 'As soon as I get to the point where I think I might forget something, down it goes.'

He starts to giggle. 'I've even written "diarrhoea" in it,' the giggle develops into a belly laugh, 'but I can't remember why.'

Again, this is what I love about these two. As the conversation shifts, you go through all the emotions with them. One minute you're crying and the next you are spitting out your tea. It quickly shifts from diarrhoea to something far more serious.

'Haven't you got Alzheimer's written on the first page, Dad?' says Nick.

'Yes,' says Paul, sighing. 'That's because I can't sometimes remember what I've got. It's not the nicest thing to be reminded of, but I suppose it's important to know.'

The conversation jumps again. 'I love snooker, Dan,' says Paul. 'I was watching the snooker with Ronnie, and I couldn't remember his surname. I could remember The Two Ronnies, but I couldn't get Ronnie . . . Ronnie . . . and then it came and I wrote it in the book because I don't want to forget that.' He checks the book. 'Ronnie O'Sullivan. Usain Bolt too! I forgot his name and you can't have that, so I wrote it down straightaway. I knew I was going to forget. The book is very helpful.'

'Do you remember when you asked me who wrote Bernstein's *West Side Story*?' says Nick, giggling again.

'No,' says Paul, but he seems to know it's funny.

'I just said "Bernstein"' says Nick, 'and you said, "That's it!"'

They are laughing again.

'It doesn't annoy me that I forget,' says Paul. 'Even Beethoven, who was deaf, sawed the legs off his grand piano so he could feel the vibrations through his feet!'

'Did he?' says Nick. 'Do you want me to do that for you?'

'Don't be daft,' says Paul.

'Do you remember playing "Four Notes" and all the things you did on the television?' I ask.

'I can't really remember it at all,' says Paul.

'We watch it a lot, don't we?' offers Nick, who explains that he has all the performances and appearances saved on his YouTube channel so his dad can watch them every time he turns on the TV.

'Do you worry that you will forget how to play, Paul?' This time there is a long pause after my question.

'I don't think so,' says Paul eventually. 'We've all got to go sometime.'

'We both live in the moment, don't we, Dad,' adds his son. 'I've seen him at his worst and at his best. At his lowest, in hospital after that fall, he was spending every hour crying and confused. Look at him now! Fundamentally, he is back. This is my dad. I don't think of the future. Right now, things are ok.'

'I can't remember anything really,' says Paul.

'I think it frustrates you sometimes, doesn't it?' adds Nick.

'When you forget the names of people. He forgot my wife's name and he adores her, or the names of his grandchildren. That upsets you, doesn't it?'

'It does,' replies Paul, 'because I love them, but I am happy. Dementia robs you of so much, but I still know who I am, and I still know that music means everything to me and I'm just glad I got to share it with so many people before it was too late.'

Nick knows that the best way to keep his dad going is to keep him at the piano. They are always looking for the next piece to play, for the next challenge. 'I want to keep going until at least Christmas,' says Paul. 'I've written some carols.' He's worked with Aled Jones and would love to write something for Katherine Jenkins.

I ask the pair of them what they think about all the money they raised through the single and the donation from Tom Hunter. 'It's amazing, isn't it?' says Nick. 'All the money, Dad, you know, from "Four Notes" . . . with Grace from the charity.'

Paul's eyes light up. 'She's in the book,' he says. 'Grace is one of my special people.'

I tell Paul that Grace thinks he's amazing and that he's made such a difference to so many people. Nick reminds him about the message he got from his hero, the composer Stephen Sondheim on the day he composed the piece with the BBC Philharmonic. 'That was special,' says Paul. 'I cried a lot that day.'

The conversation moves on to how he'd like to be remembered. 'It's pretty simple really,' says Paul. 'If I brought any sort of pleasure through music, I'll be very happy.'

'What about your Dyson vacuum trick?' says Nick. 'Dan,

he can tell you the last two notes of our vacuum cleaner as it shuts down. He's got the perfect pitch. He hears a note, and he can tell you what it is. Watch this.' Paul sprints to the piano. 'Dad, don't look . . . what is this note?' Nick taps the piano key a couple of times as Paul turns away with his eyes looking into the middle distance, listening intently.

'Well . . .' he says with a fair degree of confidence. 'It's very out of tune but it's either an A or an A-flat.'

'He's right!' exclaims Nick. 'It's an A!'

As Nick sits down, I remind him that so many people love the way he cares for his dad but also celebrates his skill and wants the rest of the world to know about it.

'I've always known that Dad's music was world class. I'm so proud that, as an eighty-year-old, you got there,' he says, turning to his dad and addressing him directly.

'You never wanted to be famous, you just loved teaching, but I knew that the quality of your music deserved a bigger audience. The songs you wrote for school productions were as good as anything on the West End and you chose to be a teacher and . . . they were so lucky to have you. And then, after all that, we got you out there and you broadcast your talent to everyone. That meant the world to me, Dad. It was wonderful. You deserve all the love.'

They embrace.

I think about Paul Harvey a lot, I think a lot of people do. I am so glad he is in this book. He is a musical giant who has allowed us all to spend a little time on his shoulders.

I love listening to the students he inspired almost as much as

I love listening to his music. I love the way his son talks about him. I love the way they poke fun at each other and laugh alongside the sadness. I love that he has done so much to change our perceptions of the cruel beast that is dementia. I love that when he was meant to be at his weakest, he showed his strength. I love that he has shown us all that although it might rob him of his memories, it cannot steal his worth.

After their long embrace, I thank them both for their time and talent.

'You are a remarkable man,' I offer.

'Thank you,' says Paul, bowing his head.

'He was talking to me,' retorts Nick and, once again, as it often does when the Harveys are around, the sound of laughter fills the air.

THE MAN WITH THE NARWHAL TUSK

When Darryn was four years old, he was bullied at school. An older boy, called Troy, pushed Darryn to one side and looked the aggressors in the eyes: 'If you want to get to him, you have to come through me.' The bullying stopped.

When Darryn was a lot older than four, he was on a train on his way to Northampton. There were two football fans harassing a young girl. They were sitting behind her making inappropriate sexual comments. She whispered, 'They just won't leave me alone.' Troy wasn't around this time, so Darryn stood up and said, 'If you want to get to her, you have to come through me.' The men were abusive but, when the rest of the carriage showed they were also ready to take action, they quickly sunk back into their seats and nothing more was said.

Darryn was in New York when he witnessed a man on a train swearing violently at the woman who the man was with. Darryn told him that it wasn't right to speak to a woman like that, especially in front of young children. The man turned his aggression towards Darryn who stood his ground. The man backed down and got off the train at the next station. An elderly lady came up to Darryn and thanked him for his bravery but warned him that the man could have easily had a gun or a knife. 'You could have been in real danger.'

Darryn has always had the instinct to protect others. Maybe it was Troy who inspired him, but it has always been something he cannot ignore. He was born in South Africa and his parents split when he was three and his father left to live in the United Kingdom for two years before coming home. His mum built a family with another man, they had another child together and Darryn was left feeling like he didn't belong anywhere. He found role models away from the family home, in other people's families.

At the age of eleven, he was sent to an all-boys' school – the Jeppe High School – in Johannesburg, South Africa. Darryn says he became a man in that school. At the start, he couldn't look anyone in the eye. He had no self-confidence and no idea what he wanted to do with his life. He had to fend for himself, defend himself when the senior boys would launch night-time raids on the newbies. Shoes were stuffed into pillowcases, rule came via the fist, but Darryn learned that in challenging times, you form strong bonds with others who are going through the same experiences. At Jeppe he learned what it meant to protect others, even if that meant putting yourself in harm's way. The school's motto was, 'For the brave, nothing is too difficult.'

All this prepared Darryn for what happened at Fishmongers' Hall, at the northern end of London Bridge, on 19 November 2019 – a day that changed his life forever.

* * *

Darryn was a communication's manager with the Prison and Probation Service in London. On that day, he was attending a conference on prisoner rehabilitation which was celebrating the fifth anniversary of Learning Together – a programme run by the Cambridge Institute of Criminology. It was all about re-integrating offenders into society. Jack Merritt, a twenty-five-year-old law and criminology graduate, was at the conference that day. He was working for Learning Together. It was also a significant day for Steve Gallant; a convicted murderer who was serving a life sentence. It was his first day outside a prison in fourteen years. Usman Khan was also at Fishmongers' Hall on that sunny November morning. He had been invited to the conference as a former participant in the Learning Together programme. He had been convicted of trying to launch a terror attack in 2012 and sentenced to eight years in jail. He was allowed to leave Belmarsh prison on a temporary release licence in 2018. One of the conditions of his release was that he was banned from entering London, but he was given special dispensation to attend the rehabilitation conference.

Usman Khan attacked five people with a knife that day. He killed two of them. One of them was Jack Merritt.

Over the course of this chapter, you'll hear from Darryn and Steve, two of the men who took on the terrorist, and from Dave and Anne Merritt, Jack's parents. I don't know if you have experience of the prison system in this country. I don't know how you feel about rehabilitation. I don't know whether you think someone can change. Is there a way back for someone like Usman Khan? Could someone or some sort of programme have convinced him not to do what he did? How do you judge Steve Gallant? Do his actions, which you will read about at Fishmongers' Hall, in any way atone for the murder he committed in 2005? Can he ever be forgiven? Can he change? I hope this chapter, and the accounts of the people involved, help you to answer some of those questions.

'I wasn't meant to be there at all,' remembers Darryn. 'My line manager was meant to be the one attending, but she was in Cardiff, so I went in her place. The event was due to start at 11 a.m. but I got there nice and early at 10. I was taking some photos of Fishmongers' Hall as it's such a beautiful building. I recorded some videos looking at the history on the walls and just the scale of it. I was meant to be writing an article about the day so I took in as much as I could. Little did I know at the time, but I was surveying the battle scene and all that information would become invaluable in the hours to come.'

Just like Darryn, Steve Gallant's attendance was also a surprise. Steve was jailed for seventeen years in 2005 for the murder of ex-firefighter Barrie Jackson. As a convicted murderer, Steve had started his sentence in the most secure facility – a category A prison – but, over the years, had worked his way through the system, and five weeks before the event at Fishmongers' Hall he found out he was going to be moved to an open prison.

Steve picks up the story. 'When I heard the news about the open prison, I put in an application to go to the rehabilitation event at London Bridge. The prison service turned me down, but then, a week before it was meant to go ahead, I found out that I was going and that I would be escorted by a prison officer. It was a big deal for me. That day was the first day I had left prison in fourteen years.'

Steve had been working with Jack Merritt on the Learning Together project and Jack had had a huge impact on him. 'I'd been working with Jack for about two-and-a-half years. He was amazing. He was one of those people who managed to give you a sense of self-worth, no matter what you'd been through. He was passionate. He cared. He would always spend a lot of time with you, and he'd do things like bring in a professor from Cambridge to talk about human rights. Jack was always the first person on the phone when people came out of the prison. I was looking forward to seeing him that day. I walked into the hall, and it was just so beautiful. It was oozing history and opulence,' remembers Steve. 'It was almost magical. It was late November, and the sun was shining and there was this gorgeous blue sky. I remember thinking that I didn't really know what freedom felt like, so I just told myself to enjoy the day. I was meant to be involved in a discussion in the afternoon. That was the only thing I had been asked to do, so I was determined to make sure that I soaked it all in.'

While Steve was soaking in the occasion, Darryn was busy taking pictures. One of them was of the elaborate dining hall where they would all be served fish pie for lunch. When Darryn looks back on that photograph now, he can see one other man, sitting at the table . . . it was Usman Khan, the terrorist.

In the first session of the day, the attendees were asked to think of three negative things to describe themselves, followed by three positive ones. 'I'm never sure if these sessions actually work,' says Darryn. 'I played along, and we were then asked to think about the first time we had felt that negative emotion. For me, like most people I suppose, it all went back to being a kid and the person leading the session made us think about the lesson we would give ourselves as a child. I remember thinking that I would tell myself that parents are not idols, but they are lessons in right and wrong, and they are often wrong.' After that session, there was a break where Steve decided to take the opportunity to go to the toilet.

'I was meant to be involved in the discussion during the afternoon,' recalls Steve. 'I was about to nip downstairs to the toilet, and one of the co-directors from Learning Together pulled me to one side to talk about the question I was going to ask. I found out later that, at that precise moment, Jack (Merritt) was going to the toilet, but Usman Khan was also in there. He was busy preparing himself for what was about to happen and strapping the knives to his hands.'

Steve went back into the hall to re-join the officer who was escorting him for the day for the next session. Darryn was already in there. 'I was at the table,' says Darryn, 'second row from the stage. I was right by the windows at the front of the building. All of a sudden, we could hear some shouting, and someone asked us all to stay in the room. If I'm honest, at first, it sounded like some teenagers or skateboarders had got in the foyer and were causing a bit of a disturbance. Then I heard the scream and the prisoner next to me turned and said, "That's not a teenager messing around!" I stood up and, on the adjacent table, Steve stood up at exactly the same time.'

'I knew it was someone screaming properly,' remembers Steve. 'I knew it was serious and I wanted to investigate, but it was my first day out of prison and my prison officer told me to stay where I was while he went and had a look. A moment later someone from Learning Together shouted, "Everyone stay there . . . it's Usman!" and I knew I had to help.'

Steve and Darryn arrived at the top of the spiral staircase at the same time. 'I tried to survey the scene,' says Darryn. 'There was a woman startled, running up the stairs saying, "Oh my God!" and when I looked over the edge of the banister, I saw Saskia on the stairs.'

Saskia Jones was a volunteer with the Learning Together programme. Two hours before she was stabbed and killed by Khan, she had sat down at his table and chatted to him. Saskia knew him because the Cambridge University Learning Together programme taught students and prisoners side by side. Khan joined when he was in prison and was seen as a success story. They had put him on their promotional leaflets and given him a computer.

'I started to move down the stairs,' says Steve, 'and I saw my prison officer with his hands pressed on Saskia's neck, trying to help her.'

At this point, Khan was attacking people in the foyer of the hall. One of them was a student at Anglia Ruskin University and was working part-time at Learning Together as an office manager. Understandably, for some people the events of the day are still too raw and chapters like this are hard to read. Some individuals have requested that their names be changed, so we'll refer to the part-time office manager as 'Jane'.

Saskia Jones was the second person Khan attacked. Jane later described at the inquest that she had watched as Jack Merritt stumbled out of the toilet after being stabbed twelve times. She screamed, 'No, Usman! Please don't!' before he attacked her. She was one of three people who survived.

Steve was one of those watching on in horror. 'They were on the stairs and there was another girl (Jane) on the floor too. I could see Usman Khan and it was obvious he was responsible. I could see the blood. He had the knives on him, and he was in the middle of a killing spree. My thought processes were working quickly: I knew I needed to slow him down until the police arrived, so I made my way down the stairs.'

Darryn was about to make his way down the other side of the double staircase. 'Steve was on the move. I didn't know what was down there, but I knew I needed to find something to defend people from whatever was attacking them below. I thought about a chair or maybe a big serving lid and a ladle from the dining hall. As I was running back towards the hall to get something, I saw a short corridor with a couple of 2-metre-long tusks hanging each side of the door from the wall. I took one and ran back down the stairs where I could see Steve taking on the terrorist with a chair.'

'I just launched something at his head,' recalls Steve. 'He came towards me and opened his jacket and showed me his bomb.'

'I was looking at Steve holding off the terrorist,' says Darryn, 'and behind them Jane was lying on the floor. This might sound strange, but the room behind was backlit by the sun which was streaming in through the stained-glass windows. The sun is shining off the blood on the floor. As I make my way down there, I meet Usman Khan.' Darryn pauses. 'I don't like saying his name. Do you mind if I don't use his name, Dan? Can I just call him "the terrorist"?' I tell him that's fine and he continues.

'He has thickset eyebrows which I can see just beneath his balaclava. There are two 8-inch kitchen knives strapped to his hands and, just like the blood on the floor, they are glistening. Behind him, I could see Jane on the floor. She looked like an angel who had fallen to the ground. She was motionless. I was convinced she was already dead. There was so much to take in, but I know I had to try and stop him, so I position the tusk at his belly button. As I manoeuvre myself into position, he stops for a moment and looks at me. "I'm not here for you," he says. "I'm here for the police." He was negotiating with me. Behind me on the stairs, one of the course coordinators is also looking after Saskia and says, in disbelief, "Oh my God, he's got a bomb!"

'He hears it too and widens his arms a little to show me what he has strapped to his chest. "I have a bomb," he said. What do I do? What is my next move? There are more than a hundred people in the room directly above him. I have to do something before the police arrive. Steve is propping a door open and throws a chair at the terrorist, hitting him on the shoulder. The terrorist turns towards Steve and starts advancing. I look at Steve, our eyes meet, and I pass him the tusk while trying to keep it pointed at the terrorist's stomach. Now I'm empty-handed and within striking distance of his blades, so I turn and run back up the stairs, passing Saskia and those caring for her, to try and get the second tusk. As I'm trying to get it off the wall without breaking it, my colleague, Tracy, is trying to stop me. She tells me to stay where I am, but I push her away to the wall. "I won't let him hurt anyone else," I tell her and make my way back down the stairs, past another girl who is bleeding from a wound to her arm. I know I have to get back to Steve.'

'There was no need to talk to this guy,' says Steve. 'I just thrust the tusk at his chest. It seemed to bounce off. It almost had no effect at all. I snapped it across his arm and then he runs at me with his knives. I ran back into the foyer and people are throwing things at him and I hit him with another chair. "I'm waiting for the police," he says, but I know I can't let him rest. I can't let him recover. I watch him as he tries to make his way outside and he tries to stab someone on the way. Thankfully, he misses. I follow him out onto London Bridge, and I can see a woman walking towards him, with no idea what has just happened inside. "GET BACK!" I scream at the top of my voice. "HE'S A TERRORIST!" People start to run and panic, and he turns back towards me.' Steve pauses. 'And do you know what, Dan? I have no further memory of the next few minutes. I had to learn it all from the public inquiry. I have just blanked it out.'

Darryn is sprinting down the stairs with the second tusk. 'I can see the shattered tusk on the floor, and I remember thinking that the worst has happened to Steve. He has become the latest victim. I see that the huge front door is closing but I see a foot going out. "LET ME OUT!" I scream. They open the door and I make my way through carefully with the tusk and try and assess the scene from the top of the stairs. For the first time in my life, I go into a state of complete tunnel vision. I can see the terrorist moving towards the bridge. He is running. I make my way down the stairs, and, to my right, a fire extinguisher goes off. It's being held by John Crilly.'

John was another former prisoner who decided to take on the terrorist. 'There is a huge puff of smoke and on the other side of that smoke, is Steve,' recalls Darryn. 'For a moment, I come out of the tunnel vision. He's alive! He's ok.'

Very quickly, the focus returns and all three men are chasing the terrorist onto London Bridge. Darryn is leading the charge. 'He is running towards a crowd of people with knives above his head. It was pure chaos. My focus is completely on the terrorist. Cars are stopping. People are screaming. I thought that Steve and John must have been behind me somewhere so when I approach the terrorist, I think I am on my own. He turns and comes towards me. As he runs, he raises the knives and I see a tiny piece of flesh on his left side, below his clothes. It was over in a heartbeat, but it feels like twenty seconds to me. Everything was in slow motion. I was fighting for my life. I aimed this 2-metre tusk into 1 centimetre of flesh. The impact buckled him over. He didn't cry out and, when I pulled it out, he buckled over again.'

Darryn wasn't on his own. 'John let off his fire extinguisher again and the smoke covered Steve. It worked because the terrorist didn't see Steve running along the bridge. He got past him and behind him and then grabbed his left shoulder and managed to drag or pull him on the floor. I dropped the tusk and jumped on his back and thrust his wrists up as high as I could go to keep his arms up above his head. He had these protective gloves on. I was holding on to him with all the strength I had in my body.'

Just like Darryn, Steve was determined to make sure that the terrorist couldn't get back up off the floor. 'I shouted at Darryn to grab his hands and we are both on top of him on the floor. I remember people shouting, "Give him a kicking!" We thought we had stopped him but, somehow, he gets back on his feet! I landed a few uppercuts to his face and he's back on the ground. I think that's when the police turned up.'

Darryn was still holding the terrorist's hands. 'I was shouting at people to not hit him. I shifted my weight to protect his head. I was screaming at people to get the knives out of his hands, but they were so heavily strapped. He wasn't saying anything at all. I remember someone with tan-coloured boots standing on my hands. It was hurting so much but it was also a relief because it meant I didn't have to apply the same pressure to restrain him. Moments later, the police arrived.'

The problem for Darryn was that he knew the terrorist was waiting for the police to turn up. He knew that this was the moment he was looking for, the moment to detonate the bomb. 'The police are shouting at me to "get back", to "move away". They are tugging at my jumper trying to pull me off, but I won't let go. Steve comes back and says, "Come on, mate, the police are here, let him go." I'm pretty sure that Steve came back to try and save my life. I've still got his hands. I won't let him kill anyone else. Just at that moment, he relaxes his arms. I thought he was giving up, but he looked at the nearest officer and said, "I'VE GOT A BOMB!"'

Darryn pauses, seemingly to reflect on the intensity of the situation. 'The officer screams, "HE'S GOT A BOMB!" and his voice breaks as he does it. My face is 10 centimetres away from this bomb. There was a tiny gap in one of the boxes strapped to the TNT-shaped sticks around his body. I was so close that I could see a 1-millimetre gap and the box looked hollow, but I also saw something that looked like a calculator, or a mobile phone attached. I was wondering, "Is this bomb real? Can I stop it by restraining his hands? Is it remote activated? Or am I going to get shot and we'll all die anyway?" While all this was racing through my head, one of the officers pulls my hands away and I thought that was the moment the bomb was going to go off. I ran off with my hands over my ears. I heard three pops but there was no smoke coming off the device. I thought they must have shot him, but I didn't want him to die. It might sound strange after what he had done but I didn't want him to have the satisfaction of his choice. He wanted to die that day. That was his plan all along, it seemed to me: to kill as many as he could and then blow himself up. I didn't want his plan to work, especially after what he'd done.'

At this point, Darryn's mind went blank for a few minutes. He has no recollection of what happened. The next thing he remembers is being back on the stairs in Fishmongers' Hall looking down on the scene of devastation and still holding a metre section of the tusk in his hand. He called his partner and told her what had happened. While he was on the phone there was another volley of shots and everyone started screaming again. The police had killed the terrorist on the bridge. Darryn was halfway up the staircase standing next to Steve. The pair of them were watching the paramedics trying to resuscitate Saskia. Between them, they'd helped protect hundreds of people. Steve turned to Darryn and shook his hand.

'Hi. I'm Steve Gallant. I'm a prisoner and today is my first day out of prison in fourteen years.'

I remember hearing about the initial incident while I was driving around that day. Like millions of others, I watched the video of the fire extinguisher going off on the bridge and the men fighting with the terrorist. I heard about the casualties and about the Polish chef, Lukasz, who took on Khan after hearing screams when he was down in the kitchen. Lukasz fought him, suffering five wounds to his arm, but giving many others the opportunity to escape. He was one of many heroes that day.

For weeks, details were sketchy, as police continued their investigations. There were rumours that Lukasz was the man with the narwhal tusk and precious little was known about Darryn, Steve and the others who had helped stop the terrorist taking more lives.

I first met Darryn on the *BBC Breakfast* sofa. I remember being fascinated reading about him the day before he came on, because he had hardly spoken to anyone. His account was captivating but, as soon as you start talking to Darryn, you realise it has taken a huge toll on him. Yes, he is a hero. Yes, he saved lives that day. Yes, he could have been killed. Yes, his life will never be the same again.

'I took medication before I spoke to you that morning,' he says, as we meet again. 'Propranolol lowers your heart rate and helps to stop the sweating. I take the drugs to deal with people. Whenever I am in large groups or if I ever have to talk about what happened at Fishmongers' Hall. It helps me to cope with the anxiety.'

Much of that anxiety goes back to the day of the attack and what happened afterwards. While Darryn and Steve were talking on the stairs, the police came in and started shouting and telling everyone to put everything down.

Darryn was taken to the triage centre and separated from everyone else. 'I kept asking about the girl who had been stabbed, Jane. In those early days, she was the one I would have night terrors about. I listened to the news reports, and they said that one man and one woman had been killed and I was convinced they had it wrong. I thought I had watched her die. I thought it might be part of the trauma. The more I asked about her, the fewer answers I got. I kept reliving it time and time again in my head, over and over. It was only the day before Jack Merritt's funeral that I found out that she had survived and then listening to her testimony at the inquiry helped me enormously. I heard Jane say that the attack just felt like a series of dull blows, like punches. That really helped me to know that she wasn't suffering the sort of pain that I thought she was going through at the time. I couldn't bear the idea of her going through that. It was too much.'

Steve also remembers the moment when his brain suddenly clicked back into gear, standing on those steps with Darryn. 'I looked around me and I realised how many people had been injured. The Polish chap (Lukasz) was sitting on the steps and bleeding. I assumed Jane was dead. I can still see the paramedics shaking their heads over the body of Saskia Jones. I asked a friend where Jack was, and he couldn't tell me what had happened; he was too traumatised.' Steve later discovered the truth about Jack visiting the toilet at the same time the terrorist was preparing himself for the attack. It was tragic timing. He was the first victim. Witnesses remember seeing Jack stumbling out of the toilet with his white shirt 'covered in blood'. He tried to take refuge in the nearby reception office but never recovered from his wounds.

Steve found the prison officer who was meant to be looking after him that day. 'There wasn't much to say. We were both just processing information. I was coming to terms with what had happened; with what I had done. My first day of freedom in fourteen years and here I was chasing a terrorist. And, more than that, the first time I'd used violence since the crime which put me in jail. Darryn took me to one side and told me that I'd saved so many lives, but I was thinking about all the opportunities I'd had to use violence in prison and rejected it. Here I was, having to make a snap decision to attack someone to stop them from hurting someone else. I suppose that is rehabilitation. That is what Jack was so passionate about. We spoke about that a lot.'

Steve lost a friend that day. Dave and Anne Merritt lost a son. 'Jack was one of those people who attracted others,' says his dad. 'He was intelligent, he was a thinker, but he was also committed to his work and his friends. He was loyal. It's one of those strange situations where we only found out just how much people loved him, and how much of a difference he made to people, after he'd gone.'

I ask his mum when his interest in rehabilitation started. 'He studied politics at A level,' says Anne. 'He was always interested in social justice; maybe because we discussed that sort of thing as a family. He did some volunteering when he was at university in Manchester and was interested in ethics. He did the Learning Together course at Cambridge University, after his degree, and started to learn alongside prisoners, people who were serving sentences for serious crimes. I think that was a big eye-opener for him. He realised what a privileged upbringing he'd had, and I think he just wanted to help.'

After his Masters, Jack started working for Learning Together. 'He could see how much injustice there was in the justice system,' says Dave. 'He was desperate to have an influence on that but didn't think he could do that if he went into a job as a criminal barrister. A lot of people have said to us that he saw the person rather than the crime and I am proud of him for that.'

'He understood people,' adds Anne. 'He had an understanding of the circumstances that had led them to the choices they had made in their lives and some of the bad decisions they had made. He connected with people, people who most of us would give up on. People like Steve Gallant.'

When you stop and think about it, it's amazing that Darryn and Steve were working in tandem that day. A man who knows that many in society will never forgive him for the crime he committed, face to face with the man who, just like Jack, feels very deeply that people can change.

When Darryn first came to the UK to work, he visited HMP Kirkham, an open prison. 'I was walking in from the front gate and a guy came up to me to escort me through the prison,' recalls Darryn. 'I asked him how long he'd been working there, and he laughed and said, "I'm a prisoner, mate." I never knew that was possible. He was just a normal guy, walking freely around the prison. I thought he was an off-duty officer. It was incredible.

'I met another man later that day who was so keen to engage. He was telling me that he was looking forward to a chance of having what he called a "real life". He had never worked before he was in prison and arrived there after committing a murder at the age of eighteen. It hit me, here I was standing 20 centimetres away from a guy who had murdered someone, and yet he posed no threat to me. He spoke really well and just wanted to live a normal life. As I listened to him, I realised that I had to challenge my preconceptions. I had thought that all murderers were just monsters and would always be that way, but as I spent more time in prison and met more people, I learned there is always more to every story. I was one of those individuals who thought "these people can't change" but I was learning that I was the one who needed to change.'

Ask yourself this question. The same question I have asked

myself as I wrote and read this chapter: what do you think of Steve Gallant? You have met a man who committed a murder and spent, in total, sixteen years and two months behind bars for it. Steve went back to jail after the incident at Fishmongers' Hall and eventually had his seventeen-year sentence reduced by Royal Prerogative of Mercy by ten months after the Secretary of State for Justice, Robert Buckland, went to see the Queen. You have also met a man who put his own life on the line to save others on his first day of freedom.

Do you see Steve as his solicitor, Neil Hudgell, described him? 'When I first met Steve, he struck me as a hugely articulate and reflective person with a wealth of insight into the prison system. He is a shining example of reformation, not only for himself, but others he has helped.'

If you ever get the chance to speak to Steve, you'll find a man who understands what people think of him. He knows there are some opinions he will never change, and he knows there are some who can't, and won't forgive. I find his determination to keep going admirable.

'London Bridge doesn't negate what I did,' he says, in reflective mood. 'I paid the price for what I did. For me, I never wanted to be seen as benefiting from it. I feel guilty about it even now. London Bridge did contradict the narrative that people can't change. I think it might have made some people think. For once we had a story of something happening that people didn't expect. We gave a voice to another side of the system. Humans are far more complex than a single act and that is something I have learned the hard way. My stepdad was violent, you know,

Dan. I'm not making an excuse but, everywhere I looked, I saw aggression and violence as a way to resolve almost every situation. My partner was attacked in my home, and I reacted to that in, at the time, the only way I knew. I went to prison. I was very loyal to my friends. I protected people and the only ones who stood by me in those early days were my family.'

I've visited plenty of prisons through my work but, thankfully, I've never spent a night in one and I hope that remains the case. Steve has spent years behind bars and has learned a lot along the way.

'I realised that violence had actually caused all my problems and that I had become a person that I didn't want to be. Very early in my sentence, I made a decision to change. My problem was, I still had a life sentence to serve. I started studying. I was trying to shatter my previous way of thinking; I suppose you could call it a flawed belief system, a belief system that had led me to murder. Nothing can change you if you don't want to change, but I'd like to think I spent a lot of my time wisely. The system shouldn't be a barrier to rehabilitation. During my time inside, I've seen all sorts of things cause problems for people who genuinely want to change ... staffing issues, resources, gangs, violence, limited access to courses and too much access to drugs. There are often so many things in the way of progress and it's much easier to just stay as you are.'

I ask Steve if people find it hard to trust him. He pauses and carefully considers his answer. 'When I speak to people, Dan, you know, the 'hang 'em and flog 'em' brigade, you can sometimes be speaking to a brick wall but, when people see the facts or actually spend time with you, they can see a bit of the real you. I don't think it helps when politicians talk about stiffer sentences all the time and a lack of mercy. I think that adds fuel to the fire and, you know how it works, things get whipped up by the media. It's just incredibly complex. I know there is no easy option but so much of it is about perception. I don't advocate a soft approach to crime. I think there should be a zero-tolerance approach to violence. I should have been behind bars for what I did, but I do think we need to look at the way we treat prisoners. They, we, have got to be dealt with humanely. That is something that Jack understood more than most.'

Jack's parents still find it hard to speak about what happened to their son. It hurts and you can see it when you talk to them. Dave is currently working on a memoir, his account of what happened. He was getting ready to leave work and cycle home on that Friday evening in November 2019. He looked at his Twitter account before he got on his bike and saw a link to the *Guardian* website and a story about a terror attack in London. 'Oh no, not again,' he thought as he read about two people being feared dead. His mind jumped back to the terrorist attacks on Westminster Bridge and around Borough Market two years before.

'My life had already changed forever, but I didn't know it yet,' says Dave. 'In a little over six hours' time, I would be in a windowless room in a hospital in East London, being told by people I didn't know that my son Jack was dead, murdered by a man I had never heard of, at an event I didn't know he was attending.'

When Dave arrived home from work, Anne was frantically asking why he hadn't answered his phone. 'Get in the car!' she shouted. 'We need to go to London now, I will explain on the way.'

Anne told her husband that she'd had a phone call from Jack's girlfriend, Leanne. She had explained that Jack had been injured, possibly stabbed, in an incident at Fishmongers' Hall near London Bridge. Casualties were being taken to the Royal London Hospital in East London. That was all the information they had. They got to Cambridge train station and jumped on a train to the capital. They both started scanning websites for news about their son.

'Almost immediately we saw "Two Dead" on the BBC,' says Dave. 'We thought, "It couldn't be Jack", because we'd have heard about it by now. It was 18.15 and the incident had happened at 13.00. We thought that it must have been someone else, but why hadn't we heard anything from Jack? Maybe he was injured? Why hadn't he called us? We kept checking the websites. Refresh. Refresh. We had no calls from the police or anyone else which we thought was a good sign. We thought that, even if he had been stabbed, he was young and fit and could recover. Our minds were racing so we closed all the websites down and just concentrated on getting to the hospital.'

Dave and Anne did get to the hospital where they met the police family liaison officers and, a few hours later, they were given the worst possible news: their son was dead, killed by a terrorist. Dave's knees gave way when he was told. Jack's girlfriend collapsed on the floor and was sobbing. Everyone was sobbing. No one could believe what they were hearing.

Everyone who loses someone they love speaks of the numbness that invades the body when you're trying to process the enormity of what has happened. Dave and Anne felt that as they travelled home. Where do you even start after hearing that news? How do you rebuild? There are so many things to do. So many people to talk to. So many journalists asking questions. Dave was worried about politicians making capital from the death of his son. He didn't want Jack's murder to be used as justification for draconian sentences.

When you speak to Dave and Anne now, it's clear how incredibly proud of their son they are. When I first reached out to them, Dave sent me an email which told me that, if I wanted to understand who Jack was, I should read the attachment. The attachment was what his mum read out at the start of the inquest into what happened at Fishmonger's Hall.

'Jack Merritt was a good person. Jack was a force for good in the world, someone who made other people's lives better for knowing him. We have said many things about Jack, our son, but we felt the best way to paint a picture of him was through the words of those who knew and loved him.'

What followed was a beautifully powerful testimony from a huge range of people: the landlady at Jack's local, his primary school teacher, his friends, his former housemates, his colleagues, his girlfriend and his brother Joe. They all paint a picture of a remarkable young man and Anne read them all. She also read some of Jack's own words about the importance of the work he was doing and why it meant so much to him.

'When you learn in an atmosphere of mutuality, support

and positive expectation, where the peaks are celebrated and the pains are permitted and shared, it can be transformative, for the individuals involved and for the society they form together. This description of the Learning Together experience rings true of my own experiences on the course and is exactly what I want for all of our students. This is why this work is so important to me.'

Dave and Anne will never recover from what happened to Jack but they take great comfort from the man he became, the principles he lived by and the impact he had on others. Anne's closing words at the inquest remain incredibly powerful: 'We are hugely proud of who Jack was and what he stood for. His death was a tragedy, but his life was a triumph.'

Just like the Merritts, Darryn Frost still struggles with the aftermath of that day. He has bouts of depression and has issues with his short-term memory. He says he has learned to be more accepting of this new version of himself through therapy. To this day, he still takes sleeping tablets. If he doesn't, the night terrors come back. He still finds it hard to talk about.

'I can tell if people just want to know the gory details and I switch off. I feel uncomfortable when people try and make me feel or sound like a hero. We need to remember Saskia and Jack. Saskia was focused on understanding and tackling sexual violence and developing effective, survivor-focused strategies to prevent it. Jack was talking about helping prisoners from minorities and he lived his life trying to make a difference. I've been doing this job for fifteen years and I still don't have the same depth of understanding as they did. We should be celebrating their lives.'

I ask Darryn want he now thinks of the man he calls 'the terrorist'; what he thinks of the man who took the lives of two people who would have defended his rights to the ends of the earth.

'I want to understand him better,' says Darryn, after a moment to reflect. 'I don't believe that people or terrorists are born hateful. There is a journey towards that place. I saw the fear in his eyes. He became almost childlike in his negotiations with me. It was like he was begging, not threatening. I wonder how we lost him. I wonder how he was treated as a child. Then I think about how he was treated in prison and whether we have the resources to tackle terrorist ideology. We all have a duty to stop people becoming what he became. Where does terror come from? That's a question I ask myself a lot. How often are we responsible for planting the seeds of hate? How do we engage? Do we understand that sometimes we are the terrorists? Do we question the wars we have waged and the bombs we have dropped? Are we willing to ask tough questions about our own actions? Do we look at the blood which is on our hands? Learning Together was attempting great things, truly transformative. It allowed people like Jack and Saskia to shine, really helping people like Steve, John and many others. It is a real shame that one horrid man can undo all this and cause so much pain. There should have been more scrutiny about who was allowed to attend the programme and the event that day. I feel this is a joint responsibility between the authorities and Cambridge University who ultimately have a duty of care.'

Darryn feels uncomfortable when people call him a 'hero'. He feels uncomfortable because he has thought long and hard about what prison officers put themselves through every day. He'll accept that he put his own life at risk, but he'll also point towards the landings of prisons all over the country where officers are doing the same thing every single day behind locked doors. Fishmongers' Hall brought that risk into a much sharper focus.

Darryn's primary concern now is the way we treat prisoners in this country. He wants to try and use the events at Fishmongers' Hall to help us all understand a little more about the process of rehabilitation.

'You know, nobody has thanked Steve or John (Crilly) for what they did that day. They prevented a massacre. I was asked how I felt about receiving a Ministry of Justice award for what I did, but I told them that I only wanted it if the men who acted alongside me – the two prisoners – got the same thing. You can imagine how that went down! It is unpalatable to give someone like Steve an award for what he did when I can't think of a better example of bravery. People like Steve are seen as lesser humans. Their lives have less value because of their previous actions. We, as a country, keep judging people without giving them credit for who they are or who they have become. Their criminal records follow them forever. Even shorter stints in prison are a life sentence. They have fewer opportunities and can never overcome the social judgement. The more we punish and stigmatise people, the more likely they are to turn back to crime. Perpetual punishment is proven not to work, but we keep going back to it because it wins votes. It's popular but it's also incredibly expensive and ineffective.'

After Steve's sentence was reduced by ten months for what he did at London Bridge, he was released from jail on 3 August 2021. He spent his first day of freedom with Darryn. They went for a drive and had a McDonalds in Oxford.

Steve still lives with the guilt and regret of the crime he committed that landed him in jail. Barrie Jackson had been enjoying a night out in a pub in Hull in 2005. On his way home, he was attacked and beaten so badly that when the paramedics tried to revive him they could not find his mouth. One of the men who attacked him was Steve Gallant. He believed that Jackson had attacked his girlfriend. Steve knows that some people will never forgive him for what he did and, every time they hear about his bravery at Fishmongers' Hall, it brings back all those painful memories. Can anyone ever really change?

'I refuse to define myself as a convicted murderer,' says Steve. 'I used to see kids come into jail all the time and they'd say, "I'm an armed robber" or "I'm a killer". You can still take responsibility for your actions without being defined by them. I'm not a hero for what I did on London Bridge, but does one horrific act of violence follow me around for the rest of my life? That's not who I am.'

Steve is now a mentor to others. He has a lot of knowledge to share. He and Darryn are working together on an idea called Own Merit which is a housing scheme for those who are released from prison and are trying to find their way back into society.

As a Christian, redemption is fundamental to my faith. I always believe there is a way back. I have seen people change and, speaking to Steve, even though I understand the depth of feeling, it seems clear that he is a different man from the one who took the life of another. Steve has written much more about this in his own book which comes out in 2023. I look forward to reading it. It was people like Jack Merritt who helped him to get where he is now, who helped him to see a little further than he would on his own.

It's incredible to think that Jack made such an impact on Steve, and many others, and he was only twenty-five years old. He was only two years out of university but had already done so much with his life. His parents knew he was a firm believer in life after prison, but they question whether someone like Usman Khan could ever be rehabilitated under our current system.

'We firmly believe that people can change,' says Dave, 'but we don't know enough about de-radicalisation. When you look at what happened to Khan, there were fundamental issues which were never addressed, so he came out of prison more dangerous than when he went in. I can't tell you what Jack would have thought about Khan going through prisoner rehabilitation, but I do know he was a believer in due process. Learning Together was never going to help someone like Khan. The only options we seem to have in this country are custodial sentences and then monitoring afterwards. It's laughably incompetent. If you look at the way they dealt with Usman Khan, they all got it wrong. There were so many mistakes made.'

Both Dave and Anne attended the inquest into the Fishmongers' Hall attack. They were trying to find out not only why their son died but also get some answers about why Usman Khan was allowed to be at the event where he took Jack's life. It was a frustratingly difficult listen.

'In some ways I found it easier that it wasn't just one mistake,' continues Dave. 'If it was one decision that led to Jack's death, then I would find it harder, but all the agencies that dealt with Usman Khan made mistakes. We got fed up with hearing phrases like "I didn't consider that my job" or "I assumed someone else was doing that" or "I assumed someone else was watching him". It was hard, but we found the inquest helpful because people had to step up and accept accountability. They couldn't just hide behind the excuse of national security.'

I ask Anne if she thinks lessons have been learned. 'I'd like to think that's the case, but I'm not convinced,' she says. 'The one witness who really impressed us was the head of the probation service who said measures that they put in place were not fit for purpose. When it came to the work of MAPPA (Multi Agency Public Protection Arrangements), the body responsible for looking after sexual and/or violent offenders like Khan, I don't think I will ever get over some of the incompetence. They manage some of the most dangerous people that we have in this country and I'm not confident that the measures are any better now than they were then. The whole attitude seemed to be one of "there is nothing to see here".'

'You know we have never had an apology,' says Dave. 'Certain individuals have been kind and considerate, but we've also seen staggering levels of arrogance and unwillingness to accept responsibility.'

I ask them how they are now, nearly two-and-a-half years on. They glance at each other, and Dave speaks. 'Birthdays and Christmases will always be hard. The anniversary of the incident, the anniversary of his funeral; October through to Christmas every year remains tough. Daft as it may seem, as horrible as losing Jack has been, there has been an awful lot of publicity for the good work that he was doing, and the person that he was, and that has been a real source of comfort. I often think that if Jack had just been run over by a car, then there would have been none of this, we would never have known or learned so much about him. It's amazing that he was such a help to so many and that continues to help us through.

'People continue to do nice things,' says Dave. 'Cambridge United invited us all along to a football match and did a minute's silence for Jack and they invited us again recently. We have also tried something called Creating With Jack Merritt where we encourage people to do something creative on the anniversary of his death. That certainly makes the day itself a little easier. We find that if you tackle days like that head on, try and fill them with at least something, then the heartache is a little easier to come to terms with. It's lovely that so many people continue to be inspired by what he did. We know that, as time goes by, people's memories of him will fade . . . but ours never will.'

Darryn will continue to wrestle with the demons of that day. He firmly believes, as Jack did, that rehabilitation is possible. The actions of the terrorist he attacked have not changed that. For him, 19 November 2019 is the perfect example of just how blurred the picture is in this country when it comes to issues like race, immigration and rehabilitation.

Speaking to Darryn, Steve and Jack's mum and dad has given me much to think about and I hope it has done the same for you. It has also helped me to frame one of the biggest breaking news stories of the last few years.

The story of that day has so many layers. It's about Lukasz, a Polish immigrant, who put his life at risk. It's about Steve, a convicted murderer, who wants to be part of society again. It's about Saskia and Jack, two brilliant, gifted young people who were convinced that there should and could be life after prison . . . even for the man who took theirs. There are so many elements which make us look at what we believe, what we hold dear and force us to ask ourselves the most difficult questions. I suppose the key to all of this is just how determined we are to find the answers.

JIMI

During my time on television, I have announced a number of deaths and read hundreds of tributes. It is a tough part of the job. Most of those tributes talk about amazing people, great friends and big ambitions. I occasionally wonder how true all those words are and how many are affected by our determination to never speak ill of the dead.

On the morning of 26 April 2021, I remember reading out a series of glowing tributes to Folajimi Olubunmi-Adewole. Jimi, as he was known to his friends, was the young man – twenty years old – who jumped into the River Thames to try and save a woman who had fallen from London Bridge around midnight on Saturday 24 April.

I remember being struck by the depth of feeling from his family and friends. We spoke to the owner of The Cinnamon Club, the restaurant where he worked, and he talked about a young man who inspired all those around him. His parents spoke of his 'precious heart', Tim's youth pastor at church mentioned the boy who was 'always looking out for others', and his friends, through the tears, paid tribute to someone who they all 'looked up to'.

No one seemed surprised that he jumped into the river. No one seemed surprised that he lost his own life trying to save someone else's. One of his closest friends was with him on the steps at the bottom of London Bridge that night. Bernard Kosia had taken his top off and was ready to jump in. 'No, bro,' said Jimi, preparing himself to hand Bernard his phone. 'You can't swim! Talk to the police.' Jimi jumped into the pitch-black Thames and that was the last Bernard ever saw of him.

The two boys met when they were eleven years old. Jimi had arrived from Nigeria at the age of ten, Bernard from Sierra Leone when he was four. Bernard was doing his usual thing of playing football in the park at 7 o'clock in the morning. He was a trainee at Chelsea at the time, in the same year group as Callum Hudson Odoi and Tariq Lamptey. He was highly fancied. Jimi was also a footballer, but he was out running in the park, as he always did.

Jimi saw Bernard working on his skills and walked over and introduced himself. 'He was so confident,' remembers Bernard. 'He said "hello" and we started talking. He told me about the school he went to and his family. I didn't know it then, but this was the start of the best friendship of my life. We trained together, we laughed together and then we walked home together.'

It was when they got back to their flats that the two lads realised they were neighbours. Bernard lived on the Vauban estate in Bermondsey and Jimi was directly across the road in the Neckinger estate.

'We were best friends from that moment,' says Bernard, 'from that first session in the park. We had a regular routine. We would train at 7 o'clock in the morning and, even at that early age, he was always encouraging me and telling me how far I could go. We went to different schools, but we spent most of our spare time together. As we got older, we just got closer.'

The boys would go to the cinema together. They loved watching films there. If it wasn't the cinema they were down at the local arcade. At the age of sixteen, Bernard was released from Chelsea. It was a crushing blow but there was an opportunity to go to America and play for Columbus Crew.

'Jimi would contact me all the time,' remembers Bernard with a smile. 'That's what he was like, he was confident, but he knew I was shy. We were so tight. I would come back from training late at night and send him a message to ask if he was up and he would come straight back and then we'd be up for hours, on *FIFA*, just chatting. We talked about everything. He was always looking out for me, but it wasn't just me, Jimi looked out for everyone.'

While Bernard was in America, Jimi was back in the UK studying business. He was a young man with big ambitions and big plans. He was the youngest of three brothers but was always telling his family that one day he would be a superstar musician and buy everyone a house.

'He was just different from the rest of us,' says his eldest brother Ayodeji. 'We were all nice boys, but Jimi was special. He was kind and generous. He would give his last penny to someone if they needed it and he would never think of the consequences for himself. I can't really remember him ever saying "no" if someone asked him for something. He was the ultimate servant.'

Jimi's family had arrived from Nigeria in stages. Jimi came to the UK in 2011 and Ayodeji and his middle brother, BJ, arrived much later.

'Jimi loved it when we were together as a family,' says Ayodeji. 'We would sometimes talk about how we could make things better, easier, for our parents. Jimi wanted to buy a big family house where we could all get together at Christmas.' Ayodeji laughs as he remembers his brother's bold promises. '"When I'm rich," he would say, and then tell us all how he would help everyone with his money. I'm the oldest brother but Jimi was a leader. "I will sort this family out," he'd say and we believed him. He was a great footballer, but his real talent was music.' Ayodeji stops for a moment.

'Is everything ok?' I ask tentatively.

'I was just remembering that he passed away a week before the official release of his first single. Did you know that? He had the whole outfit ready for the shoot. We laid him to rest in the brand-new Air Force One trainers he had bought.'

Both his brother and his best friend are full of stories about Jimi. They are bursting with examples of his care and generosity of spirit. 'There was this one time,' says Bernard, 'when we were kids, our parents would give us pocket money for food. We were always hungry after our football training and, one day, we decided to head down to Morley's (the local chicken shop). I only had £1, and Jimi had £2. He took my pound and said, "We are going to share this." He bought five wings and chips and we had a feast. What was his was mine and mine was his. He was always being that guy. He was one of the most welcoming people you will ever meet. His heart was pure, and he would always be loyal and supportive. Jimi also had the talent to make you laugh, however bad you were feeling. You could never be angry with him. I realised that I could talk to him about anything, and he would always give me advice. I would talk about missing home when I was in America. He was the only one who understood, and he would remind me of my purpose for being there and tell me that I just needed to finish things off. "You just need to try your best," he would say, and he was always encouraging me to keep pushing. He believed in me. It's hard for me to explain how much that meant to me. He was just special.'

Bernard came back from the United States because of the Covid pandemic. He needed a job but was really struggling to find one. Guess who came to his aid?

'I was getting desperate. I needed some money to live, and I put it all down in a group chat on WhatsApp. Jimi was working in a restaurant called The Cinnamon Club at the time and called me straightaway and said, "There is a job going here. Come to the restaurant, act like you don't know me, I will open the door so make sure you act professional." I did exactly like he said,' explains Bernard. 'During the interview I spotted Jimi walking past the room to check that it was going well. At the end, he met me on the stairs around the back and I told him the manager had asked for me to come in the next day. He was so happy for

Martin Hibbert and his daughter, Eve, at their favourite restaurant (San Carlo in Manchester) on the night of the bomb. This was four hours before they were injured.

The X-ray showing the lumps of metal in Martin's body after the blast.

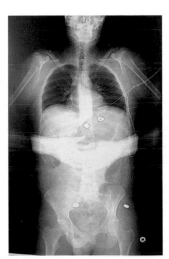

The rehab starts here. It has been an incredibly long road but Martin has had brilliant care throughout.

Sizing up the Kilimanjaro challenge.

The sunrise I told Martin to look out for. I'm so glad he got to see it too.

The summit . . . and the Manchester United flag. Only the second paraplegic to make it to the top of Africa's highest mountain.

Baby Rose with her mum, Donna. Rose was deaf from birth but her mum has always fought for her to have the same opportunities as others.

The nation took her to their hearts and voted her *Strictly* winner alongside Giovanni.

This is the shot I posted the night after the final which went viral. Mum and daughter: they didn't say much but the hug meant everything.

Mike's daughter Beth.   Andy's daughter Sophie.   Tim's daughter Emily.

Mike (left), Andy (middle) and Tim (right). The 3 Dads: ready to start their walk to raise awareness and money for suicide prevention.

It was a long walk but, as Mike, Tim and Andy explain in the book, they met some amazing people along the way and inspired millions.

Start them young! Paul Harvey with his son, Nick, at the piano.

The famous red top, the legendary piano and the genius Paul.

Father and son. Paul's talent was wonderful to watch but so many people were touched by his beautiful relationship with his son.

Darryn Frost (left) and Steve Gallant have remained good friends since the Fishmongers' Hall terrorist attack. What they both did that day was remarkable.

'His death was a tragedy, his life was a triumph'. Dave and Anne Merritt with their son, Jack, who lost his life in the attack.

Jimi (right) continues to inspire his friend Bernard, and many others, after he died jumping into the River Thames to save a drowning woman.

Two-time world champion Nadiya Bychkova with her mum, Larisa.

No piano but this was the rumba with that red backless dress.

Heather Stewart with her husband Stephen. They had been together since they were teenagers but he sadly died from Covid.

Ahsan-ul-Haq Chaudry (second from the right) and his family. Left to right: Saleyha, Saima, Fauzia, Shoaib and Safiyah.

With Shoaib and grandsons Ismaeel and Yusuf.

It's always a pleasure chatting with Maggie Keenan and May Parsons.

As May tells us in the book, the pandemic made her look at nursing in a completely different way.

Giving Tony Foulds a lift. He always makes me laugh. This was the day he told me about his favourite drink – fiddy fiddy – which is half tea and half coffee. Yuck!

He can often be found in Endcliffe Park, blowing the leaves off the path. Apparently, he'll be 'doing the M1' next.

The boat Figen Murray was talking about, with 'Ubuntu' on one side and '#BEMOREMARTYN' on the other.

Figen with her well-deserved OBE. The fight for change continues.

Paula and Tony Hudgell still going strong. You can read an update on them in the 'Still Remarkable' chapter.

Lisa Ashton continues her great work for the Winnie Mabaso Foundation. Palesa is flying at hairdressing college and the kids at Ilamula House were very supportive during *Strictly*.

Tamar Pollard standing next to the memorial to her dad in Hungary.

Jo Pollard (Tamar's mum) with Istvan Dudas – the man she forgave for killing her husband.

me. "I told you you'd get the job," he said. Those are memories you have to keep in your heart.'

Jimi and Bernard were working together at The Cinnamon Club on Saturday 24 April 2021. I ask Bernard to tell me what he can remember about that night and there is a long pause, and he pushes the air out of his mouth.

'It's still hard, you know,' says Bernard. 'I don't like to go over it. I'll see what I can say. I don't like to relive it because it's all so real, but I also want people to see the man he was.' I told Bernard that we could stop whenever he wanted. He said that he finds talking about being on London Bridge that night incredibly painful. 'Let's see how we get on,' he says.

'That day was a normal day in the restaurant,' remembers Bernard. 'The only difference was that we finished early. Normally we would finish work about 1 or 2 o'clock in the morning but, because of Covid restrictions, we got everything done before midnight. "Let's go home, man," Jimi said, so we tidied everything up, cleaned the place and headed out. It was one of those nights where we were just walking and talking.' Bernard laughs . . . 'There was never a day you couldn't have a deep conversation with Jimi. He loved to go deep. We talked about life and what we wanted to do. We talked about our families and the sacrifices our parents had made to build us the life that we wanted. Jimi mentioned again that he wanted to move his mum out of the area; to give her a better life. He was telling me about his missus, and we were, you know, bouncing off each other and laughing

'Do you know what?' says Bernard. 'I heard him say "I love

you, bro" and I was so happy he did that. It allowed me to say it back. I started getting deep. I told him that I was so grateful that I could have conversations with him that were so open. I told him I was grateful that he was in my life and that it was great to have such a cool adviser; that is what he was like . . . Jimi the adviser.'

I tell Bernard that it's incredible that the pair of them were talking about sacrifice when you think about what he was about to do. 'It's something we talked about a lot,' says Bernard. 'Both our parents had done so much just to put food on the table. My mum was always working two jobs. She would get up at 4 a.m. to work in a bakery and then do a shift at a shop. Jimi was the same. He had that in him. He was the breadwinner in his family. He would even take some of my shifts sometimes and work double. You could learn so much from his attitude. Let me tell you, when I was in the academy at Chelsea, I felt on top of the world. I had everything at my feet. People look up to you and then, one day, you are released and the dream shatters in front of you. When I got that job at the restaurant, Jimi showed me what it was to be humble and how there is great reward in working hard and serving others. I would watch him clean the spoons. How can anyone clean hundreds of spoons with such a big smile on their face? But Jimi loved it. He had that servant nature built into him.'

I ask Bernard if he feels comfortable to keep talking about the night and what happened after their conversation. He says he does. 'We got to London Bridge around midnight,' he recalls, 'and two people ran up to us. We were around about the halfway point of the bridge. They told us that someone had jumped into the river. They had a video of it. We were looking at the video and Jimi called the police. I ran back and found the steps down to the river. The tide was really high. I could hear a woman screaming but she was already on the other side of the bridge. The current was taking her down the river. We made our way down the stairs on the other side of the bridge, and we could just about see her, right in the middle of the river. Jimi was still on the phone to the police. He was trying to tell them exactly where we were. It was really hard to see anything. It was so dark. We were doing our best to talk to her, and she kept screaming, "I'm going to die! I'm going to die!" I watched Jimi come to life.'

'The only way I can describe it is that he felt the woman's pain,' says Bernard. 'You could see it on his face. I had taken my top off and was ready to go in. There was another guy with us, Joaquin (Garcia) who was also getting ready. Joaquin and Jimi both took off their clothes and Jimi gave me his phone, but I wanted to go too. He said, 'No, bro, you can't swim! You talk to the police.' They both jumped in. They were side by side. I was trying to talk to the police and tell them what was happening and where we were, but I was also trying to listen to Jimi.

'I could just hear his voice echoing around. He was calling my name.

"'BERNZ! BERNZ! BERNZ!" He was desperate.

'I thought I could see something in the shadows, but I was talking and shouting at the river. I couldn't see him, but I knew he was there somewhere. I shouted out to him . . . "HOLD ON

BRO! HOLD ON!" His voice just floated away and then it was gone.'

A few minutes later the police arrived. Joaquin, an Argentinian-born chef, had reached the woman in the Thames and saved her life. I know that this chapter is focusing on Jimi, but Joaquin's actions are also worthy of the highest praise. In a TV interview near the time, he talked about meeting Jimi and being asked by the Londoner if he was ready to 'jump with me'. Joaquin said they counted down from three and leapt into the river. He had just finished his shift at a Mexican restaurant near the Thames and was walking over the bridge at the time. Despite the strong currents, he managed to reach the woman in the middle of the river. As she lay on top of him, struggling for air, Joaquin managed to stay afloat and keep them both alive. They were later rescued from the water by the coastguard and the Metropolitan Police Marine Unit. Jimi never made it to her and never made it back.

'It still haunts me, hearing that voice,' says Bernard. 'I think about that woman a lot. I don't blame her at all. I just hope she is ok. What I remember, more than anything else, is that I just knew Jimi had gone. I could feel it. I was overwhelmed with it all and just in a state of shock. I didn't know what to do. I am not the type to cry but the whole of London heard me that night.'

The police turned up at Jimi's house in the early hours of the morning to break the news to his broken parents.

'My mum called me,' remembers Jimi's brother, Ayodeji. 'My phone went off around 1.30 in the morning. I wasn't in London. I was in the West Midlands. Mum was screaming but not making much sense . . . "THE POLICE!" she said, "THE POLICE ARE HERE!" and she just kept saying his name: "JIMI! JIMI! JIMI!" I could hear the police in the background saying, "We are still searching for him." I knew they wouldn't be there to arrest him because that wasn't Jimi. "JIMI IS IN THE WATER!" Mum was shouting and repeating herself. "What are you talking about?" I said. She was shouting, "LONDON BRIDGE!" Something spoke to me. It was all so confused, but I knew he had gone. Something wasn't right. I think maybe they were trying to give her some hope because she was so emotional. I got the first train down to London in the morning and, just as I got home, the police came round and said they had found his body at Poplar. A few days later we went down, as a family, to identify him.'

What Jimi did that night had a huge impact on so many people. In the days and weeks following, his was a name on so many lips. He was praised by politicians, lauded by community leaders and held up as an example everywhere you looked.

I often think about how I would react in that situation. I appreciate it's hard to know unless you've been there. Are you able to keep your head when everyone is losing theirs? How would you respond if you had to put your own life at risk to help someone else? Would you give it a second thought? Do your actions and words up to that point in your life dictate how you will react or is it just an impulse?

I've never had to think about jumping into a river. The closest I have ever come to something similar was when a friend of mine got hit by a car when we were on mopeds in Benidorm. He didn't look left or right at the final crossroads as we headed out of the city, and he was hit by a car travelling at about 35 mph. I was on the moped behind him and saw it all happen. His bike and body flew into the air and as he landed, he suffered a compound fracture of one of his legs. There was blood and bone everywhere and Stuart was in shock, trying to lift himself off the boiling hot tarmac. One of my mum's jobs was to be a first-aid trainer and it all came flooding back to me. While some of our other friends were being sick on the side of the road, I remembered the basics and looked after Stuart until the ambulance arrived and, on the way to hospital, I rang his mum back in the UK to let her know that he was hurt but he was ok. I am glad I didn't panic. I am glad that I was able to stay calm and think clearly but, the difference is, I was never in danger. There was never any chance of me being hurt or worse. There was no sacrifice. Stuart's mum thanked me for looking after her son and Stuart was happy, he never lost his leg and I know my actions didn't live long in the memory. The difference with Bernard is that, even though he lost a dear friend to the River Thames that night, he lives in the light of Jimi's example and his friend continues to inspire him.

'I still think about what he said to me, Dan,' says Bernard. 'You know, on the steps, when he told me that I couldn't swim and that I shouldn't jump in. Even in his last moments, he still had me, he was looking after me, protecting me. How do you go about replacing a friend like that? There aren't any other Jimi's out there. Let me try and explain. I'm not just saying this because he isn't around anymore, but I never argued with him. I never disagreed with him. The only thing we would ever get heated over was politics!' Bernard giggles remembering some of their conversations. 'We would keep talking about it until we laughed about it.'

When you speak to Bernard, it's obvious that he finds life without Jimi difficult. They were a partnership and Jimi watched out for him, as he seemingly did for everyone. 'Before he died, he sent me some of his music on files,' says Bernard. 'I started playing his songs the day after he died, and it was the story of us. It was the life he lived. It was our life. It meant so much. When I listen to his music, he comes back to me. I just wish he could have lived to drop the songs that he wanted to drop.'

On the first anniversary of Jimi's death, Bernard and some of their mutual friends got together to release one of Jimi's unfinished songs. It was called 'Let You Know'. They enlisted the help of musicians Psychs and C4 and Bernard was so happy with the finished single. I ask him why he is willing to go to such lengths to continue Jimi's legacy.

'The boy still means the world to me,' explains Bernard. 'When someone has been that loyal, all you can do is be loyal in return. I don't live my life for one anymore, I live it for two. I want people to see how much of a heart he had, how he cared about the community. It was an honour to spend time with someone like Jimi and I have to pay him back, pay the world back for the time I had with him. I had someone who taught me life lessons. He motivated me and I like to think I motivated him too. It was a deep friendship and we made sure that nothing would ever come in between us.'

The impact of Jimi's death is felt just as strongly by his family as it is by his friends. His mum, dad and his brothers plan on writing a book about Jimi and their experiences together in 2023, but his eldest brother, Ayodeji, was happy to talk to me about Jimi for *Standing on the Shoulders*. 'I cannot quantify it,' says Ayodeji. 'His loss was huge for our family. We lost our best. Imagine a team losing their best player. My mum and dad have been through therapy, but he leaves a huge hole in all our hearts. I think we would all do anything to bring him back. Anything.'

It was in the months after the incident on London Bridge that Ayodeji realised the extent of Jimi's influence. 'I knew my brother was friendly, but I didn't know he was that popular in London,' says a proud sibling. 'When I say I want to do something for Jimi, thousands of people turn up . . . and I mean thousands. The whole of Southwark and Bermondsey come out for my brother; people even take a day off work for him, even now! I love to hear about the people that he helped. So many people say to me, "Jimi did this for me", "Jimi advised me to go to school", "Jimi helped me at work", "Jimi supported me when no one else would". He would go to any lengths to support people.'

Ayodeji hasn't been through therapy like his parents, but, just like Bernard, he keeps coming back to Jimi's music when he needs a lift. 'I go back to his songs and I still feel his presence,' says his brother. 'I picture myself in a good way. I think about Jimi in the future. I wonder what Jimi would say. When things aren't going well, or I'm having a tough time, I know he would push me forward, I know he would pat me on the back. He's not here anymore but I still feed off his positive energy. I picture him in the future, and he makes me smile. I don't think that will ever change. It's strange because he's my brother, but so many other people know him so well. He has inspired so many. Our house is always open, and it is amazing how many people want to come around and talk about him. We have had so many testimonies. Let me give you an example. We had one event for Jimi and a white lady came up to me and said, "I never knew a black man could have this heart." I know that what she said was clumsy, but all she had ever seen was black kids in gangs. All she knew was stabbings, robberies and crime. Jimi showed her something else, something different. Jimi changed the stereotype.'

This is going to sound strange, but when you hear about Jimi, he doesn't sound real. It's hard to imagine someone so kind, so outgoing, so selfless, so sacrificial, so giving, so caring, and yet there is a familiar thread whenever you ask anyone about him. It's almost other-worldly. I ask his brother if Jimi was a man of faith.

'He was,' says Ayodeji nodding. 'A few days before he died, he called the youth pastor at our church, and they prayed together. I know that he rededicated his life to Jesus Christ in the week of his death. I'm sure that was all in his mind when he jumped in that river to save that woman.'

Sacrifice is one element of the Christian faith that I have always found fascinating. It is a theme throughout the Bible with all the Old Testament practices and sacrifices pointing towards the ultimate example of Jesus' death on the cross. 'Greater love has no one than this, than to lay down one's life for one's friends.' For Christians, sacrifice is at the very heart of the gospel message, a message that Jimi would have known only too well.

And it's a message that evokes such a powerful response wherever you see it. It's no surprise that it has long been used by storytellers and film-makers. Jimi loved going to the cinema with Bernard and I am sure he saw plenty of those examples himself.

I remember my own children all in tears because of the actions of Groot in *Guardians of the Galaxy*. The creators of the Marvel Cinematic Universe were able to make a tree, who only ever speaks the same three words, become one of their most beloved characters. As his friends are about to die, Groot spreads out his branches and covers them in a protective ball of wood. Rocket, his best friend, begs him to stop and Groot simply wipes away his tears and says, 'WE . . . are . . . Groot.' The scene ends, we hear the ship crash and all Groot's branches are shattered, broken and scattered all over the ground.

Cast your mind back to Arnold Schwarzenegger's character in *Terminator 2* muttering, 'I know now why you cry' before lowering himself into the molten metal to save mankind. Tom Hanks as Captain Miller in *Saving Private Ryan* who tells Matt Damon to 'earn' the sacrifice of those who have died so that he would make it back safely. Obi Wan Kenobi in *Star Wars*, Boromir in *Lord of the Rings* and Tony Stark in *Avengers: End-game* . . . the list is endless. Nothing stirs the heart like sacrifice and that is why I think Jimi's story is so powerful and has made such a lasting impact. There is no Hollywood gloss here. His sacrifice was true and real and pure, and he paid the ultimate price.

When I was thinking about who to put in this book, Folajimi Olubunmi-Adewole was an obvious candidate. Right back at the start, I told you I wanted to write about people who lifted others up. I wanted to write about people who give us a different perspective, help us to see more clearly and encourage us to follow their example. Jimi was all of those things and more and, thankfully, there are many people willing to share his incredible legacy.

'I was so fortunate to have crossed paths with him,' says Bernard. 'Jimi was everybody's favourite person, so I feel blessed to have spent so much time with him. He was adamant that he was going to save that woman; nothing was going to stop him doing what he did to stop her from drowning. Like I said, I am sure he felt her tears and that's why he did what he did. That tells you a lot about Jimi. He brought a light into my life; he brought life into our neighbourhood; he brought energy. There was never any negativity with him. Even if it took a while to find it, Jimi would always get to the good stuff. When I was released by Chelsea, you can imagine I was in a dark place. That was my life. All my dreams were wrapped up in playing football, but Jimi showed me what reality was. I was still living in the past, but he showed me what my future could look like. He was there at the peak of my life, and he was there when I had nothing. That is the sign of a true friend and everyone who shared a path with him would say exactly the same thing.'

It was a real privilege to get to speak to some of those who 'shared a path' with Jimi for this chapter. I caught up with Joseph, Marvellous, David, Adiatu and Yinka after a fitness class, run by Joseph, at a primary school in Peckham. Their words echo much of what Bernard said about his friend, full of life and full of fun.

'We arrived from Nigeria at the same time,' says Joseph. 'We were friends from year seven. We had what I would describe as love fights,' he says, laughing. 'As we got older, we got much closer and we had great talks. He was such a selfless person and he always talked about his family. The timing of everything was just so sad. He had found his passion in music, and it was all about to happen for him. I should tell you, he was annoying too, Dan. I always used to get more attention from the girls when we were younger and then Jimi got taller and more handsome. We always had that banter together.'

Joseph is sat next to David. The pair of them are giggling away as they share stories about their friend. David also came from Nigeria. 'Me and Jimi shared the same skin tone,' he says. 'We had an understanding, brothers in arms. We went to the same sixth form and I could always relate to him. He had so much compassion and was full of the right advice. It sounds strange but, whenever I spoke to Jimi, he would always make me feel calm.'

'Jimi was a flirt,' jumps in Marvellous, as the others erupt in laughter. 'We were always chasing each other, fighting together, struggling together. We shared an immigration story, and he took care of me; of everybody. I used to work in a shop and

Jimi would come and see me on the same day, at the same time, every week, just to check up on me. He would talk to me for thirty minutes; until I was told to get back to work.'

Yinka is the next to join the conversation. 'We were entrepreneurs. Jimi was at the forefront of business. He would go to Morrisons each day before school and buy ice-creams, donuts and cookies. I still don't know how he kept those ice-creams cold until lunchtime . . . but he did. He would sell them all and we would have silly arguments about territory and what we were selling. I loved the fact that he didn't care about negativity . . . about what people said about him. That gave me confidence too. He changed my attitude. I watched him grow so much when he did National Citizen Service after GCSEs.' The NCS was set up by the coalition government in 2010 as part of the Big Society initiative. It normally took place in the school holidays and would see teenagers – aged between fifteen and seventeen – go on a residential visit, usually to an activity centre in the countryside. 'If I'm honest with you, he was so annoying,' says Yinka, 'but we all loved him . . . everyone loved him. I admired the fact that, even if he had done nothing wrong, he was always the first to apologise. That is one of the many things I learned from Jimi. He was always teaching us all.'

'And what about you, Adiatu? How were you and Jimi?' I ask.

'Love/hate,' she says through a giant grin. 'I met him in sixth form, and we would always go home together on the same bus. He could be a pain, but he brought light into the whole place. He made everyone laugh and he made everyone happy. You needed his presence to have a good day and there aren't many people like that in the world. Jimi is the reason I continued with sixth form.'

'Really?' says one of the others in amazement.

'Yeah, for real,' replies Adiatu. 'I was down after my exams because I knew I wouldn't see him around much anymore. We would talk on the bus and sometimes he would open up to me. I loved being around him. The sixth form would have been nothing without Jimi.'

'He was the common-room clown,' shouts Marvellous from the back of the group. From this point on, our discussion became much more of a free-for-all with people jumping in and sharing stories of Jimi but also their own lives. We touched on friendship, sacrifice, education, love, government policy, compassion, immigration, racism and everything in between. It was fascinating and, for me, an incredibly educational half an hour.

Marvellous, who also arrived in the UK from Nigeria and first met Jimi in secondary school, continues as the conversation moves to how Jimi changed perceptions of what it was to be young and black. 'When I came here, I knew what I wanted to do. I wanted to do well. So many people helped me along the way: teachers, friends . . . I had years of growth because of those people. It hurts that people don't understand, don't know the heart that we have. Being black . . . I am proud to be black.' The rest of the group nod in agreement. 'We are welcoming and loving. What Jimi did was nothing to do with race. It was just about being a person and looking after your other people.'

'I remember hearing about what happened,' says David. 'Joseph called me, and I thought it was a joke. I heard him crying on the phone. I got a cab down there straightaway. I knew that it was something that Jimi would do, but I was praying that he would somehow survive.'

'David is always the bearer of bad news,' says Marvellous. 'What?' responds David, in mock shock. 'Really?' The rest of the group are laughing. 'You know it,' cackles Marvellous. The conversation settles again as she continues. 'I was in denial at first when he told me but then I thought to myself, "What would Jimi do?" and Jimi would have called everyone, so they heard it from him first. I didn't want them to see it on social media so that's what I did. I called as many people as I could.'

'Bernard was the one who told me,' says Joseph. 'I have thought about this a lot, but I think, if Jimi had another chance, I don't think he would do it again. I think he should have considered the people he left behind. He left his family behind.' He bows his head. 'He left us behind. He had so many plans for the future, he was a hero, he was like my brother. I don't think he was thinking straight. He allowed his heart to take over. I know that I couldn't have done what he did, none of us could,' says Joseph, looking around. 'It breaks me, but I love the way that he died, if you know what I mean . . . trying to save someone else. He died doing the holy thing.'

Yinka hasn't spoken for a while, but I have been watching him carefully listening to his friends. I ask him how he found out. 'Another friend of ours called Princess told me Jimi was dead,' he says. 'My first thought was knife crime. That's what came into my head straightaway. When she told me, I was actually relieved because there wasn't going to be a big discussion

about knives and gang culture. Instead, it was all about a celebration of Jimi, who he was and what he did. The next day, we
all met up at his house, do you remember?' The rest of the group
again nod. 'He was always bringing us together, even in death.
Look at us now, here we are again, because of Jimi.'

'Dan,' says Joseph. 'Can I be honest with you?'

'Of course,' I respond. 'What do you want to say?'

'The struggle is real.'

'What do you mean, Joseph?'

'The life of a black immigrant in this country. I don't know
if you want me to tell you about it, but it's hard, it was hard for
Jimi. It's hard for all of us.'

I tell Joseph I would love for him to tell me about it. He
adjusts his position and looks a little unsure for the first time.

'Jimi would still be here if he'd had access to university.'
Everyone falls silent for the first time. Bernard, who has been
kicking a ball about in the background for much of the conversation, stops and walks in behind Joseph to listen as he
continues.

'That's what he wanted to do. He wanted to go to university after sixth form, but he wasn't able to. He didn't have his
biometric.'

A 'biometric', or Biometric Residency Permit (BRP), is a card
that contains your name, date and place of birth, fingerprints,
photograph, immigration status and says whether you have
access to public funds.

Joseph continues. 'You can only go to university three years
after you get your leave to remain. I arrived here in 2011. I have

worked so hard since then. I want to do medicine; I want to be a doctor, but I can't get in the system even though I have the grades. I have just got my biometric but my friends from school are in their third year of medical training. I was robbed of that opportunity.'

'We love this country,' adds Yinka. 'We work hard here, and we pay our taxes, but life is unfair, particularly as an immigrant. None of us have been able to go to university.'

'If feels like we are money-making machines sometimes,' says Joseph as Marvellous joins the conversation too. 'We have to spend thousands of pounds each time we apply for leave to remain,' Marvellous adds. 'We have to do that every two-and-a-half years and, in all that time, you have no access to public funds.'

'That is why Jimi had to set up an empire at school,' interjects Joseph. 'We have to find other ways of making money. It's no surprise that some are working for cash before the legal age. There is pressure to support your family, send money back home to help others. That is what Jimi was doing. We have got to do a lot of things just to survive.'

Yinka jumps in again. 'Education becomes the last thing on your list, even though it should be the most important thing! When you think that you have no prospect of going to university or maybe getting the job you want, you have to change your dreams. You can't really think about the future, you can't look forward because you feel like everything is set up to make it as hard as possible.'

Bernard has never heard his friends talk about this before.

He wants to add something. 'It was different for me, Dan. I was given access to everything because I was a trainee at Chelsea. All this was taken care of. I was ignorant of the struggle. That all changed when I left the football system. I was cast aside, but these guys, and Jimi, had that from the start. That's why Jimi was so important. He made me realise what it was to be a hard worker. That was his way out of poverty. He was already used to it when we worked in that restaurant. He'd watched his parents work every hour and I watched him do the same. He never stopped going, he never stopped working.'

David picks up on Bernard's thoughts. 'And remember, when you clock eighteen, you have to pay more for all the immigration processes because you are then an adult. You can see why people are forced to wash plates at parties when they are underage or pack chairs away for cash. On top of all that, we are all painted as scroungers who are just out for benefits. We want to work; we want to contribute.' He points at his friends. 'Marvellous and Joseph both want to be doctors, but they can't get into the system. Jimi was in that struggle his whole life. There is so much that happened to him that you think would make him hate the world and hate the society that pushed him to the side and is set up against his family . . . but he still jumped in the river. He still tried to save that woman. That is the mark of the man.'

Marvellous is one of those currently lost in the system. 'I applied for my biometric eight months ago,' she says, clearly exasperated. 'I can't apply for a medical course until I get it and it's only after that, that I can apply for student finance. I expect to get the minimum amount and that means I will not be able to go to university anyway. We all know they can process your application quickly because, if you pay them £800, they can do it in a day! That shows you it can be done. We are doing our A levels and doing twelve-hour shifts at the same time! Your life is in limbo. There is complete uncertainty at every turn. You can't plan for anything. Think about the emotional damage and what that does to you, trying to look after your loved ones. My mum hasn't slept for ten years!'

'It feels like we are in a cage, Dan,' says Joseph. 'All we can do is work our backsides off to get out of that cage, but sometimes, no matter what you do, it won't open.'

'There are no excuses,' adds Yinka, 'but, you can see, can't you, why people stop caring about their education. You can see why it's easy just to mess about in school and start mixing with the wrong people. If you rob people of their prospects; if you cancel their future, if you know you can only go so far and there is no help, sometimes you can see why people give up.'

'And that's why we all love Jimi,' says Joseph. 'He never gave up and we are trying to follow his example.'

It was a real pleasure to listen to Jimi's friends. They opened my eyes to a struggle that I had very little knowledge of beyond newspaper headlines. It made me understand a little more of what Jimi was facing in life and, as David said, made me appreciate his sacrifice even more. They spoke to me after all attending one of Joseph's fitness training camps. It's one of the many things Joseph is doing to keep going while he waits to see if he's successful in his attempt to get into medical school. It's all part of the process of trying to get out of the cage.

Before we finish, Marvellous, who one day hopes to join Joseph in the medical profession, has one last thing to say about her friend Jimi. 'He was a good man and could have given so much to so many. That lady in the river, her life came above everything else for Jimi. He was a great friend, a great son. He was great in all that he did, and he left the world in a great way.'

It's not just Jimi's friends that like to talk about Jimi, his family are just the same. They don't really have a choice because everyone talks to them about Jimi.

'The hardest thing is accepting that he's not here anymore,' says Ayodeji, who was nine years older than Jimi. 'Sometimes I like to imagine he is still with us. Every now and again I like to go down to London Bridge and look at the water. That is the last place that he was alive on this earth, and I can just picture him there. It's just a few minutes but it's enough. We would like to get a plaque there on the bridge, to remember him. I'm sure people will keep talking about him, but his music lives on too,' reflects Ayodeji. 'That is my therapy. He gets me back to where I need to be. He has at least left us all with something. I wish he could see how much he is helping me with his music.'

At the end of my conversation with Bernard, I thank him for his time and his openness. We talk about how close he still feels to Jimi, and he tells me that he hopes that never stops. 'Dan,' says Bernard, 'I have a voice note on my phone from Jimi. It's from 8 April 2021.' That was two weeks before Jimi died.

'I had sent him this video of me in a jacket I'd got from Zara. I was pretending to be a model and I finished it with "Bro, what do you think?" Jimi sent me a voice note back and he is laughing so hard in it. "Bernard" he says, "I love you so much. You know how to make me laugh" I do the same with our old conversations on social media. I have saved them all and sometimes I'll just go through them and remind myself of how we used to talk to each other. I miss that and it keeps me close to him.'

At the time of writing this, Bernard is only twenty-one years old. He has his whole life in front of him. A few days after I spoke to him for the first time, he and Joaquin – the other man who jumped in the Thames that night – were going to pick up a bravery award from the Humane Society. The recognition for what Jimi did just keeps coming. Joaquin, who met Jimi on the bridge that night, has always pushed for Jimi to get the same level of recognition that he has received. He too seems like a remarkable individual.

Bernard is currently a freelance camera assistant at ITV. He is studying Sports Management and Sports Media, but his dream job is still to play football. He is looking for a club. I remind him that Ian Wright didn't make it until his mid-twenties and Bernard laughs and says, 'I know. Never stop believing.'

Whatever happens to Bernard, it's quite clear that the time he spent with Jimi will have a lifelong impact on him. When you speak to him about his friend, you notice that he quite often speaks about him in the present tense. I ask him if he knows he does that.

'I feel like he's still here,' says Bernard. 'His mindset and self-motivation, I take all of that onboard every day. Even if something was going wrong, Jimi could find the light in the darkness. That's why I like going around to his mum and dad's house almost every weekend. His mum cooks the best jollof rice but it's also great just to share stories about him. We all loved him deeply and I feel like one of the reasons I am still here is to let people know that good people live among us. His story has touched so many people. Jimi was special. Jimi was a one-off, so that's why I sometimes talk about him like he's still around because I feel like he is. He still walks with me. I am still learning from him every day.'

STRICTLY NADIYA

'Be honest, is this a bit of a disappointment?'

Those were some of the first words I uttered to the two-time World Ten-Dance Champion, Nadiya Bychkova, when we met for the first time at Wembley Stadium in September 2021.

'The thing is,' laughs Nadiya, 'I really wanted to get you. Call it intuition. I didn't know that much about you before I heard you were doing the series, so I looked through all your posts and stories on Instagram and you seemed different from all the other partners I'd had. You were always talking about other people, and I liked that. I knew you were tall so I assumed we'd be put together, but then the production team confused me: they told me I would be driving to the country-side to meet my partner and that I wasn't allowed to wear heels so I thought . . . it can't be you. Then I arrived at Wembley and, when I saw you up in the stands with your hands over your face, I was so happy. We did our filming, and I went off for lunch with my family and I told my mum I was delighted with my new student.'

I am not a dancer. I have avoided dance floors for much of my life. At school discos I was the kid who told jokes and messed about, anything to avoid actually having to move in time to the music. The frustrating thing is, I've always wanted to love it.

I adore music. I feel like I understand music. I love watching other people dance. I love the idea of dancing, but it has always felt like something that other people do. It's actually very hard for me to explain because it makes no sense whatsoever.

I am a confident person. I think you need a bit of that to do the job that I do. When I walk into a TV studio, I feel like I own the place. It's not in an arrogant way, I just love live television. I love that feeling of presenting something that millions of people are watching. I love knowing that everything could go wrong and it's your job to hold it together. I love the rush. Those few seconds before you go live are truly wonderful. It's at that moment that I feel like I reach out and grab the steering wheel.

I love the time just before you go out on stage to host a big event or speak to a live audience. I love it when they call your name and say, 'Ladies and gentlemen, please welcome your host for the evening . . . Dan Walker.' I love the idea of having an audience in the palm of your hand. The pressure, the intensity, the expectation . . . I think I might be addicted to it.

Before *Strictly*, I felt none of these things when it came to dancing. In fact, it's probably the only time in my life when I felt the complete opposite. I had no idea what I was doing. I would cover it with humour, silliness and an endless desire to take the kids to the toilet, get someone a drink or tie a shoelace. Walking onto a dance floor I could also feel my stomach twist and my head would be screaming, 'WHAT ARE YOU DOING?'

I have never sat in a room with a psychologist or a therapist, but I assume they would probably trace it back to my childhood and the fact that I am so huge. In later life, I have learned to embrace my massiveness, but when you are well over 6 feet tall in your early teens, it's hard not to feel like an awkward giant. I would always buy extra-large clothes which would hang around me like a giant blanket. When all your mates are frequenting the trendy shoe shops and you get told, 'Sorry, mate, we only do that size in Hi-Tec Silver Shadow,' it can be a little disconcerting.

I should probably explain that Hi-Tec Silver Shadow were not the coolest trainers when I was growing up. My dad wore them for most of my childhood and, let me put it this way, being seen in a pair of those bad boys didn't add much to your street credibility.

It's much easier to find clothes that fit tall slim men now, but when I was growing up, my mum had to take me to a shop called High and Mighty to find a shirt that fitted my orangutan arms. When you have arms of that length, combined with a 35-inch inside leg, you assume it's impossible to get everything moving in the right direction in time with the music, so I never bothered. Incidentally, one of the first things that Nadiya Bychkova said to me at Wembley was 'Don't worry about being too tall. That is our secret weapon. Your long arms are an advantage.' As you read this chapter, you'll come to understand that Nadiya has a wonderful talent for saying just the right thing at just the right time.

Limb length and concerning degrees of awkwardness were some of the reasons I continually said 'No, thanks' when the lovely team at *Strictly Come Dancing* came knocking. I love the show, lots of my friends have been on it and I've been a regular guest on the spin-off show *It Takes Two* for many years. I had been asked to go on *Strictly* every year since 2017 but always gave a very clear, very early, very resolute 'no'. This time, 2021, was a little different.

My three children approached me just after Christmas and said, 'Dad, can we ask you something?' I thought it was going to be one of their normal complaints about what time they go to bed, me embarrassing them by singing in public or my inability to stop eating their chocolate supplies. Before I go on, I should explain that the chocolate thing is down to the fact that I think that is a legitimate parental tax which I am entitled to collect at any time to level out the amount of time I spend driving them around, the amount of money spent on after-school clubs, clothes and miscellaneous items and the sheer number of nappies I had to change during their early years.

Anyway, it was none of these. They explained that they'd had a tough time of it during the pandemic (like many kids of their age) and we talked about some of the things they would like to do in 2021 to make up for a miserable 2020. The subject matter turned to television and the petition was made for me to cheer them all up by making a commitment to go on two TV shows. The first was *Saturday Mash-Up* and the second was *Strictly Come Dancing*. I could tell from their faces they were deadly serious.

I had already been asked to go on *Saturday Mash-Up* so that part of the request was relatively easy. The second part was a little more tricky. I had a really long think about it, spoke to my wife about it and rang a few people who had done *Strictly* to gauge just how much of your life it devours. Zoe Ball, Carol Kirkwood, Anita Rani, Mike Bushell, Jason Bell, Ranvir Singh and a few others all gave excellent advice and – interestingly – every single one of them said, 'You have to do it. You'd be amazing.' Crucially, none of them had ever seen me dance.

Mike was the only one who had ever seen me anywhere near a dance floor at Louise Minchin's fiftieth birthday party. On that occasion, I decided to disguise my issues by engaging a well-trodden path at large functions of never going on the dance floor without carrying at least one large food item and a drink. Having your hands full allows you to cover all sorts of potential awkwardness and, if all else fails, you can take a bite. On this occasion, Louise's decision to hire in a late-night pancake stall provided the perfect cover.

In addition to the family request, there was also a desire to do something that was just fun after a long slog of covering coronavirus on *BBC Breakfast*. Every morning we were talking about face masks and variants. We were constantly discussing death tolls and predicted infection rates. Every other guest was a virologist, and the only relief came from the occasional ray of light like Captain Tom. I love having fun on TV and *Strictly* began to look like the perfect opportunity to enjoy making a show without having to interview any politicians. The other piece to the puzzle was *Football Focus*. I'd presented the programme for twelve years and, in that time, I'd only ever missed two shows – both for family weddings. I'd finally taken the decision to find a new challenge so, for the first time in a very long time, my Saturdays would be free of football and available for footwork.

In early February 2021, my agent called. It was a request to talk to the team at *Strictly*. For the first time, I agreed. I spoke to Stef Aleksander, who books the guests, and Sarah James, the Executive Producer – both significant cheeses. We had a lovely chat about the programme, what my expectations were, what my dance experience was (a very short part of the discussion) and whether I was a good student. I was given the opportunity to go away and think about it. Within a few weeks, I was signed up and now had about four months of mild panic and regret before the team at *Strictly* made the official announcement.

'When are you doing *Strictly*?' is a question I think I've been asked about 804 times every month for the last few years. Until 2021, I was always able to laugh it off and say 'Never' or 'Have you seen the length of these arms? They'd need a bigger dance floor', but now it was actually happening there were quite a few delicate conversations to navigate.

My wife knew. My agent knew. Zoe Ball knew and that was about it. There was one spectacularly awkward moment when we were all sitting down as a family to watch a film on YouTube. My daughter had the remote control and, as I was making a cup of tea, she said, 'Er, Dad . . . what's this?' My recent search history was on the screen, and top of the list was *Ballroom Dancing For Beginners*. My wife looked at me as if to say, 'You're on your own with this one' and I tried my best to divert attention with some chocolate treats, but our eldest later revealed that that was the moment she started to get excited.

Strictly ended up being one of the greatest experiences of my life but, if I'm totally honest, it started out as one of the worst. Let me explain. I consider myself quite good at putting on a brave face and that's what I was determined to do when we had our first 'studio' day. This is before any of the cast of 2021 had been told about our partners. At this point, we were all still flying solo. We were all invited down to *Strictly* HQ at Elstree Studios in London for our first interview and a full fitting with the wardrobe team.

The fitting came first for me and that was great fun. I basically just had a giggle with Vicky (Gill), Esra (Gungor) and Meg (Sterry) as I tried on various shirts, trousers and shoes while having every inch of my body measured. This was also the day I discovered the magic of 'shants'. Vicky, Esra and Meg explained that, to keep your shirt pulled down when you dance, they sew it into your pants – shirt, into pants . . . 'shants'.

The clothing revelation was quickly followed by a ninety-minute interview in front of various glitter balls and glitter walls. I enjoyed the interview talking about the past, work, family, hopes, the dances I was looking forward to, what I was hoping for from a partner and all the normal stuff. Then came the phrase I had been dreading. 'And now, Dan, we'd love to see you dance.' I felt an uncomfortable chill across my entire body. I went into 'dance mode' and instantly made a joke to try and settle the impending doom. I even looked around to see if they had any large food items I could hold. I was in trouble.

We walked about ten steps across the studio and the lovely producer said, 'All you have to do is stand behind these glitter balls and when you hear the music, walk out and start dancing.' I am a grown man in my forties, and I can honestly tell you that I have never felt more uncomfortable. I knew the show would be primarily conducted in a different postcode to my comfort zone, but I didn't expect my mouth to go so instantly dry at the prospect of being asked to dance. I closed my eyes, told myself that it was going to be ok, and tried to enjoy it. Some ABBA came on and out I came. I can't bring myself to watch the footage back. I think I was smiling, but inside I was melting.

After about thirty seconds of Theresa May-style movement, I decided that I would attempt the old trick of trying to look super confident to cover my awkwardness and embarrassment. For some reason I don't think I will ever be able to explain, I felt it would be a good time in my life to try and moonwalk for the first time. Why not? I had never attempted it before but became convinced that this was the time to give it a go during filming for a clip which would be watched by 10 million people. If we're looking for positives, I definitely moved backwards. The best way to describe it would be if you imagine someone moonwalking with one leg in a welly filled with concrete and the other in a large orthopaedic boot. Thankfully, the whole thing was over in a flash as, two strides in, I collided with a glitter ball and tripped over.

'We'll do some close-ups now, Dan,' said the eternally posi-tive producer. 'Great,' I said in the least convincing fashion ever. It was during the 'close-up' section that I started looking for the exit. There were about five or six people watching me do what some people would describe loosely as 'dance' and about another fifteen or so were viewing the televised carnage on screens behind a black curtain. In my mind, those behind the veil were quickly scouring their list of back-up contestants. Thankfully, one of those producers was Joe Wheatley. Joe made a timely intervention. There was one point during the close-up section when the team were asking me to do something different. I have blanked out much of this time because of the trauma, but apparently, all I produced, for a solid five minutes, was pointing my finger down the camera. I had two options. Either sob gently and tell them I had no idea what I was doing, or run for the fire exit, which I had spotted in the corner of the studio, call my agent, and get him to tell *Strictly* that I'd made a terrible error. At that precise moment, obviously sensing my dancing dilemma, Joe emerged from behind the curtain and said, 'Dan, just wanted to say that the last point looked really cool.'

Now, I know what he said isn't much but, at that point, I was down to my final shred of dignity. The green exit sign was calling my name but that one sentence from Joe brought me back from the brink. I remembered one of the golden rules of TV: it never looks as bad as you think it does when you watch it back. This rule has a 99.9 per cent accuracy rate. The only time I have proved it to be incorrect was when I passed a rugby ball to a child on live television. He wasn't looking. It caught him square in the mouth and he started crying just as the regional news programme finished. I remember thinking, 'It can't have looked that bad' . . . only to watch it back and realise it was in fact at least 500 times worse than I thought it was. There was blood and there were tears.

The *Strictly* studio day was a bruising experience, but it did help to prepare me for what was to come. I felt like I learned an awful lot about the headspace I was going to have to inhabit if it was going to last longer than a couple of weeks. The important thing you have remember about *Strictly* is that you are not alone. The lovely people in charge are kind enough to give you a professional dancer to guide you, teach you and hold your hand through the whole thing. In my case, they decided to give me one of the most amazing humans I have ever met: two-time world champion, Nadiya Bychkova.

'Now remember, Daniel,' she said as we sat down to discuss our *Strictly* experience, 'I can't lie.' She is correct. I have never known anyone so straight-down-the-line as Nadiya. She tells it like it is, with very little fluff attached. She is brilliant but can also be brutal.

'You know there was a reason I asked you to do that little waltz with me when we met at Wembley? I was watching to see how good you were. I was like, ok, he has a little movement. I was wondering why you were so worried. In my head, even that early, I was like . . . ballroom will be great. I wasn't worried about that at all, and I was confident I could teach you Latin. You were worried. I was very happy.'

When I had my initial meeting with the team at *Strictly*, they made it clear that I got no say in who I got as a partner, but they did ask me if there was anything I was worried about. I assumed

I was going to get a tall professional, so I just said I hoped I got someone I was able to get on with. My *Strictly* strategy was quite a simple one: I wanted to enjoy the experience as much as possible. I love being on TV and shows don't come any bigger than *Strictly Come Dancing*. The sheer size of it means it's very easy to become consumed and I've watched it happen to others. You start worrying about all the little things that are going on and forget about enjoying it. I have spoken to people in the past who, once it's all over, say they wish they'd enjoyed it more at the time. I was determined not to be in that position.

After our initial meeting, Nadiya and I sat down in the seats at Wembley and had a chance to chat to each other for about fifteen minutes. I told her when we were sat there that I wanted to make sure that she enjoyed it as much as I did and that, although I had no idea about talent, I wouldn't go out of the competition for lack of effort.

'I knew you were going to work hard from that moment, Daniel. I could see it in your eyes. You know what I am like. I'm a simple person. I can't be friends with anyone who doesn't like food and, within a few minutes, I found it very reassuring that you were already telling me about your favourite biscuits. You promised me I would enjoy it and you were true to your word. I didn't know it then, but we laughed so much, probably I laughed as much in those three months with you as I did in the rest of my life altogether. We talked and cried about important things but, more than anything else, you showed me you were a hard worker and I saw that every week – apart from when you fell asleep while I was talking to you.' A smile cracks across my face. 'You see,' says Nadiya, laughing, 'that's the other thing. You get my jokes! I have to explain to most people that I'm just kidding, but you understood me from day one.'

I could tell from that first meeting that we were going to get on. I love people who work hard to get to the top and Nadiya has always been a grafter. It might not surprise you to learn that the dance world is quite a political one. When it comes to winning championships and top prizes, a lot of it is down to who your teacher is, how well you know the judges (who in some cases can also be the teachers) and which country you are representing. Nadiya does not come from a rich family and there was no dancing pedigree in her genes. Her story is one of dedication. It's a story of hard work, fighting against the odds and overcoming huge obstacles. It is an incredible story of success but, most importantly, it is a love story. It's all about how a five-year-old Ukrainian fell in love with dancing after watching a professional for the very first time. She knew at that moment that she didn't just want to dance, she wanted to be the best dancer. She wanted to be world champion.

Nadiya was born in Luhansk, Ukraine, in 1989 to Larisa and Alexander Bychkov. Her mother was a professional pentathlete but worked on the local market to make ends meet. Her dad trained as a lawyer but, after the collapse of the Soviet Union, he used the family market stall to brings goods in from other places and sell them on.

Nadiya's grandmother, who lived with them in their tiny

house, was a huge part of her life. Babushka Zoya was the one who introduced her to dancing by taking her to a local arts centre as a young girl.

'I loved it from the first moment I saw the dresses,' remembers Nadiya. 'It was all so mesmerising and so beautiful. I wasn't old enough to join in. They said you had to be five, so I waited for a year and spent the whole time stretching to make sure I was ready.'

The following year Nadiya went back, and it wasn't long before she was in her first competition.

'She was incredibly stubborn,' remembers her mum. 'She always wanted to have things a certain way from a very early age. Dancing became everything to her very quickly. She was either at dancing or at school and that was about it. She came home to sleep.'

'I needed a dress, but we had no money for one,' says Nadiya. 'I asked my mum and, in the end, my godmother made it for me. I entered my first competition with a chubby lad called Stasik. He had a bakery in his house, and he was always eating. I think that's why we got on. We won. He celebrated with food!'

Nadiya was spotted even at this tender age and her mum realised she was going to have to start taking things seriously. 'Everyone kept telling her she was talented and gifted, but I knew that from the start,' says Larisa with a smile. 'I watched as she would come alive as soon as she stepped on the dance floor. It was magical to see and very exciting for a parent when a dance teacher takes you to one side and tells you your daughter could be really special. She was very young when her teacher told me that he'd never seen someone with no shyness about performing and who was in their own world as soon as the music started. I could see how much she was enjoying it and, as a parent, I just wanted her to be happy.'

Nadiya started dancing with older boys and got to the final of the Ukrainian championships when she was only seven years old. Her parents wanted to make sure that Nadiya's grades didn't suffer at school, so she was given an ultimatum: she could only go to dance lessons if she got the top grades. She worked harder than ever at both.

'It was getting to that stage where I needed to start making big decisions if I was going to take dancing seriously. At the age of ten, I moved to the city of Harkow. It was about 220 miles from our home, but I needed to be there to dance with my new partner.'

It was that same year that Nadiya came to the UK for the first time to take part in the Blackpool Festival. 'I remember standing in that famous ballroom and just looking around in wonder. What a place. I told my mum while we were standing there that one day I would live in the UK. I think she thought I was a bit mad, but I knew from that moment that I would make it happen. It was just going to be a matter of time.'

At the age of ten, Nadiya and her partner made it to the under-16 final and, wherever she went, success followed success. Her first World Championship title arrived in 2002 in the under-21 competition; she was only twelve years old. The little Ukrainian had arrived on the global stage.

'One of the greatest moments of my young life came in a dance class run by one of the legends of dancing, Espen Salberg,' explains Nadiya. 'He was a teacher that everyone looked up to. There were some really talented dancers in the room, and I was just a kid, twelve years old, not even a teenager. He was trying to teach us all how to do a samba walk. After a few minutes, he stopped the class. "There is only one person in this room who is not doing what I have told you to do . . . but it is a perfect samba walk." He pointed at me, out of everyone. That was an amazing moment. Things like that do make other people jealous, but that is something you just have to accept in dancing.'

Nadiya's growing reputation meant she had to move again, this time to Odessa to train with a new partner. She was now over 600 miles away from her family. Her next stop was Slovenia at the age of fourteen. She was doing all her schoolwork while she was travelling and then, every two months, she would go back to Luhansk to sit exams on what she was learning. She got top marks every time.

The dancing wasn't going quite so smoothly. Nadiya's partner wanted her to be his girlfriend, so she quickly looked for someone else who wanted to compete rather than kiss! When she was sixteen, she met eighteen-year-old Miha Vodicar.

'I could tell from the moment he walked into the room that we could be amazing,' she remembers. 'We had like a perfect dancing connection. I was able to follow him as if we'd been dancing for years without even really thinking about it. We had our first competition after just two weeks, which is almost impossible. We went to the UK and were placed in the top two couples straightaway.'

Nadiya and Miha had the talent to win everything. They

made both the Latin and ballroom finals in Blackpool in their first year together, but with increased notoriety came increased attention and, for the first time, Nadiya saw the power of politics in her sport.

'We simply didn't have enough money to get the right results. You needed to play the game and we didn't have the cash to do it. If you don't have the lessons with the right people, then you can't win the big competitions. We started to struggle with results. We weren't making finals, and you start to question what you love.'

I ask her if she ever thought about giving up. She stares right through me before a huge smile comes across her face. 'Never, Daniel,' she says. 'That little five-year-old didn't dream of just getting good at dancing. That little five-year-old was going to be a world champion and that battle wasn't won. Quitting was never even an option.'

At the same time as the political power games, Nadiya found out that her dad had been living a completely different life with another woman back in Luhansk. He told Nadiya he was going to stop supporting her financially, so the little girl with big dreams had nothing.

During our months together on *Strictly*, I got to spend some time with Nadiya's gorgeous daughter, Mila, and her mum, Larisa. Mila is Nadiya's pride and joy. She wants to give her the same opportunities that her mum gave her. Larisa remains her great inspiration because, throughout her life, her mum made the sacrifices to keep the dancing door open.

'I was determined that nothing would be closed off to my daughter,' says Larisa. 'It wasn't just me making the sacrifices.

She was missing out on parties, friends and a normal childhood. We were both working towards the same goal. I could see that Nadiya had the talent to go to the very top, and all I wanted to do was help her get there.'

Larisa decided to sell everything they had to get her daughter into the right dance school in Italy. She had just 5 euros remaining when Nadiya left for yet another new start, in another country, even further from home.

'My mum risked everything,' says Nadiya with tears in her eyes. 'Everything. She was selling the dresses she had made me to make ends meet, to pay for rent and food. I saw in her an amazing work ethic, and it was all for me. She inspired me to work hard too. I started teaching when I was twelve years old and, by the time I was eighteen, I was teaching for money. I was modelling part-time; I was training whenever I could, and we were travelling to compete at weekends. It was non-stop.'

Funded by her mum's hard work, Nadiya and Miha got in a car and drove to Italy. She had a bold strategy: Nadiya told the dance teacher – the famous Davide Cacciari – that they could be world champions. Thankfully he agreed, but his dance lessons cost 200 euros a time. Nadiya was earning 20 euros an hour for her teaching, so she had to work for 10 hours to pay for one of his lessons. It was worth it. At their first World Championships with Davide as their teacher, they finished second. A year later, in 2013, they were second again. Nadiya and Miha were dancing for Slovenia and, desperate to avoid accusations of bias, it is alleged that the Slovenian judge didn't give them the one extra mark they needed to take the title.

They returned the following year and this time 'everything on the floor was just perfect,' recalls Nadiya. 'I could tell from the first dance that it was going to be our year.' The dreams of that little five-year-old came true. Nadiya was a world champion. The European Championships followed, and in 2015 they were crowned world champions again.

But, even when bathing in success, there was heartache. At the end of 2014, when they were the best dancers on the planet, Miha and Nadiya had a professional falling-out. The dancing relationship came under incredible strain. 'He thought I was the worst person in the world,' explains Nadiya.

There were suspicions of jealousy and rivalry and when they went to the 2015 World Championships, they only saw each other on the dance floor. Miha didn't even want to be in the same room as her.

'I still don't really understand what was behind it all,' says Nadiya, 'but I used to get a lot of attention and I was always in the spotlight. That is often the case with a partnership like ours. It would have been easy to walk away from it all, but my love of dance kept us together. We were brilliant but broken.'

Away from the dance floor, Nadiya was in a relationship with the Slovenian footballer, Matija Skarabot. After her second world title, Nadiya found out she was pregnant. After her daughter was born, she wanted to return to dance together with Miha, but he decided that he would find someone else. 'I told him it wouldn't be easy because, even though we didn't get on, there was no one else like us, but he wouldn't listen.' He went back to the World Championships the following year with a new partner but didn't make the final twenty-four.

The World Championship win in 2015 was to be Nadiya's final competition and it wasn't long before the world of TV came calling. In 2017, she joined the cast of *Strictly Come Dancing*.

Fast forward to 2021 and our meeting at Wembley. Nadiya and I swapped numbers and were warned we had a few more weeks to keep our secret before the launch show. 'I think you'll get Nadiya,' said virtually everyone during those weeks. 'She's the only one tall enough for you.' I perfected the 'you'll have to wait and see' smile.

And while the *Strictly* fans waited, we started on the quick-step. 'Why did no one ever tell me dancing was this much fun?' I told Nadiya on day one.

'I enjoyed week one, Daniel,' remembers Nadiya. 'You surprised everyone. I was trying to teach you quickstep, which is a lot. There is so much to learn but I knew you could be amazing. You were so busy so we couldn't do as much practice as everyone else, but I just loved the way you dealt with it.'

I loved everything about it. The hard work, the technique, the language and the fact that you could eat as much cake as you wanted because of all the exercise. I was learning how to dance and Nadiya was expanding her snack game. She was opening my eyes to the world of dance, and I was teaching her about the powers of flapjack. I think it was a fair trade.

One of the great privileges of my job has been getting to see brilliant people up close and personal. I have stood next to Tiger Woods while he was hitting golf balls. I have watched Cristiano Ronaldo take perfect free-kick after perfect free-kick on a football pitch. I will never forget sitting within a metre of one of the world's great cellists as he played the solo in Karl Jenkins' 'The Armed Man', backed by the London Philharmonic Orchestra. I could feel the notes through my body. I can still feel them now when I close my eyes and listen to that piece of music.

That is what it was like to watch Nadiya. My appreciation of dancers and dance went through the roof in the space of just a few days. I always knew they were talented, but I had never seen the control of the body, the skill, the ability to channel power and feeling through movement. It was all so alien to me at the start. I saw it as a form of communication that I had closed myself off from my whole life. I was desperate to learn it. Thankfully, I was alongside someone who spoke it fluently. Some professional dancers specialise in ballroom and some in Latin, but Nadiya was a 10-Dance World Champion which meant she was a master of both. I couldn't have been in better hands.

'I loved the fact that you understood the work it took to be a professional dancer,' she says. 'Some people think it's easy but, when you have someone who can see it and appreciate it, you just want to teach them everything.'

The most important thing that happened in those early weeks took place at a London hotel and the Borehamwood Accident & Emergency Department. My workload was a little on the hefty side during *Strictly*. I never expected to be in it for more than a month, so I decided to just keep doing all my normal jobs. I was getting up at 3 a.m. on Monday, Tuesday and Wednesday to present *BBC Breakfast*, and then going to London on a Thursday night to film the *NFL Show* on a Friday morning. I would always arrive at Elstree a few hours after everyone else for the Friday run-through, so we were constantly playing catch-up. Looking back now, it was a crazy decision but it worked.

Nadiya told me quite a few times during *Strictly* that she would never complain about being tired again. 'I don't know how it was possible, Daniel. You would wake up at 3, travel to work while I was sleeping, and then I'd watch you on TV with a coffee and, an hour later, you were learning something you'd never done before! The more you worked, the better you got.'

But, when you've got too much on, you start to forget things. You leave your wallet on the back seat of a taxi while you're rushing into a hotel and, when you run back out to catch the driver before he leaves, you don't see a giant revolving glass door and nearly knock yourself out. Your teeth go through your lips and the blood pours down your face and a lump forms on your head. The next day you struggle through a TV show trying to tell yourself you're ok as your head throbs and then, when you get to training and meet your partner, she can see how white you are and that you can't stand without swaying.

A medic is called, and you're told there is no way you can train. You're ordered to go to A&E to get a brain scan. Your partner is told she can't go with you because of Covid restrictions, and you can't be seen together because it's meant to be a secret until launch night.

She grabs your hand and says there is no way you're going anywhere without her. You wait for hours at A&E and are eventually told your brain is ok, but you have concussion, and you can't dance for three days. Your partner has waited the whole time for you in the car park and, in the fog of tiredness, a constant headache and mild delirium (mixed with delight that the dancing isn't over before it's begun) you tell her that her actions will never be forgotten and you know that, on that day, in that A&E car park, the friendship has been cemented. That was the day that the bond was sealed. That was the day I decided to throw everything at *Strictly* for as long as it lasted.

'I remember that day well,' laughs Nadiya. 'That was simple for me. I didn't do it for any reason other than that was the only thing I could do. I needed to be there for you even if that meant I would lose my job. I was really worried for you and there was no way I would let you go on your own. We were a team and that wasn't acceptable for me. I think we both learned a lot about each other that day. That was the start of something special.'

The quickstep was our first dance. I surprised myself, my family and most of the watching public with a half-decent, middle of the scoreboard performance. The judges seemed genuinely impressed. Week two was the paso doble and then it was foxtrot in movie week. Each dance required something different. I was loving every minute of it but also expecting it to end every Sunday night. In week four, Nadiya and I went back to my old primary school in Crawley in West Sussex to try and find some school disco inspiration for our cha cha cha to MC Hammer's 'You Can't Touch This'. It was seen by the judges as something of a performance breakthrough. 'You need to start believing you can actually dance,' said Nadiya at the start of the following week. 'I believe in you. I see it every week. You need to start believing in yourself.'

By this stage I was loving the process of learning to dance. It's easy to be crippled with nerves as Saturday night approaches, but I just love being on telly. I knew that I would put the hours in, so the only thing holding me back was the speed at which I could catch the others up in terms of talent. There were so many great dancers in the class of 2021, but we were still determined to enjoy it as much as ever.

Week five was a major turning point. We were doing a Viennese waltz to Billy Joel's 'She's Always A Woman', one of my wife's favourites. 'You were always asking me questions,' recalls Nadiya. 'It was lovely to see how much you wanted to know. Remember the week of Viennese waltz you asked me where the joy came from in ballroom dancing?'

I could see that during some of the Latin dances you could whoop, holler and scream, but during the ballroom, I was struggling to see how you could show that same enjoyment while maintaining your posture and composure. While Nadiya was busy teaching me the practical elements of high elbows, vertical lines and unsplayed fingers, she was also trying to convey the deeper elements of dance: the connection.

'I told you that joy in ballroom comes from two people moving together in harmony. When it works perfectly, it's like two moving as one . . . almost breathing together.'

I had very little idea what Nadiya was on about until one

Thursday afternoon in week five. During our three months on *Strictly* I can honestly tell you that we never had a cross word, an argument or one of those 'toys out, storms out' moments that often happen. But that Thursday afternoon was a frustrating one. We were dancing in a beautiful old hall with stained-glass windows in North London, but nothing was clicking.

'Come with me, Daniel,' said an eternally patient Nadiya. We grabbed our coats and wandered outside into the little garden behind the hall. During that five-minute chat we talked about the importance of me learning to let go a little. We had a laugh about flapjack and the two-time world champion reminded me that I had to trust her and trust myself. I was enjoying *Strictly* so much, but every now and again there were these little moments where I would doubt myself.

'What on earth are you doing?'

'How did you expect to be any good at this?'

'This isn't for you, is it?'

'You look ridiculous, don't you?'

'Everyone is laughing at you, right?'

Nadiya always answered all those questions, but it was frustrating for me not to be better than I was by week five. I think my expectations were writing cheques my talent couldn't afford. I reminded myself of why I signed up to *Strictly* and thanked Nadiya for her wisdom and kindness. We ate some biscuits, cracked a few gags and, when we walked back into that hall, everything was different.

We Viennese waltzed around the room and as we did, the afternoon sun burst through the clouds and streamed through the stained-glass windows at the far end of the hall. It burnt our faces as we turned and spun down the dance floor. It felt, for the first time, just as Nadiya had described. 'I don't want to get ahead of myself, partner,' I said as the music stopped, 'but was that what you were talking about?'

For the first time it didn't feel like Nadiya was dragging me around the floor. For the first time she hadn't put her hand across the small of her back after a run of the dance or had to stretch her neck out. 'That was it, Daniel!' she screamed with a huge smile across her face. 'That was it! Keep that feeling!'

Nadiya was still smiling as we danced it together on that Saturday night with my wife, Sarah, in the live audience. Yes, the judges were a bit picky about my lack of drive and encouraged me to lengthen my stride but, in my head, it was perfect. As we skipped up to see Claudia I waved at my wife and whispered 'thank you' to Nadiya. I tried to explain to Claudia how surreal it was to be watching myself back on the big screen in the 'Clauditorium' and think 'Who is that guy? He's not too bad.' It really didn't feel like I was watching myself.

During our interview, Nadiya said something that I'm not ashamed to say was the closest I came to bursting into tears on *Strictly*.

'Claudia, do you know what, there are two things I really love about this show. I love to teach, and I love to dance, and this week I managed to do both because, as a professional dancer, you are always worried about your celebrity, making sure that they are ok, but tonight, I was able to dance myself. So, thank you very much for this, Daniel.'

I know how much that meant to Nadiya because the one thing you realise about her very quickly is that she just loves dancing. Her face lights up when she talks about technique, performance or just anything to do with something that is so close to her heart. When you spend time with someone who loves something that much, it's impossible for a little of that magic not to rub off on you. She can even convince you to dress up like a giant lobster!

We survived the jive and that was quickly followed by our Couple's Choice of 'Classic' by MKTO. Each week we survived the red lights and avoided the bottom two and the dreaded dance-off. That didn't stop a small section of the press writing the 'how on earth are they still in it?' articles, but brushing them to one side became part of the weekly ritual. Nadiya has always had her fair share of negative headlines to deal with – normally about her private life – and it's interesting to see the way she deals with all the rumours, rubbish and lies. She would walk into training on a Monday and say, 'We take the negative stuff, we laugh, we put it in our hands, and we simply blow it away.' She would then start to teach me another dance. I was very much of the same opinion, so each week it was onwards and upwards.

The week of the American Smooth to 'King Of The Road' was a tricky one. I had picked up a bit of an injury the week before during the Couple's Choice and I couldn't put any weight on my left foot on the Monday, Tuesday or Wednesday. I had physio, acupuncture and was on some heavy-duty prescription painkillers and anti-inflammatories. When I turned up to

226

training on Thursday morning – our final day to get it sorted – I could tell Nadiya was a little concerned.

'How long have we got to learn this dance?' I asked her.

'It's 10 a.m. now and we leave for *It Takes Two* at 4 p.m., so we have six hours,' she said.

'Well, let's learn the dance in six hours then,' I proclaimed. It's amazing what the brain can do when you are all out of alternative options.

'That was a big week, Daniel,' Nadiya recalls as we look back on the series together. 'I remember you promised me that, no matter what, you would learn it and deliver. I saw your brain take over your body and I saw the presenter come out of you. By that stage, you were so much more technically and mechanically aware of your body. I knew we were going to be ok.'

We were struggling with the final lift that week. I had to push Nadiya high above my head and then let her slide down my back before the big finish. Five minutes before we were due on telly, we were practising the lift backstage. Every time we did it, Nadiya's dress went over my head or her heavily beaded sleeves would whack me in the face. There was an emergency call to the brilliant wardrobe department. While they attacked her outfit with a pair of scissors, we just turned to each other and said, 'We don't need to practise this. It's going to be great.' The brain took over the body.

When we walked onto the dance floor a few minutes later, Nadiya noticed something was different and it wasn't just the high-strength painkillers.

'Are you ok?' she said, as we made our way to the stairs at the top of the stage. She was in a gorgeous ballgown – with slightly shorter and less deadly sleeves – and I was in a full tail-suit.

'You've got "TV Dan" from now on, Nadiya,' I said with a smile.

'I like him,' she said. 'What happened to the other fella?'

'He's long gone. TV Dan is as comfortable out here as he is in the studio.'

'Is there anything I need to do?' she said as the *Strictly* voice-over king, Alan Dedicoat, started to introduce us.

'Just keep up!' I whispered. The music started and we were off to our first score above 30.

The American Smooth was followed by musicals week, which was so special. It was one of our favourite weeks of the competition and dancing a Charleston to 'Good Morning' will remain one of my enduring memories of being on *Strictly*. Nadiya always said that, if we'd made it to the final, she would have chosen to do that Charleston again. Getting through that week took us to week ten and to a dance with added significance.

One afternoon, early in the competition, I was eating lunch and Nadiya was dancing around the floor on her own. It wasn't a dance I was familiar with, but I could see how much she was enjoying it. She was totally lost in the movement as she floated effortlessly around the room. I asked her what it was. 'That, Daniel . . . is rumba. My favourite dance.'

The following week I played Nadiya a piece of music I said I would love to dance to – 'Desperado' by The Eagles. The story behind it goes back a long way. I always wanted to play the piano growing up, but our house was too small to fit one in. I still want to learn the piano just so I can play 'Desperado'. I told this to Nadiya and, as she listened, she sat upright in the chair in the training room. 'We can dance a rumba to this.' She also explained that she had also always wanted to play the piano and had dreamed of doing it in a red backless dress. It's very peculiar that we have both had the same piano dream with the only difference being the wardrobe choices! I played her the end of the song, where it all gets stripped back to the piano again, and said 'Wouldn't it be great if you started the routine on the piano – in a red backless dress – and I finish it on the piano?'

'Like James Bond in a tuxedo!' she jumped in.

'Yes, a tuxedo sounds great, and we can dance your favourite dance, to one of my favourite songs, wearing a dress you've always dreamed of.'

Nadiya was excited but told me that even the possibility of the rumba was a long way off. Given that it was week two at the time we discussed this, I didn't think there was much chance of it ever happening, but that became my reason to work harder than ever: to stay in *Strictly* long enough to fulfil both our dancing dreams with a rumba, in a red backless dress, to 'Desperado' on a giant piano.

It was week six when Nadiya came skipping into the training room and told me that, if we stayed in until week ten, we'd get to dance a rumba and we'd get to do it to 'Desperado'! That's why we both let out a little squeal when our names were called out at the end of week nine after our Charleston. We knew rumba was next and that 'Desperado' was on the horizon. As we walked off the stage that night, Nadiya had a little sob because I don't think she ever thought it would happen. It was time to dig out the red backless dress.

Rumba week was to become even more special because our film was going to be all about Nadiya's love of dance. I'll come back to that in a minute but, at this point, I'm now going to let you into a *Strictly* secret. I've watched the show for years and have now taken part and I think there are essentially four crucial elements to doing well on *Strictly*.

Obviously, the dance itself is essential. It lasts for ninety seconds every Saturday night, but each couple also gets a ninety-second film (or VT) and another ninety seconds with Claudia. Those are the three key elements, and the fourth is the stuff you do outside the confines of the show, both on social media, and on programmes like *It Takes Two*, the *Strictly* spin-off.

I have always thought that all those elements are just as important as each other and yet most people seem to spend four days learning the dance and hardly put any effort into the VT, the interview or the extra bits. Obviously, viewers want to know if you can dance and are getting better, but the other elements are the only opportunity they get to see who you are, what makes you tick, how well you get on as a couple and whether you're actually someone they want to see dance again. The other elements are just as important as those ninety seconds on the dance floor.

That week, the plan for our VT was for me to speak to Nadiya about how she got into dance and explain her love of rumba. When you hear her talk about it, it's easy to see why it means so much to her. I asked her what makes rumba so special. A huge smile broke out across her face.

She looks up momentarily, as if she is watching one of the great performances from her stellar career ... 'The rumba is so beautiful, so intense, so feminine. For me, it is the perfect expression of what it is to be a woman. You have the time to express yourself and feel the movement but, not independently or only in certain areas, your whole body is involved. You feel the dance in every part of you. Everything is engaged, every muscle matters, everything is working towards something special, and everything is important. Rumba is the essential Latin discipline, the queen of the dances. The rumba walk is how you warm up your body and it is at the very centre of dancing. If you told me I could only choose one dance for the rest of my life, it would be the rumba.'

She pauses and looks up, back to that perfect routine in her mind. She smiles again and then comes back to me.

'Every step matters, Daniel. Every look, every gesture, every movement, however subtle,' she says rolling her wrists and stretching her fingers. 'Everything has a meaning and a purpose. There is no waste. That, Daniel, is the rumba.'

'And was it always rumba, Nadiya?' I ask her.

'In the beginning it was just dance. I fell in love with it from day one and that fire inside me has never died. As a young girl, I watched a man called Slavik Krykliyvyy performing in Ukraine. I knew then, at that precise moment, that I wanted to dance for the rest of my life. At times, it has been the biggest struggle of my life but also the richest reward. I've had to break down barriers, fight against the system, and dig deeper than I ever thought I could. The journey from the five-year-old, who fell in love with dancing, to the twenty-five-year-old who became world champion, is the hardest, greatest, and most rewarding thing I have done. It was my one dream, and through hard work, sacrifice, dedication, love, perseverance and sheer determination I made it to the top.'

Do you see what I mean? When someone talks about something with such care and affection you can't help but be drawn in and wonder why you've gone your whole life without being able to see it for yourself.

I have another question for the two-time world champion. 'If you love it so much, Nadiya, is it frustrating to be dragging a numptie around the floor who is so far out of your league?'

She laughs. 'That's why I love this show, Daniel. I love to teach you because, when you love something so much, the greatest gift you can give, is to pass that love on to someone else. I love that moment when someone else's eyes light up when something clicks. I love that look in your eyes when you realise that you've done something well and your body is moving in the right way. I love that smile that cracks across your face when you understand the joy that comes from dancing.'

I certainly felt that joy during our week ten rumba. That was a crazy week. It also marked the ten-year anniversary of the death of Gary Speed. I had been asked by his family to film a special piece about the importance of talking to your friends if you were struggling with mental health. Gary, who was a good friend, had taken his own life the night after we'd worked together on *Football Focus* in 2011. I was happy to do the film but, I don't mind admitting to you, I cried for most of the Friday after doing the interview. For some reason, I then foolishly decided to watch it go out live on the Saturday afternoon before our rumba. I also read through some of the incredible messages that people sent me after watching the piece on *Football Focus* and I was a complete wreck for a couple of hours. Nadiya was brilliant that day. She took care of me and helped me get my head back together. We danced our rumba and off we went to the quarter-finals.

During our time on the show, I learned an awful lot from Nadiya. She showed me that I could not only enjoy dancing but that, if I allowed myself to smile as I did it, the world would smile along with me. When I spoke to the publishers of this book, we talked at length about the title *Standing on the Shoulders* and the sort of people I wanted to include within its pages. As we discussed some of the individuals who lift you up, who inspire you, who help you to achieve things you felt were beyond you, I remember thinking that it was the perfect description of how I felt after spending time with Nadiya on *Strictly*.

As I got to know her, I realised that it was also what her mum had done for her in helping her to pursue her dream. Larisa sacrificed everything to allow her daughter to first become a professional dancer, and then rise to the top of the tree. When I spoke to Nadiya's mum, she was also keen to thank me for helping her daughter to be herself for the first time on television.

'You allowed her to blossom,' says Larisa. '*Strictly* is such a big show in this country, much bigger than back home in Ukraine, or anywhere else. I realised that when I came to the studio to watch it for the first time. I had never seen anything like it: the attention to detail, the quality of the dancing and the size of the whole thing. There was my daughter in the middle of it. She has always been a wonderful mover, but you helped to show the world that she is much more than just a beautiful blonde who can dance, and I don't think she will ever forget that.'

When we eventually went out of *Strictly*, we were both gutted. Nadiya had never made it to the final five before, but I was desperate for us to make the semi-finals and get the chance to dance twice in a week. There is not a single doubt in my mind that the best four dancers went through in Rhys, AJ, Rose and John, but having lasted such a long time, and exceeded every expectation, one more week would have been amazing.

On that Monday morning after our Sunday night exit, the alarm went off at 3 a.m. and I picked up the phone to turn it off. There were hundreds of messages on it. After reading my notes for that morning's *BBC Breakfast* I had a quick glance at social media on my way downstairs. If you just count Instagram direct messages and emails that had come through my website, there were more than 8,000 of them! It was mind-blowing that so many people had been moved to write such beautiful messages. It was a reminder of what it's like to be part of a show which means so much to so many people.

There were lots of messages from women telling me that their partners had taken up dancing for the first time. There were messages from men who said they had used me as their inspiration to dance at a wedding. There were fans of Nadiya's who – like her mum – were thankful that they had got to see the real her. There were lots of people worried that they had seen the last of the Yorkshire Barmaid. The barmaid was a little character we had invented for Nadiya during the show. We recorded a sketch each week of her perfecting her Yorkshire accent behind the bar in our training room at City Limits in Sheffield and put it on social media. By the end of the series, they were getting more views than our dances! In among all the Yorkshire Barmaid fans, there were also hundreds of videos from parents of their kids dancing around dressed as lobsters. There aren't many days that pass without someone mentioning the lobster jive or walking past me using their hands as claws.

There was one message which really cut through and that was the message which persuaded me to include Nadiya in this book. It was from a woman called Amy on Instagram.

Dear Dan,

I know you didn't win Strictly *but I hope you realise how special you and Nadiya have been on this series. We all loved watching you learn to dance but, at the same time, it was wonderful to see how much Nadiya was learning from you and how she was growing too. You were blossoming on the dance floor, and she was blossoming on the camera. You were a brilliant partnership. You were great for each other, and we loved watching it every week. That's why we kept voting for you. Keep dancing!*

This was one of the many messages I sent to Nadiya during that horrible week when the show is still on but you're not involved anymore. There is no training, no interviews, no VT to film, no taxis to get in, no trains to catch and no kit to wash. All you have left are the memories of three amazing months on the biggest show on telly.

'I matured a lot during our season on *Strictly*,' says Nadiya, reflecting on our time together while preparing for her next dancing tour of the UK. 'I go into the next series of the show far more confident. I knew I could dance, and I knew I could teach, but being able to work with someone who was so willing and being able to get so far with a complete beginner, it gave me that confirmation that this is what I was meant to do. I see things much more clearly now and you helped me to understand the show from the outside, if that makes sense. I used to only think about the dancing, but it is much more than that. It's the entertainment, it's the fun, it's the excitement. You taught me that if I was willing to give a little bit of myself, to let go a little, I would get so much more back in return. You showed me how much people cared and you helped me to understand how people watch the show and that is going to be so special for me going forward.'

That is why *Strictly* will remain one of the most rewarding things I have ever been involved in. I didn't embarrass my children, I didn't go out in week one, I learned a new skill, I surprised myself, I didn't fall over on TV, we somehow made it all the way to the quarter-finals and, with the help of Nadiya Bychkova, I completely conquered my fear of dancing. It's not just about no longer feeling the glitter-ball-inspired terror either. I feel more confident in general. I have an entirely new walk (which Nadiya taught me in week one) and I think my time on *Strictly* has made me a better TV presenter.

'Do you mind if we use you as an example to recruit men who think they'll be rubbish?' giggled one of the senior producers on the night of the final. 'I bet you wish you'd said "yes" years ago.'

I'm more than happy for *Strictly* to use me as a recruitment tool, but I disagree about wishing I'd said 'yes' earlier. The 2021 season felt like a pretty special season to be part of. Rose, who also features in these pages, was the undoubted superstar, but the whole team of contestants were amazing. We got on so well from day one and encouraged and cheered each other right through to the end, which doesn't happen every year. If I'd done *Strictly* another year, I would have missed out on Friday-night dinners at the Borehamwood Hilton with Adam Peaty, Ugo Monye and the wonderful Sara Davies – founder members of Hotel Club – which later grew to include Judi, AJ and occasionally Rhys. If I'd done *Strictly* another year, I wouldn't have got to know Nina, Katie, John, Tilly, Tom, Robert and Greg. And, without Greg, I wouldn't have been able to talk about falafels to his wife, Emma Thompson. She used to bring them in most weeks. I showed the picture to our youngest and he shouted, 'YOU'RE EATING WITH NANNY MCPHEE!'

Most importantly, if I'd done *Strictly* another year, I might not have had Nadiya as a partner and, above everything else, she was the reason I enjoyed every second of it and put my heart and soul into it. She was the glue that held it all together.

The tango in week eleven was our final time on the *Strictly* dance floor. After the dance-off, you stand there in front of the judges and Tess asks you if there's anything you'd like to say to your partner.

I told Tess that 'sometimes people walk into your life at just the right time and switch some lights on'. I think both Nadiya and I felt that way. She was precisely the person I needed to guide me through the show, and I was precisely who she needed to give her the confidence to be herself and give her the ability to shine on the TV in the same way she always has on the dance floor.

That's why I struggled to find the words to say when we went on *It Takes Two* for our final appearance on the Monday after our tango and Rylan asked Nadiya about our partnership. She thanked me for creating an environment where she felt safe and then said, 'your friendship has given me wings to fly again'. I think that might be one of the nicest things anyone has ever said to me.

I will never forget that. If you can enable someone else to shine, if you can lift someone else up, if you can help someone achieve a little more than they would on their own, then forget the dancing, that's what it's all about.

That's what we managed to do for each other.

That's why two-time world champion, Nadiya Bychkova, is in this book.

That's why I loved my time on *Strictly Come Dancing*.

That's why we'll be friends for life.

BEYOND THE PANDEMIC

My last book, *Remarkable People*, came out right in the middle of the global coronavirus pandemic. I don't know about you, but it seems so strange to remember the sort of restrictions we were all living under for most of 2020 and the huge life and lifestyle changes that were forced upon us all.

I was very thankful to be able to work throughout lockdown, but every day in those first few months on the TV we were talking about death tolls, issues with PPE, a lack of consideration over care homes and the strain our National Health Service was under.

Remarkable People included a whole chapter about people who felt the full force of the pandemic: either surviving, raising money for others, losing a loved one or working on the frontline.

I know the vast majority of us feel that the worst is very much behind us now, but there are still so many people who stick in my mind, so many stories that I still keep coming back to it. Sitting on the *BBC Breakfast* sofa, I got to listen to stories of both tragedy and triumph, and I wanted to share some of those with you here. These are the people who I often think about;

some of the people who will never forget life in the pandemic as we all look forward to life after it.

I feel the need to offer a gentle word of warning at this point. This chapter was hard to write and I appreciate it may be hard to read. Coronavirus ripped thousands of families to pieces and that is reflected in the next few pages. I spent hours interviewing the people in this chapter and most of those were spent with tears in my eyes. This is about family, it's about love and loss, but I trust you also see the hope of a brighter tomorrow.

Margaret Keenan was born just outside Enniskillen in Northern Ireland in 1929. Her dad was a butcher, and they had a family smallholding. Margaret, or Maggie as most people call her, used to help her dad every day along with her two brothers and sisters.

'I loved the bright lights of the big city,' says Maggie, 'and I got to go to Belfast for the first time when I was nineteen or twenty – my oldest sister was having a baby and I was to look after her. I met my husband there on Easter Monday 1955. My friend and I had gone to the holiday parade, and we went to the Rainbow café. There was a fiesta going on around the corner, so we popped round, and a fella asked me if I wanted to dance. That fella was Phil Keenan.'

When Maggie met her future husband he was about to go back to Canada, but he had a brother and a brother-in-law in England, so they changed plans and moved to West Bromwich initially and then settled in Coventry when they got married in 1957.

'I was a window dresser, Dan,' says Maggie. 'It was a job that I loved but I stopped when I had children. I worked in a restaurant and then settled into a role as a shop assistant at a jeweller's. I did fifteen years at one jeweller's and then twenty-five years at the next one.'

Maggie first heard about coronavirus, like the rest of us, in those first few months of 2020. 'It frightened me, if I'm honest, from the start. I remembered back to when I was a child and we experienced scarlet fever. I remember it being horrible and, in those days, people died a lot younger than they do now, so I was incredibly cautious. Everyone I knew was cautious. I had a feeling it wasn't going to go away. I was happy to stay at home in a bubble with my daughter Sue. I was on a stool in the hall while Sue and the grandkids would sit on the wall in the garden. That's how careful we were.'

Then things took a turn for Maggie when she became ill with suspected heart failure. 'My breathing was terrible. I don't think I have ever been that ill in my life. I went into hospital (Coventry & Warwickshire) and was being looked after there. Obviously, I was following the news, but I didn't really think too much of it when someone from the hospital came round and asked if I wouldn't mind having the jab.' Maggie starts laughing. 'My daughter Sue said that they asked me because no one else on the ward was really speaking. I've had jabs before, and it didn't bother me. I never considered not having the jab. I didn't really know much about it.'

Maggie was told later that same night that she was going to be the first person in the world to have the coronavirus vaccine.

Maggie starts laughing again. 'I was on a lot of medication at the time, so I didn't really think much about it. I remember thinking that I couldn't really be the first person in the world to have it, there must be someone else having it at the same time elsewhere.

'That next morning, I went into the room and there were cameras and people all over the place. I had no idea it was going to be that big a thing. May Parsons was the nurse who did the jab, and it was all over in a flash. I went back to the ward, and they were all excited. 'You're on TV!' they all said. I rang my daughter Sue and her brother, and they were all watching too. They let me go home from hospital, but I got told to go to Sue's house because there were so many people outside mine, and I couldn't even get near the door. There are a lot of bushes near my house and one of my neighbours told me they were all hiding in there. I didn't want to give the neighbours any problems, so I just stayed at Sue's. She was working from home, and we just kept the lights off because there were people outside the door the whole time.'

Maggie got the jab on Tuesday 8 December 2020. I remember the day well. My boss at *BBC Breakfast* had called a few days before to let us know that it was going to be happening. We didn't know the name of the patient, but we were told it would take place at Coventry & Warwickshire Hospital while we were on air on that Tuesday morning. We had correspondents in place and guests ready to talk about the significance of the start of the vaccine rollout. In the previous weeks there had been so much talk about how many vaccines the UK had bought and whether they would come from Pfizer or Astra Zeneca.

'It's all in the past now,' says Maggie. 'I feel good about it now. I thank God that I came forward and had it. It is a good feeling. I came up the road yesterday and one little boy said, "Excuse me, is it true that you're ninety-four?" I told him I was ninety-two, and ninety at the time of my jab. I'm amazed people are still interested but I suppose it was so important because it was the start of the way out.'

Maggie hits the nail on the head with that one. She may just have been one ninety-year-old lady getting an injection, but she signified something special. I remember listening to various radio stations that day and there was genuine euphoria that there was a little light at the end of a very long tunnel. There had been so much talk about a possible vaccine, and scientists across the world had been working crazy hours to meet demand, and here it was, finally, before our very eyes.

A few months after the vaccine rollout, I got to visit Maggie at the Coventry & Warwickshire Hospital where she'd had the jab. I met the team from the hospital charity who gave her the famous penguin T-shirt she wore for the big moment. They have since sold thousands of them – and are still having them printed even now! Maggie became quite the celebrity.

'Do you know I won an award for that, Dan?' laughs Maggie. 'When I had my latest corona jabs, they gave me a little prize because of all the T-shirts they had sold. It took my mind back to that day. You know, I didn't watch the news that night . . . I was too tired. I kept thinking, I wished I'd brushed my hair. It wasn't to my liking at all, but I was well looked after by May.' 'May' is May Parsons, the nurse who administered that first-ever jab. We'll meet May again later in the chapter, but the two of them now have a very special bond.

'It's lovely to have a friendship with someone that you'd never met before,' says Maggie. 'I suppose we were thrown together, and we exchange cards at Christmas too.'

I tell Maggie that she was one of the answers to a question in the first pub quiz I went to after they reopened. She is dealing with the attention well. 'I'm having a photograph taken for a museum in London, which is nice. Whenever people do stop me, they are very nice and always kind. I still wear a mask when I go into public places because I'm in my nineties and I think that's just part of life for some people now. I am so glad that I did it though. People tell me that I showed them it was safe, and I have always said that, if I can do it, anyone can. My jab was the first step. It gave people hope that we could get back to normal and that there was a way back. I know that so many people have died, and I remember people being in hospital saying, "Please, can I have it now?", but it was too late. It's terrible . . . so sad when you think about the people who have died. I am very thankful that I am still here to tell the tale.'

I thank Maggie for her time and tell her it's lovely to talk to her again and she perks up. 'Before you go, Dan, two things I wanted to tell you. I had a letter last week from a broadcasting company in Korea. It was handwritten and it was thanking me and congratulating me. I'm going to write back to them and say I appreciate it all, but it was nothing to do with me. I just provided the arm. Everyone else did the work. The other thing, Dan,' says Maggie, 'I loved you on the dancing. Nadiya turned you into such a beautiful dancer. It was lovely to watch. I never miss a single show. I like to watch the dancer but I'm also a keen sewer and I'm always amazed at how those costumes are done so quickly.'

We talk for about ten minutes about Vicky Gill and her wonderful wardrobe team and the magic of sequins.

As Maggie mentioned, there were many people who did lose loved ones during the pandemic. I felt very fortunate to go through the whole period without contracting coronavirus – at least not to my knowledge. I was testing several times a week. I was permanently worried about my elderly relatives, but I'm also very thankful that no one in our family became particularly ill with the virus or required medical attention. My little sister works as a nurse in Derby, and, during the pandemic, she gave our family regular updates on what she and her colleagues were going through. She was moved to intensive care and would send through selfies to our WhatsApp group showing the creases and sores on her face after twelve hours in uncomfortable PPE. She, like many other nursing staff, saw some terrible things during those eighteen months: stretched colleagues, dwindling resources, dying patients and bereaved families. Every single one of those families has a grim story to tell, but there were some that I will never forget. One of them was the story of Heather Stewart and her husband Stephen.

'If anyone in our family was going to struggle with the virus, I thought it would be me,' says Heather. She was meant to start her new job at the Scottish Association for Mental Health on the first day of lockdown.

She and her husband had been together for thirty-two years and married for almost twenty-six. They lived in Motherwell and Stephen worked as a lab technician at the local cement works. He was classed as an essential worker and all he did during those early days of the pandemic was to go to work and then come home. 'He didn't do anything else,' says Heather. 'He was as careful as he could possibly be. We were concerned when it first hit. I could see things happening all over the world. I thought we should be closing our borders and I thought we could have kept ourselves safer. We followed the news closely and followed all the restrictions. My mum lived in a different council area, so we didn't see her for a good nine months. It was just WhatsApp and video calls like the vast majority of people.'

Stephen went to work on Monday 18 January 2021. He'd been back at work after Christmas, and he phoned home and told Heather that he didn't feel 100 per cent. Some colleagues had tested positive, so he did a test and came home.

'Stephen was one of those people who, when he was ill, he'd just go to bed and sleep it off,' says Heather. 'He isolated himself in the bedroom and the test said he was positive. Test and Trace spoke to us, and they said I was also positive after my test. Stephen was being physically sick, and I phoned the NHS, and they sent a car over to take him to the Covid assessment centre on the Thursday of that week. He got an injection, came home and went back upstairs to bed. The first week I wasn't too bad. I was working from home. At the weekend, Stephen asked me to come upstairs. I put the oxygen reading on and it was 71 per cent, which I knew was a long way below what it should be. I called for an ambulance, and they came and took him to the hospital.'

That was the last time Heather spoke to her husband in person.

Stephen went to the University Hospital Wishaw. He was there for ten days and during that time he was too ill to reply to a text message and Heather wasn't able to visit. She would call the hospital for an update on her husband, and they would simply tell her the dose he was on and what his oxygen levels were. Stephen got moved onto a ward but still needed help to breathe. Heather got a call on Valentine's Day from an ICU doctor to say that her husband was struggling, and they were going to monitor him closely and that he was going to go on a ventilator because he had Covid pneumonia. Stephen was on hefty antibiotics but managed to text Heather to let her know that he was hoping to go back to the ward. That sounded like positive news to Heather. That message arrived on the Sunday.

'The following Tuesday, the doctor called again,' says Heather. 'I was told that Stephen was exhausted, and they decided to ventilate him to give him a rest. He said he wanted to "let the machine be his lungs". Again, I wasn't allowed up to the hospital. Stephen was having panic attacks but still I couldn't go up there. Just before he was ventilated, they tried to set up a video call, but it didn't work and we did it on FaceTime instead.

It was all a bit frantic. We had two minutes with him. Stephen was wearing a hooded mask. We couldn't hear each other but at least I got to see him. I told him I loved him, and he mouthed it back and he made a heart with his hands. I told him I would see him on the other side.'

It always seemed to Heather that there was no chance that could be the last goodbye. 'It was always put in a positive light. They phoned me back later that night to say he was responding and was comfortable. On 16 February, the Wednesday, I got a call at lunchtime to say that Stephen hadn't been to the toilet so they had to put him on a dialysis machine, and they had to turn him and they couldn't say if he would survive. I was told I was able to see him for about thirty minutes. He was face down on the bed, ventilated and in an induced coma. There was no communication, but I could touch him and tell him I loved him. I was then sent home and they said they had successfully turned him. They told me that if he crashed or reacted that would have been it because he was already on 100 per cent oxygen. I was able to go back for another thirty minutes. They called me that Wednesday night about 11.30 p.m., and I was told to come back because his blood pressure was all over the place.'

It's clearly emotional for Heather to recall all this. We take a break and talk about something else before returning to that night.

'I was covered in PPE. I sat with him, and he had about twenty pipes and other things coming out of him. They got his blood pressure stabilised, so I went home at 1 a.m. I went back on the Thursday and sat with him playing pieces of music that we enjoyed. He was holding on. I went home again and then I went back to the hospital at about 9 a.m. on Friday 19 February to be told that his organs were shutting down and there was nothing more they could do.' Heather is talking slowly, taking her time, crying. 'I was sitting with Stephen when he passed. I was handed two plastic bags that had all his things in them. His whole life in two plastic bags. I left the hospital in total shock.'

I am speaking to Heather almost eighteen months after the death of her husband and she says her life is still all over the place.

'I was really thankful to see him. I know that so many people weren't even able to do that. I don't think I could have coped with the idea that he was struggling, and I couldn't be there for him. That meant the world to me. It puts things into perspective. There are so many people who didn't get the chance. They couldn't even have the process of grief. The problem is that I feel like we have been together our whole lives. I have no idea how to be on my own. I just miss him. He was such a help, and we did everything together. We were only allowed twenty people at the funeral. There was no wake, no sharing of stories and memories, and then you come back to an empty house, and it hits you . . . this is my new life. A life without him. I still expect him to walk through the doors even now. The world is going about like it's gone, but it still worries me, and I can't shake those memories. I know that we are getting over it, but it's so hard for anyone who has lost someone like Stephen.'

I ask Heather about those people who still claim that the whole pandemic was a hoax and there were empty hospital wards and unused ventilators. She sighs.

'I would tell those people to go and walk along the memorial wall by the Thames in London. We were able to go in August 2021 and visit it. We touched up Stephen's heart and rewrote the words. His heart is on panel 17 and there are now twenty-five panels. He passed away at the height of the second wave and another 70–80,000 people have died since Stephen. I would ask them to go and walk along the Thames and read some of those names and those messages and to think about the devastation that each one leaves behind.'

On the day I spoke to Heather there was another revelation about the parties that went on at Downing Street during the pandemic. She brings it up.

'I don't think you could possibly write down what I feel about that. It is beyond belief that they broke the rules. I don't know any other employer that actively encourages you to drink on the job. Why was it accepted? Why did they smuggle alcohol inside in a suitcase? I want to look up to our leaders. They should be setting the example. I feel like they let us all down. I don't want to be angry though,' says Heather. 'I want to think about Stephen, and I know I need to find a way to live with that but . . . I can't live without him. My life will never be normal. Covid took all that away.'

Heather's story is one which will always stick with me. I remember watching her on *BBC Breakfast* and hearing her powerful testimony. I also have vivid memories of talking to Saleyha and Syira Ahsan. Their father, Ahsan-ul-Haq Chaudry, died from Covid in December 2020 during the second wave, just a few weeks before he was due to get the vaccine.

He lived a remarkable life, and I will never forget the way his two daughters spoke with so much passion and love for their father who had sacrificed so much for them to succeed. His story was made even more remarkable by the fact that all six of his children were working on the NHS frontline during the pandemic. He and his wife, Fauzia, had raised an ITU doctor, two GPs, a junior doctor, a consultant and a pharmacist. A remarkable family mourning the loss of a remarkable dad.

The proud father came to the UK in the 1950s as a nineteen-year-old after fleeing partition violence in India. He was crammed into one of the many trains which left India for Pakistan and his route, through countries like Iran and Turkey, eventually brought him to England.

Syira is his second eldest daughter and still works in the hospital where her dad died at the age of eighty-one. 'My dad was six-foot-two and really overwhelming in stature. All my friends used to think he was really strict, but that was my mum,' she laughs. 'I can only remember my dad shouting at us once in my whole childhood. He was desperate to sleep, and we were making too much noise. He was always laughing. Always having fun. He was like the BFG.'

I ask Syira what her dad did for a living. 'Everything,' she says, 'absolutely everything. Let me see if I can remember. He was trained as a chemical engineer, but he was a civil servant, a maths teacher, a computer science teacher, he worked for the council, and he was a part-time security guard as a second job in the evenings and weekends. He loved teaching and learning. He would always give you a history or a politics lesson when you were with him. He knew so much about the world around him, and he loved to share that with people. He started a lot of his conversations with "Now look here", before launching into something he had observed or picked up. His love of learning never stopped, he even did a degree in Astrophysics in his seventies!'

Syira has one older sister. It's probably worth giving you a little family rundown in age order:

Saleyha: A&E Registrar

Syira: GP and urgent care doctor at Queen's Hospital

Shazlee: Pharmacist

Saima: Consultant Paediatrician

Safiyah: GP and a Sports Physician

Shoaib: ITU doctor

Saleyha also learned so much from her dad's thirst for knowledge. 'He was the man who made me care about news and current affairs. He was all about social justice. He had a hearing problem so he would sit on the floor, watching the news, and we would all sit with him. It was the same every evening – sometimes the BBC and occasionally ITN. We used to love those bongs. We didn't just watch it either. He would talk to us about the stories and the impact it was all having on the world around us. My mum was a royalist, and my dad wasn't quite so supportive of the royal family and we used to have these big differences of opinion, but we all talked about it together. I remember during the war in Bosnia we were watching a report about refugees, and my dad turned to us and said, "I was a refugee once." That was the first time he ever mentioned about coming from India during partition. He saw some truly terrible things, things he never really spoke about to anyone.'

Saleyha got into medicine relatively late after retraining at the age of thirty. Because of what her dad had been through, she was always fascinated by a career in the armed forces. She was the first British Muslim woman to go through the army officer commissioning course at Sandhurst. She knew her dad was incredibly proud of that, particularly because of what the family had faced growing up in Essex.

'We were one of the first Asian families to move into the area of Seven Kings in Ilford,' remembers Syira. 'I remember looking out of the front window one day and asking my dad what "BNP" stood for. He asked me what I meant, and I told him that someone had written it all over our car. It's so strange, because I think Dad was actually teaching the daughter of the leader of the BNP at the time! He said she was a lovely girl. That was him. He was never angry. He would always think that if you can love someone they would come around.'

Her dad was subjected to racism during his earlier years in the UK too when he was first looking for work. Many adverts had the letters 'NCA' on them – No Coloureds Allowed. Saleyha also has clear memories of some of the difficult days. 'I remember being with Mum and our house being pelted,' she says. 'We just stayed inside and waited for Dad to come home. He would always take us for a daily walk around the community in the evening. We would sometimes meet up with another

Asian family and go together. I could sense that, whenever we walked in certain areas, we were prepared for comments or trouble. It's only now that I think about Dad having to shield us from all of that. I will always be thankful for what he did. It can't have been easy.'

Saleyha's dad was also shielding during the pandemic because of his underlying health conditions. The family kept their distance for much of 2020 and visited only to drop off food and supplies to their father, who had lost his wife the year before.

'We don't know how he caught Covid,' says Saleyha. 'Maybe it was one of the shopping drops or when his carer went out on a day off. We don't know, but when he went into hospital, he never came out. I watched a lot of people die from Covid, but it's very different when it is someone you love so much.'

'He was always thinking of other people though,' adds Syira. 'Even when he was lying in his bed, struggling to breathe, he was on the phone to his brother in America, comforting him and telling him that it was going to be ok even though he knew he was deteriorating and that his body was shutting down.'

'Right at the end, Dan,' recalls Saleyha, 'when he was in pain, he had his mask on and he said, "I had six children." He was acknowledging his legacy, I think. He was looking back at his life, all he had come through, and he was thinking about what he had achieved. He was proud of us. I think he also despaired because, you know, we make mistakes and we are far from perfect, but he was happy that we were happy and that he'd lived to see all that.'

After his death, his daughters learned a lot more about their dad from the tributes paid to him and by going through his belongings. 'I remember his teaching and working as a security guard at the same time,' says Saleyha, 'but I never realised how hard he had to fight. Most of it was to pay for our education. He was incredibly highly qualified and yet I found letters in his boxes that he was writing to so many people to get a job as a teacher. He was sending his CV everywhere and begging for any sort of role just so he could support the family. When my dad passed away, some of his former students came forward and contacted us. They are now in their fifties and many of them have successful careers as programmers and they all said they developed their love of the subject in my dad's computer science lessons. He was a pioneer in computer science when the schools didn't even have computers! He would get his pupils to start coding long before it was ever on the curriculum and he would process all that information in his own time, while trying to raise his own six children. He never stopped caring about others. I know he could have been brilliant at anything and that he didn't achieve his full potential because he prioritised us. That is one of the reasons I keep pushing myself . . . I keep trying to achieve more to make his sacrifice worth it.'

'He was just a wonderful man to have around,' says Syira. 'He handled everything really well. He was decent and always held the moral high ground, whatever people threw at him. He could never look at images of war because it always reminded him of what he saw in his childhood in India. My daughter interviewed him about partition for a school project and I think that was the only time he talked about it. He had tears in his eyes that day. I think that's why he was so full of life and always laughing. He was just so thankful that we didn't have to live through what he did.'

Both Saleyha and Syira talk about their dad's love of food. Apparently, before he left India, his mother gave him a week-long cooking course and gave him all the kitchen skills he needed to know for the rest of his life. 'I think he always loved his food because he went through real hunger,' says Syira. 'He appreciated every mouthful and food was the answer to everything. I went through a divorce, and it was getting really hard. I was on the phone to my dad, crying, and he just said, "Enough . . . enough. Come home after work, I am cooking you dinner." He did, and it was lovely. When I was pregnant he decided that he would cook me a gorgeous meal before I went to hospital. He did that and then, while he was in the waiting room, he had a heart attack! The doctors said he was the most dignified patient they had ever met. They asked him if he was having chest pains and he said "Yes" but he just didn't want to make a fuss. That was dad in a nutshell.'

I enjoyed talking to Saleyha and Syira because it was so clear they had learned so much at the feet of their father: watching the news, listening to his impromptu history lessons, sat at his dinner table or just watching the way he treated others.

'My dad was living with us for a while,' remembers Syira, 'and one night we had a takeaway. My daughter came back with the food but also with some change. "What is that?" said Dad. "You never take the change; you always give them extra because you know how hard they work" He sent her outside to give the rest of the money back! He was always buying a McDonald's breakfast for homeless people. We were a poor family ourselves but that never stopped him giving to others. He was a great example to us all.'

It seems that Ahsan-ul-Haq Chaudry had two life rules: study hard and play hard. Syira continues the life lesson.

'He saw from his own example that education was a path to a better life. It wasn't about money; it was about understanding the world that you live in. He also sent us to every sport's club going. I remember him asking me, "When are you going to the Olympics?" and laughing. He just wanted us to love learning new things, to spend time in the library, to love books, to dream big and aim high.' She pauses. I ask if she is ok.

'I'm ok,' says Syira. 'It's just that talking about him now makes me realise that I still haven't really processed the fact that he's gone. I still expect to go around his house and to see him there, cooking food, telling me about politics and making me watch the news with him.'

I thank Saleyha for sharing her dad with the rest of us and ask her what her overriding memory of him will be. She takes her time to answer.

'He was really brave, Dan,' she says eventually. 'He made sacrifices throughout his life so that we could achieve things. He put his own dreams to one side and did what he had to do as a father so that we could fly. He was a talented chef, a great teacher and he was gifted at so many things. He was passionate about education and had such a strong sense of justice. He was always inquisitive, and he had this wonderful, constantly questioning mind. He has left behind six highly qualified children, but it doesn't really matter what letters I have after my name on a piece of paper ... I am staggered by what he achieved. To leave that mess behind in India, to leave his whole life, to come here and then to fight for everything he achieved, against the odds, and to laugh and love the whole time, that is incredible. I'm glad you called your book *Standing on the Shoulders* because that is where I feel I have been my whole life.'

There is another family I want to tell you about too. Josh and Samantha Willis didn't have as many children as Ahsan-ul-Haq Chaudry, but their story is just as compelling. Whenever I think about the impact of the pandemic, my mind skips back to Josh and Samantha.

They met in Northern Ireland back in 2012 on Samantha's birthday, 15 May. Her friends had made her go and Josh was bored. They met up regularly and eventually moved in together and decided to get married in March 2019 in Derry. Their daughter, Lilyanna, was born in April 2017 and Samantha was due to give birth to their second child in August 2021.

'I remember hearing about coronavirus around Christmas time in 2019,' recalls Josh. 'It was all getting hyped up and then, a few months later, it was everywhere. The bars and restaurants in Derry actually closed a week before the rest of the UK. I was working at the Northern Ireland Housing Executive and was off on a week's holiday. I didn't get sent home from work for the first lockdown, I never went back from my break.'

Samantha was working in community care in people's houses and worked right the way through lockdown. 'She had to pass police checkpoints and prove she was an essential worker quite a bit,' remembers Josh.

It was Friday night, 30 July 2021, when Josh got a call from his sister. 'She told me she was positive and we'd been with her that day. We both did the tests, and we came back as positive on the Sunday. Samantha was getting worse with her breathing, and it got to the point that she could barely get out of bed. At this point she was about thirty-six weeks pregnant, so I was a little worried. I called the doctor and told them what was happening, and it took them five hours to come back to me. I got told to bring her over to the hospital, so I did that. They checked her oxygen and then said they wanted to keep her there to get some extra checks done, because of the baby.'

Samantha was put into a wheelchair when Josh dropped her off. He had Covid himself at the time, so it all took place in the ambulance bay outside the hospital. He told his wife he would see her soon.

'There was no kiss and no hug,' says Josh. 'It was a super-quick drop-off. I just left her outside A&E. I went home, finished off packing her baby bag and then went back to the hospital and dropped her bag off at the same place outside the emergency department.'

On Wednesday 4 August, Josh heard that they were going to perform a C-section on his wife for the safety of their child. This was three weeks before the due date.

'I had sent our iPad up in her baby bag so that is what we

used for the birth of our little daughter, Evie Grace. Me and Lilyanna watched it all from our sofa in the house. It was bad, because Samantha never wanted a section. It was one of her fears, and the other one was having to give birth on her own. I'm glad that Lilyanna got to see the birth of her sister, but I knew it was awful for Samantha. That would have been her worst nightmare. She just gave in on the C-section because of the safety of the baby. It was all a bit surreal to be sat watching it on the sofa.'

As soon as Evie Grace was born, she was whipped into the next room. Her mum still had Covid, and she never got the chance to hold, or even touch, her new baby. Samantha went straight to the intensive care unit.

'She was sitting up in bed ok, but she couldn't really finish a sentence. We were FaceTiming her, but she was just exhausted. I would text her and it would take her hours to respond because she had so little energy. I kept asking if she could maybe hold the baby because I thought that would help her, but they just kept saying "no". I understand why. She was out of isolation, but she was still showing symptoms.'

Samantha went back onto the Covid ward, was turned, spent another week in ICU and then, tragically, after sixteen days in hospital, she died in the early hours on Friday 20 August.

'I was ringing twice a day,' says Josh. 'I was worried about her, but I also knew she was only thirty-five years old with no underlying health conditions. At points it looked like she was getting better but, in the end, her body just gave up. She never had the vaccination, because we found out she was pregnant on Boxing Day in 2020 and the advice at the time was for pregnant mums to avoid the jab. She was going to have it after the baby was born.'

Josh recalls getting the call he was dreading on Thursday 19 August. 'They rang and asked if I wanted to come over and see her. They had told me before when I'd asked to go in, that the only way that would happen would be if things got really serious. I knew it wasn't good. I went in to see her with this huge Covid suit on. I was there for about an hour. I was just talking to her. When I left, her oxygen level had gone up a little, which was good news, but she was unresponsive. She was in an induced coma. They called again that night. I was at my manager's house updating him in the garden and I was told I needed to bring my family. There could only be four of us there so I rang her mother, her sisters and her brother and thought, we can decide when we get there. I remember sitting in the office of the hospital and the staff were asking me about a "do not resuscitate" order. I couldn't bring myself to say the words. How can you say that you don't want them to try and save your wife's life?'

In the end, it was decided that Josh would go in to see his wife along with her mum and her two children from a previous relationship – her fourteen-year-old daughter Holly and Shay, who was seventeen.

'I walked into the room,' says Josh, 'and there was a priest there. I looked at the oxygen machine and it was in the sixties. I knew that was bad and I asked the nurse, just checking really, how serious it was, and she looked at me and told me that my wife had just that minute passed away.' Josh is recounting the events at a much slower rate now. He is understandably taking his time.

'I was glad I was there; I was glad I got to see her earlier that day. I hope she heard me when I was talking to her. I asked if she could hear, and I just talked about our family and I told her to keep fighting. For most of it I just held her hand. It sounds stupid, but I remember, while I was there, thinking about the people saying that Covid was a hoax. Here I was, saying goodbye to my wife.'

Josh went home in the early hours of Friday 20 August to collect some clothes to put Samantha in. He went back with a lock of Evie Grace's hair and Lilyanna's hair, and the nurses dressed her.

'I brought some photographs with me, to go in the coffin. I had some of the girls' toys and I brought the perfume that she had for our wedding. Normally, we would have had an open coffin in the house for a few days but, because of Covid, that wouldn't be happening, so I knew this was the last time I would ever see her face. I sprayed her with the perfume. I told her kids to tell her whatever they needed to tell her, and I said to them that all they could do now was make her proud of them. I kissed her through my visor and tried to leave. I knew they needed her bed for another patient, but I just couldn't walk away. I knew that I was never going to see her again. I tried to go about five times but just kept circling back to her side. I knew that as soon as I walked past that curtain . . . that was it. As I drove away in the car, I remember thinking that we should have been together for the best part of fifty years. I thought we would have all the time in the world to do the things we wanted to do. We were in the process of buying a house, I had just had a job interview for a promotion and, if I'd got that job, we were hoping that she wouldn't have to go back to work. There was so much to look forward to.'

Josh's uncle, Joe Clifford, was a priest in America. He was the one who had married them, and he was coming over for the funeral. He arrived at the house on the Sunday after Samantha's death and Josh asked him if he would be able to christen Evie Grace in the short time he'd be in the country.

'He looked at me,' remembers Josh, 'and said, "I don't know if you're allowed to do this, but do you think we could christen her at Samantha's funeral?" I just said "yes" straightaway without thinking about it. I wanted her to be there. I know she had gone, but I didn't want her to miss it. The chapel said it was ok, so we decided we would do it.'

Josh hasn't watched the funeral back. He doesn't think he ever will. 'It wasn't a big thing,' says Josh. 'We didn't publicise it to the people who were there. It was just something we wanted to do, so it just happened at the side of the church. I think it brightened things up a little bit. Evie Grace was christened because I wanted them to feel close to each other. I wasn't really thinking about what I was doing, but I just wanted Samantha to be there. It felt special to have them both together.'

Life remains hard for Josh and his two daughters. The enormity of the loss still hasn't really set in. He is so busy with the girls, and he still visits the cemetery every day. 'I just tell her what is happening,' says Josh, 'you know, the date, the weather, any news, what the girls are up to. They are always up to something. It's hard to know what Lilyanna will remember. There is endless information on Google which I can't really protect her from forever. I have put pictures up of her mum everywhere, so she remembers her. I have kept newspapers, pictures, and put them all in a box. One day she can read them all and see what an amazing person her mum was.'

Josh put a post about his wife on Facebook on the Friday of her death. That weekend was a big vaccine weekend in Ireland and the circumstances of Samantha's last few days had a huge impact people.

'It took off,' remembers Josh. 'I wasn't making a political point. I don't think I even said "Get the vaccine" . . . I just told our story. There were people queuing for hours to get the jab. It's strange to think about it now because hardly anyone talks about Covid anymore. I don't blame anybody. I am just sad. I can't change it. I wish it hadn't happened, but I can't do anything to bring her back.'

I ask Josh how he will remember his wife. He tells me about a video on his phone.

'We were together for just over nine years, and I've got loads of videos and photos but there is one that stands out,' he smiles. 'She was out dancing, blowing me kisses, you know . . . laughing. She was happy, she cared, she loved people, she had goodness in her. She was my best friend as well as my wife.' Josh laughs before telling the next part . . .

'I've got to tell you, Dan, when she got into bed at night it was like her feet had been in the freezer but . . . I miss all that . . . you know, the annoying stuff. I miss all the stuff we never got to do, the stuff we were planning. The two little ones keep me going so I'll just keep going forward, one day at a time. One of the last things she texted me was from hospital. She was talking about cutting the drama out of her life. She wanted no negativity. She wanted to keep moving, to keep being positive, so that's what I need to keep doing for her. I know that now, she is just a number. One of thousands of people who died with Covid. I just hope her story lives on, and kids can read about her. To me, she will never be a number. I would rather her be named than just a pregnant person who had a baby. She would have hated every part of that, but I want people to know who she was, and how special she was. She was great at what she did, and everybody loved her.'

I thank Josh for his time. He is round at his sister's house, and I've made him late for a fried breakfast.

'Don't you worry, Dan,' he says. 'This is important. Can I just tell you one more thing?' he asks, almost whispering.

'I feel that she's around a lot of the time. There was one night, back in November, I felt like she walked me down to her graveside. I could feel the weight of her arm on mine. I know it sounds daft and maybe it's in my head but, believe me, I felt it. She was with me as I walked back up the hill and then, as I stepped out of the graveyard, it was like she stayed inside, and I left. It's one of the weirdest things I have ever felt. I don't know if my mind is playing with me, but there are little things that I feel, like she is trying to send me a message sometimes.

I hope she's happy with what I am trying to do with the kids. I hope she knows I'm trying to stay positive and keep going. She always said that if she went first, she would haunt me. Maybe that's what is happening. I just hope she stays around for as long as possible.'

Earlier in the chapter, we met Maggie Keenan who received the end of the needle containing the first coronavirus vaccine in the world. As promised, it's time to introduce the person who was on the other end of that syringe: May Parsons.

May's official title is Modern Matron for Respiratory. She trained as a nurse in the Philippines, graduated in 2000 and arrived in the UK in 2003. She has been working at Coventry & Warwickshire Hospital ever since.

I caught up with her the morning after another long shift. May has always been brutally honest about what it was like to work in a hospital during the pandemic and she paints a pretty grim picture of those early months of 2020.

'From the very start of it all, I volunteered to go into the intensive care unit. That was a time when we didn't have any-thing to protect ourselves. We were just catching people who needed ventilation. There were days when you had a group of people none of whom would be there the next day, they had all passed away. I can still remember the youngest person we saw; she was only twenty-two years old. There were young, fit, mus-cular men from the BAME community who would come into the ward and die overnight. It felt like our job was just sending people off, you know, making their deaths as comfortable as we could. It was hard to call a family member and tell someone that their loved one is going to die, and it just kept happening, day after day, after day.'

I ask her how she coped with that.

'I just don't know. You can see that people are scared, they are terrified of dying, worried about going on a ventilator and never coming off it. I was dealing with health workers terrified of catching the virus themselves and taking it home to their families and loved ones. I remember I told my husband and my kids that I would live in a hotel, but I just couldn't do it. I couldn't have survived without them. I would shower after work and scrub all my stuff before I went home. I was getting undressed in the garden to protect them and then, in the house, I would sit in the same chair. I couldn't hug my own son. He was crying, I was crying. It was awful.'

Did she ever think about her own mortality when she was surrounded by so much death?

'I tried not to think about it, you know, "What if I get it?", "What if I die?" I think that would have stopped me from doing my job properly. I've never thought about that in my twenty-four years of nursing before Covid. I was just trying to keep myself safe, keep my family safe and keep people alive. That was my motivation every day but, the longer it went on, the more you realised that we were losing the battle time after time. I felt a sense of helplessness for months. I knew that I couldn't save someone, but I could make sure that they didn't die on their own. It wasn't why I signed up to be a nurse. Have you ever tried holding someone's hand when they are dying? My colleagues were terrified. We just felt like sitting ducks with no protection from what we saw all around us.'

I ask May whether she and her colleagues spoke about what they were seeing and what they were going through, or was it just a case of ploughing on? May starts to cry. She doesn't stop. She apologises and tells me that it is still so raw and her colleagues are still so deeply affected by it.

She continues, 'There were a lot of conversations with colleagues about death. As a senior nurse, I just wanted to make sure that people knew that there was help when they needed it. We had what we called a "wobble room" – if you needed five or ten minutes to cry or scream then that was available for everyone. Some people chose to speak to the hospital chaplain. He was a busy man, but he did a great job for so many people. You can imagine that we formed a close bond and we became very protective of each other. That was the one real benefit from all of this . . . that bond between us became such a strong one. We had to rely on each other and help one another. I could see that some people were really struggling. There was a lot of trying to keep people's heads above the water.' May is still crying and takes a deep breath before continuing.

'I couldn't even tell my family what I was going through at work. How do you even begin to talk about that? All I know is that I am not prepared to do it again in this lifetime.'

'Did you ever think of leaving, May?' I ask. She replies immediately.

'Never. I never thought of leaving. I just wanted to focus

on the job in hand and fulfil my nursing duties. As a leader, I needed to show my colleagues how to be a nurse even when the job seems impossible. How can you ask people to risk their lives when you are not doing it yourself? I had no other option than to just carry on. I remember when I did my oath in nursing school. We promised to do our best for our patients. It didn't matter what I needed because someone else needed me more.'

May is keen to talk about the everyday stresses of working through a pandemic.

'You have to imagine what is going through the heads of a workforce that is under more pressure than they have ever forced before. Every day there are more patients dying and more patients arriving. At the start, there was not enough PPE and there was a race to get the equipment to treat patients. Every day you are thinking, "Is today the day that I get it?" You are under intense strain, people are dying around you, you are calling relatives, trying to look after yourself and others, you are all thinking about PTSD, and you are scared to go to work. If you cough at work, you are stared at by everyone and you're asked to test, test, test all the time. That is why I still wear a mask now,' says May. 'I think it's the legacy of everything that we went through. That was the one piece of protection that we felt we had.'

It's when you consider all that, you begin to realise why that morning with Maggie Keenan was such a big one for people like May. It marked what she hoped would be the beginning of the end of the nightmare.

'I gave Maggie the jab on a Tuesday morning, and they asked me about it at the end of the week before, I seem to remember,' says May. 'I had been part of the steering group for the delivery of the vaccination. I remember I was told that there "might be a few cameras" but I had no idea it would be as huge as it turned out. There were fifty NHS trusts rolling it out on the same day and I didn't know ours was the first. I met Maggie on the Monday before the jab. We talked about the fact that she didn't want to wear her hospital gown, so I went to buy her some clothes and I think that is where the famous T-shirt came from. I came and woke her up at 5 a.m. so that she would have plenty of time to prepare. I know it was hectic and there were TV crews everywhere, but I wasn't really looking at the cameras. I was just focused on Maggie. I knew she was ninety and I just wanted her to be ok.'

The significance of that day was certainly not lost on May and the rest of the staff at the hospital.

'I know that the pictures were important, but that day felt like a big one. I have done thousands of injections and I never thought that just one of them would cause such a stir. Covid had made us all feel like we were in the firing line, but the vaccine was our way of fighting back. It felt like a big step forward. Until then, we were feeling hopeless. We were looking after people with our hands tied behind our backs. I will never forget that day.'

I don't know if you lost someone close during the pandemic, but I do know that whatever you went through, it is something we will never forget.

And I hope that it stays that way but I wonder how society will look back on it all in ten, fifteen, fifty years. What will our children tell their children? How will history remember the death of so many? How many pages will it get in a textbook? As time passes I imagine it will be more about numbers and less about names. The individual stories will quickly fade.

That's why I'm so thankful to have had the chance to meet the people in this chapter and to learn from their experiences, sacrifices and heartache. I trust that you have been able to learn something too, and that you won't forget them.

STILL REMARKABLE

When the publishers of this tome first approached me to write a book in 2018, they wanted me to write an autobiography. I really didn't want to go down that road, because there are only so many copies my mum can buy. I asked if I could write about other people and that was the start of *Remarkable People*. I loved writing about some of the individuals who have made a lasting impact on me and I am still amazed by not only the number of people who wanted to read it, but the amount who still want to talk about the people in it.

There isn't a week that goes by that I'm not asked about Tony, Terrence or the orphanage in South Africa. I am often being asked how Ilse is, or whether I'm still in contact with John Sutherland.

When the opportunity arose to write another book, I wanted to revisit some of those individuals and see how they are getting on. They were 'remarkable' a few years ago and they remain just as impressive now.

Figen Murray is one of the people I get asked about all the time. She was the mother of Martyn Hett, one of the victims of the Manchester Arena bomb. It was a real pleasure to catch up with Figen again, although she doesn't appear in this chapter. You'll be able to find her in 'The Truth About Monsters', a chapter about forgiveness, which is such a central element to her story.

Let's start with John Sutherland, the former police officer, turned author, who remains one of the wisest people I have ever met. I didn't need to catch up with John for this book because we speak regularly. He is doing wonderfully well and, if you're interested in books, John published his first novel in 2022. It's a thriller called *The Siege* and it's brilliant.

I've also managed to keep in regular contact with Paula and Tony Hudgell. Tony is the amazing young lad who had his legs amputated after being abused by his birth parents. He was adopted by Paula and she has seen him grow into a gorgeous boy who, inspired by Captain Tom, walked 10 kilometres during lockdown on his prosthetic legs and raised more than a million pounds for the Evelina Children's Hospital in London – the hospital where he has all his treatment.

'Life has been pretty hectic,' says Paula. 'Tony went on to win a Pride of Britain award, which was amazing. Ant and Dec gave him his prize in Hamleys, but it was in the middle of the pandemic so they couldn't touch each other. His walking is improving all the time and his profile is growing too. One of the most amazing things that happened was when his photo popped up during the Queen's speech at Christmas. It was one of the 100 Photos Of Lockdown. It was so strange. I was late putting the telly on, as usual. It had just gone 3 p.m., she had started and the first thing I saw was a photo of Tony! I thought it must be a mistake but then my phone started going berserk. All my friends were contacting me. I had to rewind it to make sure it was actually happening. It just made me think of how many people he has been able to reach. How remarkable is that? We only set out to raise £500 for the Evelina and I think he's near enough £1.7 million now.'

'How are his legs?' I ask. 'Has he got new ones?'

'Yes,' says his mum. 'He has kept improving his prosthetic legs – he can walk unaided to a certain extent and he has knee bends put into his legs now. He is a lot more independent and able to interact with his peers. He is the same height as his friends now, which might not sound that important, but it's a huge thing for Tony just to be on the same eyeline as them. Some days he has to spend time in his wheelchair, but being able to stand next to his peers and look them in the eye, has changed his whole outlook on life. You wouldn't recognise him, Dan,' says Paula, oozing pride. 'He is so much more confident. For the first time, he can reach the surfaces in the kitchen, so he's making his own toast and hot chocolate. His whole world has opened up. He is a normal seven-year-old. He's even able to kick a ball around with his friends.'

Tony's issues run much deeper than his prosthetic legs. There are a number of ongoing health concerns and the emotional damage will always be there too. 'He is always going to have challenges,' says Paula. 'He will always need surgery on his legs, his hip permanently dislocates and his face will need looking at soon because his jaw is very small from the blunt-force trauma. He's had surgery on his wrist because so many of his bones were broken by the abuse, and his arms are deformed from all the injuries. That is the reality of the life away from the smiles you see on TV. You know I love him to bits, but he is a troubled young man.'

One of Paula's concerns when we spoke last time was the answers she would need to give Tony when he grew up a little and started asking about his birth parents. 'He asks more questions,' she says, with something of a heavy heart. 'He thinks his issues are due to being poorly from infection. It's heart-breaking sometimes. Recently he asked me, "When I'm older, Mum, will I have my legs?" He seems to think his legs might grow back. He has seen photos of how his legs were before they were amputated. We are always honest with him. If he asks the question about his parents, I won't lie to him. The last thing I want to do is for him not to hear the truth. I owe him that. They (his abusers) are both due to be released this year. That's always going to be there. I don't know how to deal with all that really.'

I ask Paula how she feels about Tony's abusers being back in society. Paula considers her answer for a moment. 'You know, she actually sent him a couple of letters via the charity Barnardo's? They are not appropriate for Tony now. When do we give him those? All we can do is do what we feel is right at the time. It's a massive parental conundrum – when do you show him? When do we open him up to all that? What is right for one child isn't right for another – people are always saying, "you should do this". Mark and I want to do the best for Tony. That is all we have ever wanted. It was strange for me. I do wonder how much remorse and understanding there is. I'm assuming that the letter was sent as part of her rehabil-itation programme, but the real test will be when they come out in August. There are probation restrictions and there are limits and they can't make contact with him or any of us. If they break any of that they go back to prison. After five years on licence, they can do whatever they want. I do worry if she goes on to have another child. I worry about them changing their names and getting lost in the system.'

All this was the inspiration for Tony's Law, an attempt to see child abusers in England and Wales spending a lifetime behind bars. Under those changes, campaigned for by Paula, if a child survives, their abusers will spend fourteen years behind bars instead of ten and, if a child dies, the maximum sentence can be life imprisonment. Under the old system, the maximum sentence was fourteen years.

'It has been a struggle for us,' says Paula. 'Finally, Dominic Raab got it (Raab was the Justice Minister at the time). We went to his office to discuss Tony's Law and, to be fair to them, they have been really good at staying in contact. There are other things we want to do too. We want a Child Cruelty Register so that you are on there for life, even if you change your name, just like they do with sex offenders. The police can keep tabs on them then. It's about accountability. I'm also having meetings about a dedicated Child Cruelty Department within the Crown Prosecution Service. There is one for rape, one for murder, but nothing for one of the most complicated areas . . . child cruelty. Only 3 per cent of child cruelty cases actually make it to court and that has to change.'

Paula is formidable. She is a fearless campaigner who gets things done time and time again, but it has taken its toll on her health.

'I tried to get a GP appointment at the end of 2020, but we all know what that is like. I thought it was a flare-up of my IBS (Irritable Bowel Syndrome). I've suffered with it for thirty years. When it's one of our children, I just demand to see a doctor, but I'm not as pushy when it's me. I tried again in early January because it was getting much worse. I finally got to see a GP and was told I was probably alright because there were no lumps, but my blood tests were not right. I had a colonoscopy in mid-February and the doctor called me in and said he'd found a large tumour in my colon and it was cancerous. That was the biggest shock of my life. I was young at fifty-four and it had been there a long time so they needed more tests to see if it had spread. You fear the worst. I walked out thinking that my time was up. My biggest fear wasn't death but for my children and for Tony: I am his world, I do everything for him. I take him everywhere and I am his number one. If I am no longer around, who will look after him? It's not easy bringing up a disabled child. Everything moved really quickly. I had CT scans and an MRI and they found that the tumour had been there for ten years but it hadn't spread. I had it removed in March and it was far worse than giving birth to seven children. I woke up with a stoma bag and now I need a six-month course of chemotherapy because it was in my veins.'

I ask Paula how the family reacted.

'All the older children know. It's been a crazy two years with some real highs and deep lows. I lost my mum in 2019 and then my dad in 2020; both to lung cancer. The kids lost two grandparents in a short space of time and I felt a responsibility to show them that not everyone dies of cancer. I need to be around for my children. I need to be here for Tony. I am convinced he can do whatever he wants in life. There are no boundaries for this boy. He will have so many opportunities. He is bright and confident, loving and caring, and has a great sense of humour. Because of the surgery, I haven't been able to pick him up for months, but I've told him the world is his oyster. The one thing I want for him is to be happy, and he knows how to do that now.'

I remind Paula of the first time we spoke to each other for *Remarkable People* and we both cried as she told me about the consultant who was assessing all of Tony's injuries and said, 'Who would want this kid?'

'I am so grateful the consultant said that,' says Paula. 'That was the kick I needed. He made me see it. I was just doing my job and that day . . . Tony became my life and he has brightened all our lives. I don't think I would be as strong mentally if I didn't have Tony in my life. He is so positive about everything and that has made me try and take that onboard. When I had my cancer diagnosis, I was incredibly low for a while and Mark and Jess, who is sixteen, were a real mess. I remember saying, "We have to be like Tony," and that has pulled me, all of us, through so far. Tony never complains. His whole life is an uphill struggle and he just keeps on walking.'

*　　*　　*

There must be something about Tonys because we are going to move from a young superstar to a slightly older one. I am writing this chapter on a day when I have seen Tony Foulds again, back in the park where we first met in 2019.

Tony was in Endcliffe Park in Sheffield in 1944 when an American bomber called *Mi Amigo* crashed into the trees behind the current café to avoid children playing in the open field. All ten of the airmen onboard died. Tony was eight years old at the time and was one of those playing in the park. He says he has always felt guilt over their deaths and has spent many years tending the memorial in the park: sweeping leaves, planting flowers and telling anyone who will stop about the ten men he calls his 'lads'.

I met him and listened to his story just six weeks before the 75th anniversary and, with a little help from social media and a lot of help from the US Air Force, we managed to organise a flypast on the day of the anniversary and there were over 15,000 people in the park to see it as Tony stood alongside the family of some of those who had been onboard. It was a magical bit of TV watched by millions of people all over the UK and around the world. I wrote all about Tony in *Remarkable People*.

'I've had so many people come up, Dan,' says a very cheery Tony. I catch him on one of the many days he is blowing leaves off the paths around the memorial. The council have had to resurface the walkways behind the café because so many people are visiting Tony these days.

'They all tell me that they've read your book. I reckon I'm due some royalties,' he laughs. 'I hope this next one is even better. University!' he shouts at me. 'I've had people come from all these universities today. It's been lovely. There was a time that nobody walked down this side of the river. I'll have to blow all the way to the M1 soon. I can't have it dirty.'

I watch as Tony breaks off to speak to a family who have turned up with a family member who is 101 years old. They still remember the war well and Tony relives his own memories and talks about visiting the graves of the men who died in the park in 1944. Once he's finished chatting, and retold his joke about the M1 again, he returns to talk to me and give our dog Winnie a little stroke.

'You and this dog have changed my life, Dan.' I had promised my wife I would walk Winnie in the park on that day in 2019, but I was late for work, so we went a different way to normal which took us past the memorial. That led to the meeting with Tony.

'I am invited to all these events,' he says. 'The US Air Force have been great. I go and visit memorials all over the country now. I have been to, let me see, Norfolk, Bedworth, Derby, Nottingham . . . I even got invited to Edinburgh! Do you remember Dan, a few year ago, when I asked you if you thought it would all go away? You said that we'd have to wait and see, but you thought that people would always be interested. Well, you were right. It's gone mad.'

Tony has picked up a number of awards and is a regular visitor to US air bases around the UK where everyone knows his name. There was a trip to America planned to visit the home cities of the men of *Mi Amigo* but it was another casualty of lockdown.

'I was thinking of writing to (President) Biden,' says Tony. 'I wanted to ask him to look after them properly, you know, the graves. I have seen some of them on pictures. They are just a little stone, same size as two house-bricks. I would want to go and visit all the graves. I thought when we first started that they were all in the Arlington Cemetery, but they are all over the USA. I just feel so happy that so many people know about the lads now. They teach about them in schools and I get people from South Africa, Australia . . . all over the place, who come here just to see it on their trip to England. I had one last Monday from Winnipeg, in Canada. "We've come to see you, Tony," they said. Can you believe that? From Canada!'

We walk back to the memorial together. 'I want it to be the best-looking one in the country, Dan,' he says, bending down to pick up a leaf which has fallen on the path since his latest blowing session.

'If you look,' he says, pointing at the memorial, 'we now have ten vases for each lad and I buy the flowers for the vases. At the front we are full of flowers and full of colour. The shrubs are fully grown; there are ten tubs with shrubs and flowers, ten pots full of pansies and ten vases full of fresh flowers. I don't accept money and if anyone insists I send it all to Duxford where the last *Sally B* is – to look after that.' (*Mi Amigo* was a B-17 Flying Fortress and *Sally B* is the last remaining Flying Fortress in Europe and is stationed at Duxford.)

'I've even been invited to other memorials to help people look after them,' says Tony, puffing out his cheeks. 'I can't get round them all, Dan, but these last three years have been the best ever. I'm too busy down there to get poorly. The Park Run goes past the memorial now; twice every single Saturday. The organisers have given me a proper tunic so I'm now a marshall for the run. They all wished me "Happy Birthday" this year. It were great.' He pauses and looks me straight in the eye. 'April the second, by the way.'

Tony says his connection to the story and to the men who died in Endcliffe Park feels stronger than ever. 'I do feel much closer to these lads,' he says, resting his hands on some of the pictures at the memorial. 'When I come down here now, my son and my daughter say, "Are you going home?" I hate leaving them and I hate going away, but I've got a good friend who checks in on them when I'm not around.'

One thing that has changed is the Stars and Stripes that flutters in the wind above the memorial. The flagpole was erected after the flypast and was part-funded by a local school in Sheffield and the rest came from Boeing. Every time I walk past, it reminds me of just how far the story reached, touching everyone from a primary school around the corner from the park, to a multinational company. Tony loves it too.

'As far as I know, we are the only place allowed to fly the flag in the UK,' he says, with an understandable degree of pride. 'It actually came from Omaha beach in Normandy. It were flown on the anniversary of D-Day and it were flown specifically for the *Mi Amigo*. It were given to me by RAF Mildenhall and I were given permission to fly it outside a military base, which never normally happens. We only ever used to be able to fly it on the day of the anniversary (22 February), but now I just bring it down to clean it.' Tony looks up at it and the tears start to well in his eyes. 'Doesn't it look beautiful?'

One of the questions I often get asked about Tony is how he is doing healthwise. His essential tremor is slowly getting worse but he continues to look after himself.

'I am eighty-six now, Dan. There isn't much I can do. I've been told that the Chinese are making a bracelet and it does stop the tremors, but it's a bit chunky. I have now joined an essential tremor association that meets in Sheffield. That's been great, but I can't have a shirt with buttons; I can't have shoes or coats without that sticky stuff, you know . . .'

'Velcro?' I suggest.

'That's the stuff,' says Tony. 'I love that stuff. I can't use knives or hot things and it's worse in the morning and it's worse when I'm stressed. The only thing that helps is whiskey but, as you know, I don't drink. Although, I do think my milk and egg helps.'

'You what, Tony? Milk and egg?' I reply.

'Yep. When I used to be a bodybuilder, and enter competitions, I would mix raw eggs into milk and drink it all down. I have that every now and again, but most of the time I just drink fiddy fiddy.'

'You'll have to help me out with that one, Tony,' I say, laughing. 'Is that fifty fifty, as in half tea and half milk?'

'No, Dan, fiddy fiddy is half tea and half coffee. Every morning on our estate, I pop into Steve's Café for a mug of fiddy fiddy. I'm not allowed to make any hot drinks myself because of the shakes, but Steve brews one up every morning. It used to be the old toilets, you know.'

'What did?' I ask.

'Steve's Café. They turned the toilets into a café. It's great. Fiddy fiddy every day.' Tony laughs and slaps me on the back. 'He says I am the only one who drinks it.'

I tell Tony I'm not overly surprised and tell him I'll see him soon.

'You'll still come and see me, won't you, Dan?' he says.

'Of course. What do you mean?'

'Well, you're one of my best mates, and I keep being told that you've left the BBC and you've gone to Channel 5. You won't forget about me, will you?'

I give Tony a hug, assure him that I'll still see him in the park each week and tell him that, just for him, I'll try out a mug of fiddy fiddy. I did. It was awful.

Of all the interviews I have ever done, I still think that the one with Ilse Fieldsend is the one that keeps coming back to me. I spoke to her during a show on BBC Radio 5 Live in 2015. It was a special show, based at the Queen Elizabeth Hospital in Birmingham, looking at the issue of donors and transplants. Ilse came on to talk about her daughter, Georgia. In 2013, they had been on a family holiday to Egypt when Georgia collapsed with a ruptured brain aneurysm on a beach. She was rushed to hospital and eventually back to the UK where her parents had to make a decision about donating the organs of their dying child. Georgia died that night but she saved four lives with her kidney, her liver and her heart valves. There are two young men who can see because her parents took the heart-breaking decision to donate her eyes too.

Ilse's life was torn apart that night and she still lives in the shadow of that loss. She is broken but brilliant and, for all those who ask me how she is doing, that's where I started when we caught up with each other again.

'We are ok,' says Ilse. 'We are surviving. We are happy, our son Joshua is getting on with life and I am a professional dog walker.'

Ilse's son Josh is turning eleven this year. Georgia would have been twelve on 10 May 2022.

'Josh is talking to a counsellor at school which has been really helpful. He finds it hard to see happy families and he is talking to her about loss. I think he finds it hard to come to terms with why we lost Georgia and why it happened to us. We are still working through it all. In the past, I have done a proper party and invited all of Georgia's friends on her birthday. I make a rainbow cake, we crank the music up and have balloons but, on other occasions, we just keep it quiet. I am worried. I feel quite nervous, like I can't be Georgia's mum in the way I used to. People forget, which is totally understandable, but I can never forget. Once or twice a year I talk about organ donation and I go on radio stations and I think that helps me as much as it helps others. I still want people to ask me about her. That's why I was happy, sad and a bit worried when you asked me to talk to you for your new book, because I don't talk about her that much anymore. Life does go on. You have to be happy, you have to try and fit in. I have to be a happy parent for Joshua.'

The pain is still very much on the surface with Ilse. She still feels like a mother of two even though Georgia has been gone for almost a decade.

'Losing a child is like losing a limb,' she says. 'It's a part of your heart that will never be repaired. Her bedroom is still the same as it always was and I still sleep in her bed. I'm better, but it's still hard to move on. I see her friends becoming young girls and I wish I could be there for her to guide her through as a mum. I'm much better at coping with comments like "You are so lucky you don't have a girl, boys are so much easier". I never have a go at anybody, but my heart breaks every time. I have become far more tolerant with time. I used to react if someone said, "I can't wait to get rid of the kids after the holiday", but now I just smile.'

I ask her if she feels she'll ever not need to sleep in Georgia's bed.

'I know that people will read this and think that I am doing the wrong thing, but this is my way of getting through the days. I don't think I can ever get rid of her things. I still take a few of her dresses away with me when we go on holiday. I just want to feel her presence. She goes on holiday with us too. I can't see that changing any time soon. We take her ashes with us. That is how I cope. I am sure it will change. I just feel that when I wake up I can't breathe because I don't feel as close to her. I think one of the main reasons is that I can do less for her. When I did the charity song, or the coffee mornings to raise awareness, I still felt like her mum, but sometimes I feel like she is disappearing. I have to hold on to her. I know

I won't love her any less if I didn't sleep in there, but I want her to know that I am still with her.'

Ilse is right, it is very easy to judge her, but it's also impossible to know how you would act if you found yourself in that situation.

'When we go out for a meal it's hard when people say, "Is it just the three of you?" My head says, "What are you doing?" I know deep down it is all too much but, at the moment, this is where I am. I have done therapy but it hasn't really worked for me. There is only so much you can say about how sad you are. It doesn't help, because nobody can bring her back. I don't tend to bother too many people with Georgia because I know I become too much to cope with. That's why I sent you so many messages when you asked me about my daughter again, because not many people want to talk about her.'

Ilse still gives talks about the importance of organ donation and, occasionally, her son asks her about where his sister's organs went. Ilse would love to be in contact with all the people who were helped or saved by Georgia, but she knows that is a choice that the recipients have to make for themselves.

'I know that one of her kidneys went to a young boy and he is now healthy. Every now and again, we get letters to say that he has gone from being in hospital all the time to being young and healthy. That is great to hear and the point I always make is just encouraging people to talk to their loved ones. We have an opt-out donation system now, but it's still essential to discuss plans because, as we found out, nobody wants to have to make those death-bed decisions.'

Ilse often speaks to her auntie and uncle who lost their daughter, Sandy, when she was nineteen in a car accident. Her cousin's death had a huge impact on the then fourteen-year-old Ilse, who still asks her auntie and uncle how they cope, how they move on and how they managed to move house but still hold on to the memories. There are many people who have contacted her since reading about her story in *Remarkable People*.

'There was one woman,' says Ilse, 'who said that she hadn't spoken to anyone until she read the chapter about Georgia in your book. She told me that the only way she could feel close to her dead son was to sit in the bath and pour his ashes over her. It's so easy to judge, but she was completely lost. When you've been through something like that, and feel it so deeply, you inevitably lose friends. I am sure she has and I know I have. It's just part of life. I'll keep going. I'll keep loving and supporting Joshua and hopefully, the next time we speak, Dan, I'll be able to tell you that things are improving.'

I know we are all trying to move on from the pandemic, but the next person I wanted to catch up with was one of those who put a big smile on many faces while we were all worrying about coronavirus. Kia Tobin was the care-home worker whose video was watched by millions when she presented resident, and veteran, Ken Benbow, with a cushion with his late wife's photograph on it.

Kia is a fascinating woman with big plans for the future and quite a bit has changed since she went viral during a virus.

'I left the care home last year,' says Kia. 'It was a really hard decision for me but, because we had to live there at the same time, it got to the point where there was no separation from my work and home life.'

Kia now works as a healthcare assistant at The Harbour, a mental health hospital in Blackpool. 'It's weird because I always wanted to work there. It opened in 2016 and I was about fourteen or fifteen and mental health has always been something that has interested me. My goal in life is always to work with people, all different sorts of people. I find it so rewarding to help so many different individuals with different issues and I'm able to work with all sorts of different conditions. We are a hospital, so we get patients who need rehab. They are dealing with things like bi-polar, personality disorder and schizophrenia and my job is to build up good relationships with them. I don't expect them all to like me, but there is something amazing about trying to get to the bottom of people's problems and seeing them progress.'

I ask if she misses the care home where, like many employees during the pandemic, she moved in to try and keep the residents safe.

'Of course I miss aspects of the care home. I miss the residents, I miss Ken. It was a big thing for me to leave but quite a few people left. I miss that family vibe, but things change. I got myself in a place where I wasn't able to not take work home with me. I was trapped and I don't think it would be the same now. I think he found me leaving quite hard to understand, but I have to remember that it's a job and I've grown up a lot in the last two years.'

Kia turns twenty this year and still wants to eventually work in Africa. 'I would love to keep going to work, get all the qualifications I can, and then I can go to Africa when I am twenty-five with the funds, the means and the knowledge. I want to make a difference in the world and I think I can really help people there. I'm enjoying life here at the moment, though. I am managing to help a lot of my friends with their issues too and I've had problems of my own as well, but I feel like I am learning all the time.'

Kia has moved on, but does she still think back to the madness around that video which sent social media into a spin and saw her and Ken appear on TV stations around the world? 'I was on a training course the other week and the first thing someone said was "Were you on TV?" It all seems like a bit of a blur if I'm honest. It just happened, I rode it out and I look back on it with fond memories. It's more important to me that people saw what it was like for carers during the pandemic. We all did the clapping for carers and it was lovely to get a bit of recognition for people working outside the NHS too, because there are thousands of us, and it was brilliant that so many young carers progressed and saw value in their jobs even though we were all going through something that was so horrible.'

If you have an amazing memory you might recall that the first chapter in my last book was centred on the work of two women. One of them, Winnie Mabaso, is sadly no longer with us, and the other, Lisa Ashton, is the woman who was inspired by Winnie and is trying to continue her legacy.

Lisa runs the Winnie Mabaso Foundation which currently funds an orphanage in South Africa and, as she told me when we caught up with each other, they have big plans going forward.

'I actually had a cheque this morning,' says Lisa with her customary bubbliness and enthusiasm. 'A £1,200 donation from a group down in East Sussex who read about us in your book. We get so many encouraging messages and so many people who are now supporting us on a regular basis.'

Lisa takes time out every week to write back and thank the charity supporters. It's one of the many things that mark her out. When I last spoke to her, there were plans for a second home, a forever home, for girls who were moving from the main house at Ilamula into full-time employment. Lisa has some exciting news.

'We are busy preparing our new property, Tropic House. We bought it in 2020 and it was completely dilapidated. It has taken us an age to do it up because of the pandemic, but two of our staff are living there at the moment and Palesa (who we met in the last book and is now twenty-one) will be one of the first to move over there.'

Palesa was one of the shining stars in *Remarkable People*. She was from an abusive home and found love and hope at the Winnie Mabaso Foundation. When she first moved there, her sisters were still stuck in the family home, but eventually they were able to join her and the three of them have thrived under the same roof.

'Palesa is now at college studying hairdressing,' says Lisa. 'She got 88 per cent in her latest creative assignment and is doing really well. My dream is to bring her to the UK one day . . . then you can get to meet her in person.'

Palesa's two sisters, Maki and Lerato, are still at Ilamula and loving their time at high school.

'We have two new little girls in our family now,' says Lisa. 'They are our first two Muslim children so we've had to introduce halal food to Ilamula. They are both sisters, only two and four years old and they take us up to twenty-three girls in all.'

The plan, eventually, is to have twelve older girls based at Tropic House. As the numbers continue to grow, so does the size of the job for Lisa.

'I think, like all charities, the last few years have been a real struggle. A lot of people who would normally have donated have found it tough during the pandemic, but we have just about managed to ride out the storm. The joy for me is for all the girls to have the opportunities to better themselves, but it's hard to be hands-on when you're stuck here in the UK. Before Covid, I was able to spend a month here and a month in South Africa but, like everyone else, we had to rely on video calls. I was back out there in March of 2022 for the first time in two years and it was incredible to see them all again and to see them all maturing. They were safe and loved and cared for by an extraordinary team in South Africa. By the way,' asks Lisa, 'did you get to see all our videos and pictures during *Strictly*, Dan?'

I did. The girls at Ilamula sent through regular good luck messages and cards and I showed them all to Nadiya throughout our time on the show.

'They loved doing them,' says Lisa, 'and it's just one of the ways we try and keep them connected to their international family. They definitely feel it and it makes a difference to them all. They were so excited when you made it to the quarter-finals! I think this is part of what makes the Winnie Mabaso Foundation so special . . . it has always been about family.'

In that 'family', many of the girls call Lisa their mum. She provides the love and care of a mother and what I have always found so inspiring about her is the fact that she goes further than most of us. Most of us have an ability to see a need but we rarely get to the 'what am I going to do about it?' stage. Lisa is already there. She spoke so powerfully in *Remarkable People* about how she was driven to help by looking through the back window of a charity food bus to see children chasing the vehicle holding an empty bowl. That image has stayed with her because, in her mind, there is always another child somewhere who needs food, who needs help, who needs lifting up. She is managing to teach that attitude to the girls at Ilamula.

'Let me tell you about Forgiveness who is twenty-one,' says Lisa. 'This year, she has started studying law at university. She wants to be an attorney because she says she wants to be a voice to the voiceless. How cool is that? She wants to help people who haven't had the same start as her. I am always impressed by how children are so remarkably resilient; you want them to thrive but you also need to help them repair their broken lives. These girls have been through so much, but they are so happy and so positive and they are so filled with joy. Our charity house is not a place of sadness. You've seen that, Dan, for yourself. It is a place of joy.'

I first visited the orphanage, on its old site, in 2010 during the football World Cup in South Africa. It was an amazing day where we showed the children a football match for the first time on a giant TV screen. In those twelve years since that visit, the charity has been able to do so much and, even though they were slowed down by the pandemic, Lisa says they have been able to re-start all their additional activities on a nearby squatter camp.

'We are back in business,' she says with a smile. 'We did have to rethink what we did on the camp during the pandemic. All the clubs had to stop but we could still deliver food parcels. Our focus shifted from face-to-face work to practical care with basics like sanitiser and toiletries. Everyone was telling them that they needed to wash their hands for twenty seconds, but it's hard to do that when you have no soap and no running water.'

I ask Lisa to run me through all the things they are currently running for the local community. 'This may take a while,' she says laughing. 'Ok, we have a pre-school, an organic gardening scheme where one hundred families have been trained to grow their own vegetables, a library, a mobile clinic where we do smear tests, blood tests and injections, a granny club, a mother and baby group, a homework club, meals on wheels and we are still doing the basic food delivery drops too. I think that is everything.'

The workload is exhausting. In an attempt to run the charity without any overheads, Lisa remains the only employee in the UK and there are forty-three people working in South Africa.

I ask her if she ever thinks she needs to take a break from it all and she replies in typical Lisa fashion. 'You can't take a break from life, can you? It's not a job. I can't take a holiday. This is what I do!' She laughs . . . 'I know I look one hundred and four years old at the moment, but my focus at the minute is on getting Tropic House up and running as soon as possible. I want to support the girls as best we can. We invest a lot of money in their education, but we just want them to grow up and be thoughtful and loving in life too. Many of them have been through so much trauma and have missed huge chunks of their childhood. We are trying to restore all that. You can't take a break from that. They are never going to stop being my girls. They will never stop being my family.'

From Lisa, with her massive extended family, to a man who spent twenty Christmases on his own.

I first met Terrence on the *BBC Breakfast* sofa in December 2019. He was taking part in a loneliness campaign for the charity Age UK and, during our chat, he talked about the fact that he'd spent every Christmas Day on his own since the death of his mother two decades before and he didn't even have a Christmas tree.

I said we would try and help him out, and a local college in his home town of Oldham got involved and we turned up at his house that night with a tree and a choir to sing his favourite carol, 'Silent Night'. He was very teary on the doorstep and the piece that we made about our visit went around the world and was watched millions of times.

Terrence's life changed dramatically. He became something

of a local celebrity and has kept his friendship going with Oldham College. The best news is, he no longer spends Christmas on his own.

He did promise me that he was going to celebrate his eightieth birthday by doing a skydive, and that's where we started our catch-up.

'My doctor wouldn't allow me to do it at all,' says Terrence. 'He told me straight. He said I was a diabetic with asthma and he also mentioned that I'd had a heart attack. I said, "When you put it like that . . ." He told me there was no way he would sign a form to let me do it. I can't skydive, but I can still help people and that's what I love doing. I've been in the caring profession all my life. I left school at fourteen with no qualifications whatsoever but, when I eventually got into nursing when I was twenty, I took to it like a duck to water.'

Terrence has always fought for the downtrodden. When he was younger he was brutally bullied and never fought back. His father was particularly cruel about his dyslexia and Terrence has struggled with confidence his whole life. He retired at the age of fifty to become a full-time carer for his mum, but his life changed immeasurably after that appearance on *BBC Breakfast*.

'After talking to you, people started recognising me. I had a funny experience last Sunday. I was serving teas and coffees for a charity and a ninety-two-year-old said to me, "I know you from somewhere . . . you were on television!" If I was to tell you the number of people who have stopped me, you would never believe it, Dan. I couldn't understand the impact at first. It changed me a great deal. It hasn't made me a different person, but it has made me appreciate things a lot more and it has also brought the struggle of loneliness and isolation to a lot of people's mind. I was alone at Christmas, but loneliness is a three-hundred-and-sixty-five days a year problem. I know you won't put this in your book, Dan, but it's all down to you really; you are a very kind and caring man. It's always about more than just the story, you are interested in the people involved and you don't forget them'. (If this quote is still in the book, it's because the publisher wanted it kept in.)

Terrence still loves talking to other people. Nancy, the woman he spoke to every week through Age UK, died last year and Terrence really misses her. In the last two months, he has lost three good friends to cancer.

'I get my joy from volunteering and staying busy. My mother has been gone for twenty-one years and I still miss her every day. I had Christmas dinner with my friends Andrew and Simon this year and I will never forget my Christmas in 2019. I am still in contact with the kids at Oldham College. I am so thankful for their friendship. I know a lot of people out there are still struggling and need help, but I am no longer a lonely old man. Friendship has changed my life.'

It was a real treat to catch up with Terrence and with the rest of the people in this chapter who all featured in *Remarkable People*. I love the fact that they are all still carrying on quietly being amazing in their different corners of the world.

When I left *BBC Breakfast* in 2022, the production team

made a wonderful leaving film which included getting Tony and Terrence together. They spent a lovely day with each other. Terrence remembers watching the flypast and told Tony it was one of his 'favourite ever bits of TV'. Tony said it was a real pleasure to meet Terrence. When I last met up with him I asked him if they got on, and Tony answered as only a Yorkshireman can . . . 'Me and Terrence? Aye, we got on. He were a reyt lad.'

THE TRUTH ABOUT MONSTERS

How do you see forgiveness? I have always thought that it is a quality which is easy to admire in others but becomes a lot more complicated when it arrives at our own doorstep.

If you look at the clinical definition, the websites and self-help manuals will tell you that forgiveness means different things to different people. Generally, it involves letting go of resentment and thoughts of revenge. The act of forgiveness doesn't entirely remove the pain, but it helps to free you from the control of the person who you feel has wronged you. It can even lead to feelings of understanding, empathy and compassion for the person or people who hurt you in the first place.

I did a search online and found a list of eight benefits that forgiveness can lead to:

Healthier relationships

Improved mental health

Less anxiety, stress and hostility

Lower blood pressure

Fewer symptoms of depression

A stronger immune system

Improved heart health

Improved self-esteem

The manuals also speak of all the potential complications which centre around how the person you forgive reacts. What if they don't change or are repeat offenders? What if forgiveness doesn't lead to reconciliation?

As a Christian, forgiveness is a fundamental part of my relationship with God. A simple search of the word will produce verse after verse encouraging us to forgive others because God has forgiven us. The Christian's understanding is that God's forgiveness flows from Jesus' sacrifice on the cross for the sins of all of us. Forgiveness is at the heart of God's character and Christians are called to be 'loving' and 'good' and to follow that example.

That is one of the many reasons I have great admiration for people who are able to forgive others. They are the sort of people who show us all that forgiveness is not a theory, it is something that you have to practise. It's hard sometimes to get our heads around, particularly when you see it in others and you try and put yourself in their shoes. I want to focus on three women in this chapter who have all found it in their heart to forgive. I have learned so much from talking to them and they have certainly challenged some of my preconceptions.

The first of them is someone we met in my last book, *Remarkable People*. I have no idea in which order you have read the chapters of this one but, if you've read the 'Still Remarkable' chapter before this one, you'll know that I didn't include Figen in there, but I did promise to catch up with her as part of this chapter.

Figen Murray is the mother of Martyn Hett, one of those who lost their lives in the Manchester Arena bombing in 2017. Despite suffering immeasurable loss, Figen took it upon herself to try and learn about why the terrorist chose to do that to her son. It also started her on the road to forgiveness. She began studying counterterrorism and has been pushing for legislation in her son's name – Martyn's Law – to make sure venues are better prepared in the event of another attack. When I caught up with her, she had just completed her Masters.

'I must have been mad undertaking the whole thing,' she says. 'When I look back now, I had started the Masters when I was attending the trial of Hashem Abedi in London.' Hashem Abedi is the brother of Salman Abedi who actually carried out the attack. Hashem Abedi helped organise the bombing and is serving a life sentence.

'I would go to attend my Masters in Preston in the morning and then get a train to London – writing essays on trains and in hotel lobbies. I didn't want to be a special case. I just wanted to be like everyone else. I just stayed up all night sometimes with my laptop and a pizza. It's strange how you get motivation for things like that. I got through it and got it done. I was writing my dissertation in a corner of the family room of the Old Bailey, but I managed to get a distinction.'

Figen now spreads her time between speaking at conferences, going into schools, reading the occasional novel and working on the implementation of Martyn's Law.

'I am still having regular meetings with those in government. The final details are being put together. It might still take some time. I am impatient, but I also want it to be right. I have worked on it for such a long time and people need to be able to use the law properly, so I want to make sure we have thought of everything. It won't be about his name, it has always been about making sure that no one had to go through what I went through. I also thought that once Martyn's Law comes in, I could disappear but I realise I can't do that now. I expect plenty of teething problems and there are going to be a lot of issues and chaos and people wondering what they should and shouldn't do. I have embraced that role and I don't mind going and talking about security. The UK is at the forefront of good modelling and I have to keep pushing that through. I look a little bit different to the bald men in tattoos that you normally associate with the security industry . . . but I can be just as persuasive,' she says with a glint in her eye.

On the day after the anniversary of Martyn's death in 2022, Figen was going to Washington to speak at an international security conference. Her work has spread far and wide. Her guiding principle is that she wants us to be more resilient as a nation. She wants adults and young people to take part in counterterrorism training programmes. She is convinced that she can change the world around her and, while she is doing that, she is also a mother who misses her son.

'It doesn't get any easier. I don't enjoy doing all these talks, but I know it's my job even though I just feel like I'm a mum to Martyn and the rest of the family. I always feel like he is at my side and it's teamwork between him and me. I am doing it in his memory and he drives me on. I love him so much. It's hard for me to explain, because I miss him more than ever and yet I find it hard to look at photos of him sometimes. I still cannot look at his photo on the windowsill.'

Whenever I think about Figen's story, I think about the bear. One of the ways she copes with grief is to spend her time making them. She gives them names and a backstory and sells them for charity. She mentioned in *Remarkable People* that she wanted to make one very special bear using the pieces of metal that were left in her son's body after the blast. The police had always told her that she would be able to get the pieces back once the inquiry had been completed. In the early days after Martyn's death, Figen also started collecting screws and nails off the floor. Her plan was to melt all of them down and mould them into the shape of a bear with its arms outstretched. In those outstretched arms, the bear would be holding a heart shape, made out of the pieces of metal that killed her son. It would be a permanent reminder to Figen that out of the depths of hatred and pain, she could find love.

'I have everything back from the police now,' says an emotional Figen. 'It still feels very raw and the days before the anniversary are always the hardest. I find it helpful when another anniversary is over. It's almost as though a fresh year of grieving starts. The whole of May is a tough one for me. As each day approaches, it gets more and more uncomfortable. There is too much to think about. I don't want to be consumed by grief. It is there in the background and then, as soon as the anniversary goes, I have a fresh drive to carry on living and to get on with life again. I remember the day after the first anniversary I told Stuart, my husband, that I could breathe again. There are a lot of things I am doing now that I could never have done in the first twelve months, but I have fresh energy every year.'

Figen is still making the bears. 'They help me on the bad days. There are some days, Dan, when I know it's going to be a tough one, and what I tend to do is get myself a cup of tea, put on a TV show and surround myself with ribbons, wool and buttons and that is my happy place where I can recharge. I keep things very basic. I don't run away from days like that anymore. I know I have to work through them. I know those days are important for self-care. I am better at looking after myself. I knew I was talking about Martyn to you today, so I am going for a walk with my friend after this. All of that helps.'

I ask Figen if she still has plans for the bear holding the metal heart. She takes a long pause before answering. 'I do,' she says hesitantly. 'Some of my children are struggling with having too many things about Martyn around the house and I understand that. When I do get it done, I don't think I will be displaying it in the house. It will probably go in there,' she says, pointing to a cupboard. 'I will get it done because, whether I look at it or not, that is my "up yours" to terrorism. I can turn what killed my son into a heart and that is how I try and make sure that I am not eaten up by the bitterness and the hatred. I don't need to look at it every day. It is part of the whole process for me. Grieving is a journey and it's something that is so precious and important to me. It would be the end of a chapter for me, and the bear will be a symbol of love for me going forward. I can't wait for it to be done. It's on my mind a lot.'

As I prepare to ask Figen about another topic, she raises her hand. 'There is something else, Dan. You won't believe this,' she says as her eyes widen. 'I have stopped collecting screws and nuts and bolts and, ever since I made that decision, I haven't found any. For years I have just found them everywhere, without ever really looking for them. I sit down, and there would be one next to me. I cross a road, and there would be one there on the floor by the kerb. They used to just appear in front of me but, ever since I decided to stop collecting them, I haven't come across a single one.'

The bear is all part of the continuing grieving process for Figen. As a trained psychotherapist, she can see the stages she is moving through very clearly.

'The bear will complete something,' she says confidently. 'It will free up time for me to do other things. It will give me more head space. I don't need the screws anymore. I don't need that crutch. The next task for me will be to really step up the number of talks I give to school children.'

Figen tells me that the day after we talk, she is going to speak to 1,000 children about her experience. That means she has personally addressed nearly 20,000 kids since Martyn's death. I ask her what she tells them.

'The first thing I talk about is Martyn and the others who died that night. I talk about my visit to the morgue. The last thing I talk about is the power of online radicalisation. I admit that my generation has made a mess of things and remind them that theirs can sort it out. I ask them how many of them want to become parents in the future and I remind them that they have a huge responsibility to teach their children the right values. In between those two things, Dan, I talk about Ubuntu.'

Feeling a little ignorant, I ask Figen what 'Ubuntu' is all about. 'I love explaining this,' she says. 'A few months after Martyn died, a woman sent me a message on Twitter. She said that she had read all about him and it made her so upset and reminded her that life was too short. She said that it had given her the motivation to fulfil her lifetime dream of moving to the Gambia. She had made the move and, once she was there, she asked a man to build her a boat. She asked him to put some words on both sides of it. On one side there was the hashtag #BeMoreMartyn and on the other was this word, "Ubuntu". The woman explained to me that it is an African concept that means "I am because you are". As soon as I heard it, I told my husband that I had found the name for our house. You see,' explains Figen, 'all the houses on our street have a name except ours and I knew that one day I would find the right name for it; a name that summed up all the things I felt about Martyn; something that encapsulated his kindness, his empathy and his compassion, and there it was: "Ubuntu" – I am because he was. He inspires me every day. That's why I talk about Ubuntu. It is the one word that brings it all together.'

Figen remains a remarkable woman. I find her attitude to life and loss incredible. I love the way she quietly works things through at her own pace and how she is aware of her fragility and limitations at the same time as recognising her strength. I'm glad she is taking care of herself and, when we spoke, I told her I was going to write about the subject of forgiveness. One of the schools she is going to speak at is the school where the

Abedi brothers went. How does she feel about Salman Abedi, the young man who killed her son? How does she feel about forgiveness?

'His name is just a name,' she says. 'I forgave him very early on.' I am reminded of the story Figen told about seeing the face of the bomber on the front page of a newspaper for the first time a few days after the explosion. She froze on the spot and was struck by how young he was. 'He was in his early twenties. What on earth would you know about the consequences of your actions at that age? I remember wondering why he would choose to throw his life away.'

Figen also recalls the incident four weeks after Martyn's death which had a significant impact on her. 'My family had all gone home. My husband had gone back to work and the doorbell and phone stopped ringing. I suddenly found myself at home on my own. I went across to the Co-op and I bought some newspapers. I opened the front page and there was a picture of five men linking arms and a guy on the floor. It was a picture from the Finsbury Park Mosque attack in London. The guy on the floor had tried to kill them and they were there protecting him, telling people to get back until the police arrived. I had the whole day to think about that picture and it had a big impact on me. When my husband came home from work that night, I told him that I was going to go on the BBC the next morning and publicly forgive the terrorist for what he did. My husband thought I was completely mad, but I told him that when there was so much hate and anger around, it was really important for me to try and rebalance things.'

I ask Figen if that act of forgiveness has allowed her to get to where she is today. 'When you are a therapist you learn a lot of skills. I think I have told you before that I used to tell my clients to imagine a helicopter when they face what they think is an impossible situation. I tell them not to worry about not being able to fly it but to imagine getting inside and looking at what they face from as high above as possible. That's what I did for myself because, from that perspective, you can also see solutions. You will see things much more clearly. You can see people who can help you. You are also further away from the pain, the suffering and the anger. I could see the terrorist as a baby. I remember thinking, "You were not born a terrorist". My overriding emotion was always sadness that I had lost Martyn. I was never angry with the terrorist. That was helpful on my road to forgiveness.'

The other thing that helps Figen is speaking to others. She wants to reach as many people as she can with Martyn's message.

'I want us to be kinder to each other. I want to live in the UK where most adults have skills to help others because they've had the training and I want to live in a world where it's safer to go out to the theatre, to the cinema and we know that our children are safe. We talk a lot about post-traumatic stress but I firmly believe there can also be post-traumatic growth and that is what I am experiencing. I am convinced that, if I wasn't trained as a psychotherapist, I would have gone under after Martyn died. I am not spiritual, but I do believe that everything happens for a reason and I am convinced that I was given the tools, the years of training to deal with what landed in my life.' Figen stops talking. This is clearly something she has thought about a lot.

'Maybe Martyn needed to die for this law to happen. There are questions I cannot answer. There are roads I dare not even turn down. There are bridges I will never cross. I have come to the point where, even though it has broken every part of me, I can accept what happened. I will never be able to explain it, but I have learned to live with it . . . to live without him.'

I am not sure 'enjoy' is the right word, but I do enjoy every conversation with Figen. She always gives you something to think about, something to take away and use in your own life.

'Can I leave you with a poem, Dan?' she says, before we say goodbye. 'You asked me about forgiveness and, when I was studying for my Masters, I used to sit next to another mature student because, as you know, the older ones tend to stick together. He was a former police officer and we would often share our experiences. He sent me a poem one day and said, "I don't know if this will help you but, when I read it, I thought of you." It's called "The Truth About Monsters" and it has helped me because it has reminded me that my enemy is not Salman or Hashem Abedi . . . my enemy is terrorism. I don't hate those young men, I hate what they became, what they did to my son and to others and what turned them into that. The best way to defeat your enemies is to learn about them. Those are the first few steps on the road to forgiveness.'

'The Truth About Monsters' by Nikita Gill

The truth is this:
every monster
you have met
or will ever meet
was once a human being
with a soul
that was as soft
and light
as silk
Someone stole
that silk from their soul
and turned them
into this
So when you see
a monster next
always remember
do not fear
the thing before you
fear the thing
that created it
instead.

I have always wanted to talk to Mina Smallman. The first time
I heard her speak was when I watched her on television saying

that she had forgiven the man who had brutally murdered her daughters.

Mina was the Church of England's first female archdeacon from a black and minority ethnic background. She also used to be a schoolteacher.

On 6 June 2020, her life was ripped apart when two of her daughters were murdered by a stranger at Fryent Country Park in Wembley, north London. Bibaa Henry was a social worker and Nicole Smallman was a photographer. They were celebrating Bibaa's birthday in the park with friends. In the early hours of the morning, Nicole sent a message to her boyfriend saying she and her sister were still dancing. Soon after, the girls were dead, stabbed to death by Danyal Hussein, a nineteen-year-old satanist who was determined to make sacrifices which he thought would enable him to win a lottery jackpot. He stabbed the two women nearly forty times.

It was Nicole's boyfriend who discovered the bodies after the police did not search the park. To make an awful tragedy even worse, Mina was later informed that the two police officers who were guarding the crime scene, Deniz Jaffer and Jamie Lewis, took photographs of her daughters' dead bodies and posted them on WhatsApp groups where they referred to Bibaa and Nicole as 'dead birds'. Mina decided to take on the Metropolitan Police because she was convinced there was a racial element to the treatment of her daughters. She firmly felt that if they had been white women, the park would have been searched and the two officers would not have taken the photographs.

'Forgiveness is an interesting concept,' says an eternally

thoughtful Mina. 'I have spent a lifetime forgiving injustices that have been done to me. I have had to fight hard for most of my life. As a black woman you spend a lot of your life being overlooked. Sometimes it makes you angry and then you become the "angry, black woman". I have made mistakes too and I hope people can forgive me for those. I don't believe you can forgive alone. I see it as a gift of grace from God. The Lord blessed me by allowing me to let Danyal Hussein go. He is not my responsibility. As soon as I heard about his satanic motivation I knew it was not my job to judge him. It was at the point that I heard about his pact with the devil that I can say the Holy Spirit came down and filled me with peace and strength. I knew I was equipped with what I needed to forgive him. It was a feeling that I was being held and it is so hard to explain to anyone who hasn't had that experience. I released that burden. If I'm honest, I don't think about him at all. Forgiveness is a gift, but you have to be open to that gift. The gift I was given was the load being taken away from me. That is what I feel. I turned to God and asked Him to help me. "I need you," I said, and He was there.'

Mina is dual heritage. Her mother was white and Scottish, her father a black Nigerian. 'When you are from that background, you have to battle just to be heard,' says Mina. 'I went through the education system when there was a whole issue of treating black children as if they were educationally subnormal. There were individual teachers who gave me so much support and went out of their way to help me, but the system was built against me. As I got a bit older, people I was with would talk about black students in a derogatory way and say, "Present company excepted" and I would be like, "What do you mean?" They would say, "Not you, you're different, Mina". The level of ignorance was staggering at times. I remember being told that "someone like me" wasn't clever enough to do Shakespeare at school! Maybe that's what drove me on to become a teacher of English Literature and Drama. Drama was my passion.'

Teaching is where it started for Mina. She taught drama for fifteen years before feeling the call to join the church. She was ordained as a priest in 2007, served as a curate in Harrow and Stanmore and was then appointed as the Archdeacon of Southend in 2013 where she served for three years until her retirement in 2016. During her time in the church she had to take many funerals, preparing people to remember their loved ones once they had gone; skills she had to use herself. The death of her daughters was one thing, but the actions of the officers at the crime scene made her feel like she had lost them twice.

'Bibaa was a lot like me,' says Mina. 'She was "Marmite". Loud, proud and a real dynamo. She was a brilliant social worker and really streetwise. Nicole was a talented musician and super cool. She had gone to performing arts school and, even though there were a lot of years between them (Bibaa was forty-six and Nicole was twenty-seven) they were best friends. It was devastating to lose them and I hadn't even thought about what they looked like until I was told that those two officers had been taking photos. You start thinking about it, you start picturing it all in your head. You're trying to do the everyday normal things like getting up, getting dressed, but it's all you can think about. You've been robbed of normality. All you're trying to do is hold yourself together to function, but you just keep going back to why they chose to do that to my girls.'

Mina found it in her heart to forgive the killer, but it has been much harder when it comes to the police officers. She agreed to meet with them as part of a restorative justice process but that offer was withdrawn after the two officers decided to appeal against their thirty-three-month sentence for misconduct in a public office and Mina attended the hearing.

'I don't hold any malice or hatred, but I haven't forgiven them,' says Mina. 'When I was listening to their unsuccessful appeal I thought I was going to pass out from the stress. I could feel my heart pounding in my chest. I was having this incredible physical reaction to what their advocates were saying. Jaffer's defence lawyer was arguing that the photographs were only shared with close friends and didn't go any further than that. He said things like, "It was part of the culture to share photos from work" and compared it to saying, "Look at what I'm doing today." It got even worse when the barrister asked us to think about how his two teenage daughters would cope while he was in prison! That's when I thought the stress of it all was going to kill me. What about the impact his actions had had on others, on me and my family? Part of me wants to meet with them and talk to them about their attitude to women and how destructive it is, but I'm not sure I could do that at the moment.'

When you think about what Mina had to endure, you can see why it might be hard to ever think about a resolution, but she still comes back to the issue of forgiveness.

'Maybe I will be able to forgive them one day. I'm not ruling it out, because Jesus Christ is my ultimate example and perhaps I just need a little more time. I don't hate them. I feel . . .' she pauses, 'let me think . . . neutral. I am still cross about what they did and why they did it. The good thing is, I don't think about them. I wish we would focus on the victims more. Look at the Prince Andrew situation,' she says. 'You have the Archbishop of Canterbury talking about forgiveness for him, but why is our gaze on him? What we need to focus on is not the suggested, or alleged, perpetrators, but the victims. We need to concentrate on helping them to put their lives back together and helping them to find peace in this life. To my mind a lot of these cases come back to that issue of white privilege: men of a certain age feeling that they have the power to do whatever they want, to whoever they want, wherever they want. It's the same when it comes to women's safety at the moment, which is something I am passionate about. So often the people discussing it are old, grey, white men; people who have no lived experience. I don't think that only women can speak for women but representation is essential and, now I'm retired, I love the freedom to say whatever I want. It's quite liberating.'

I ask Mina what she would say to her daughters' killer now if she had the chance. 'That is a great question,' she says. 'If you'd found me ten years ago and said to me, your daughters are going to be killed by a satanist who thinks he's a member of the Aryan race, I would think I would struggle to forgive him for doing that. I think about the sort of mum I am. I would do anything for my girls. When Nikki said she wanted to go to Thailand, I told her that if anything happened to her there I would go full

Liam Neeson and come and find her. Nothing would stop me, like in those films. What are they called, Dan?'

'*Taken*,' I suggest.

'That's it! That would be me. But now, when I think about him, I don't think I would have any words for their killer. I don't know if he'd be able to hear it. I really upset him at the trial, because I think he thought he could intimidate me. I just smiled and winked at him and I think that really annoyed him. There is nothing I could say to him that would make a difference. I just hope that one day he sees the impact of what he has done. There is a verse in the Bible, in the book of Ezekiel (chapter 36, verse 26), which talks about God giving someone a new heart. It says that God can turn a "heart of stone" into a "heart of flesh" and that is my prayer for him, that God would do that for him. I hope he experiences that one day. There is nothing more powerful than God's forgiveness, than realising that the world doesn't revolve around you, that you are not at the centre of the universe, that God is in control and he has a plan for your life.'

It has been fascinating to talk to Mina. She is so open about her experiences and, just like Figen, has no issue when it comes to the things that she struggles with. Her husband deals with loss very differently. He keeps himself active and their different approaches have actually brought them closer together. They don't judge each other for the way they have chosen to grieve. Mina finds that talking about her struggles makes her stronger and those 'struggles' are not just mental. She suffers with Chronic Fatigue Syndrome and Fibromyalgia. On three separate occasions she had to postpone our chat because her energy levels were so low.

'This has all taken its toll on my body,' she says with a sigh. 'I have to balance my energies really well. I can't sign up to things because I don't want to let people down. I was diagnosed with it before, but all the stress and anxiety has definitely made it worse. I wasn't in a great place. I shy away from promising more than I can do, but I know I have a purpose and I know I can still do good in this world.'

I ask Mina what is next for her, where she wants to be in five or ten years' time.

'I just want to still be here,' she laughs. 'If I'm still here at seventy, I'll be celebrating.' Mina is currently sixty-five but worries about her family history. 'I come from a weak gene pool, Dan. I am the only one left and I shouldn't really be here. My dad died from a stroke when I was sixteen and my mum was born with cardiomyopathy (heart disease) and was always struggling. Talking about forgiveness, I'm not sure my mum could have forgiven the killer for what he did. She was of good tartan stock,' laughs Mina. 'She would be baying for blood. My brother has gone as well. He was seven years younger than me but also died from cardiomyopathy and my older sister passed away after a five-year battle with cancer. I think the murders finished my sister off. Anne was very close to Bibaa and I found it really hard to talk to her at the end of her life because she only ever wanted to talk about the girls and I couldn't bring myself to do it. It's too hard for me. I couldn't even go to Anne's funeral because it was at the same place the girls had theirs. It was too soon to go back.'

Mina says sometimes she feels like she is two different people: the campaigner who challenges bias and prejudice and who took on the Metropolitan Police, and the mother of two murdered girls. Anyone who watched Stacey Dooley's recent documentary about Mina will have seen them both: the activist and the mum. The activist, empowered and ready to take on the world; and the broken mum, who feels like she can't leave the house to go to the shops because she doesn't want to be seen. Grief is a powerful master. Mina is as fierce as she is fragile.

I tell her it's amazing that, despite all she has been through, she has been able to forgive the man who has had such a devastating impact on her family.

'Remember, I have found the strength to forgive from God. I couldn't have done it on my own. Forget about the health issues; the hatred and the anger would have killed me by now otherwise. I was able to let go of that and I am so thankful that I did.'

Does she have any advice for someone else thinking about forgiveness?

'If you have lost someone like me, the most important thing is to remind yourself that you are not letting your loved one down by letting go. If you let the anger eat you up then the murderer wins. Try, with everything you have, to let that anger go. It still hurts. I still miss my daughters more than anything, but forgiveness has given me the chance to live the rest of my life, however long that is, without the weight of bitterness.'

*   *   *

The final person I want to tell you about is Tamar Pollard. Just like Figen and Mina, Tamar lost a family member in horrific circumstances.

'Mum and Dad were in Prague in 1968. They were on a youth hostel holiday and they woke to the news that the Russians had invaded. They knew that people's lives would change overnight. They were both Christians and they thought about what it says in the Bible's 1 John chapter 3 verse 17: "If anyone has material possessions and sees a brother or sister in need but has no pity on them, how can the love of God be in that person?" They were both challenged by that and a friend said to them that they were both teachers, with long holidays, so why didn't they use them to come back each year and bring humanitarian aid? So that's what they did. That's what we all did as a family.'

From the age of seven months old, Tamar travelled around Europe with her parents. They would spend one summer in northern countries like East Germany, Czechoslovakia and Poland and the next a little more south in places like Romania, Yugoslavia and Hungary.

'We rarely spent more than a day in one place,' says Tamar. 'Our van was always loaded with basic foods like flour, sugar, coffee and tea and we would give out toys, clothes, sweets and we would sometimes take prescription glasses too. Every year we went, sometimes at Christmas, but every single summer. We started off in a Skoda; I had to sleep in a hammock pulled across the back of the car! We had camper vans, and in 1990 we had one with a shower! I remember we thought it was the height of luxury but Mum and Dad just used it for storage.'

Tamar was one of three children. She has an older sister, Rebecca, and Andrew is her younger brother. They all have some incredible stories to tell and Tamar just drops them casually into the conversation.

'The Romanian revolution was on my thirteenth birthday,' she says, very matter-of-fact. 'I remember that one. I know I stopped going on the trips in 1993 when I stayed in the UK to do my GCSEs, and we were once stuck in Yugoslavia during a war, and there was another time that there was a military coup in Kiev and we had to rush to get out of Ukraine as quickly as possible.'

Tamar was marched at gunpoint when she was eight years old on the Hungarian-Romanian border. 'My sister was twelve and Andrew was six. I remember they searched our vehicle and they found that we had food, clothing but also some Bibles which had been translated into Romanian and Bulgarian. They said it was illegal and they wanted more than £3,500 to let us go free. We went to the toilets on the border and I tore up the addresses of the people we were going to visit and flushed them away and my sister hid money in her pants. The guards said that we had to give them the camper van and they took Mum as hostage! We were marched back to the nearest town in Hungary and Dad had to spend the next few days at the local post office. He organised a loan to pay for Mum to be released, and we did get the van back but we were banned from Romania for five years. When we got Mum back, she joked that it had been the most peaceful part of her holiday. We all laughed but we also knew how serious it could have been. Lots of people back home thought Mum and Dad were mad taking us on their travels, but it was just something we did as a family. It was a bit different to a fortnight in Tenerife!'

Tamar started out resenting the long summer trips but eventually enjoyed them. 'I saw them like a *Famous Five* adventure. In some places we weren't allowed to talk in the street, we could never stay in one place for long but I saw some amazing things. I went to orphanages in Romania at the age of thirteen and I realised how much I had back home. I started to see how big a sacrifice my mum and dad were making for others. I was amazed at how much they cared and my eyes were opened to what it meant to love your neighbours without question. They saw their job as serving other people.'

From 1996 onwards, things changed. Tamar, Rebecca and Andrew would stay in the UK for their education or work and their parents travelled alone. The kids were given a rough itinerary and they would get a phone call every now and again to say the van had broken down, but there wasn't ever day-to-day contact. One night in 1997 changed everything.

'Mum and Dad were going through Slovakia and then Hungary on their way to Romania,' recalls Tamar. 'As they drove, the lights on the camper van failed. They used to try going through border crossings at night because they were much quieter, but the roads were poorly lit and really bumpy so they pulled into a lay-by. It is something they did quite regularly. It was a Monday night, 4 August. They were woken up by two men who said they were police officers. They were trying to fine them fourteen pounds for staying in the lay-by. Mum and Dad knew they weren't proper police, but they paid the fine and the officers left them alone. The problem was, they had seen inside the van and it was packed with stuff for Mum and Dad to give away. The two men came back and Dad jumped into the cab and tried to drive off. One of them got through the driver's window and beat Dad to death with an iron bar. They left again, but Mum knew they would soon be back. She tried to resuscitate Dad but he was gone and she couldn't drive away because he was slumped over the steering wheel. She hid everything valuable she could think of and she just had to wait there for them to return. They came back with someone else and beat her, strangled her and left her for dead. She woke up on the Tuesday morning and couldn't see because they had sprayed something in her eyes. Eventually, someone stopped by the side of the road and took her to hospital. She looked awful, so bad that the police translator collapsed at the sight of her. Mum's jaw had been shattered and she couldn't speak.'

The news of Michael Pollard's death was broken on Sky News on Wednesday 6 August at 6 o'clock in the morning. At the time, none of his children had been informed. Rebecca was working in Leeds in IT and she was the first to hear. Andrew was woken up by the *Daily Mail* at the family house and Tamar was doing voluntary work with children in Broadstairs in Kent.

'Someone came and got me but I wasn't told anything,' remembers Tamar. 'I was walking up the hill back to the main building thinking, "Maybe I have to take over the cooking for the day." I wondered what I had done wrong, especially when I saw there was a policeman waiting for me. He took off his helmet, which is never a good sign. In my head, I remember thinking, "Dad's dead," but he was just talking about Mum. It was like an out-of-body experience. I knew he was talking to me, but I was in total shock.'

Tamar had to call the foreign office. Tamar's mum, Jo, was in a bad way. The children all met at Heathrow and on the plane they got complimentary copies of the *Evening Standard* newspaper. Their parents were on the front page. 'I just hadn't processed it at all,' says Tamar. 'We were upgraded to business class and I was looking around watching people reading the news while they were drinking a glass of champagne. I felt like shouting at them, "THIS IS MY DAD YOU'RE ALL READING ABOUT."'

When they arrived in Hungary it was late. The next morning they had a three-hour drive to the hospital and, upon arrival, they heard that the three men who killed their dad had been arrested. One of the things their mum had successfully hidden in the van was the receipt the criminals gave them for the traffic violation. Jo had put it behind the cutlery drawer. She had planted £50 in a purse near the door in an attempt to distract them and it worked. It really was amazing clarity of thought when her husband had just been brutally murdered and she was convinced they were coming back to finish her off.

I asked Tamar why her mum didn't run away from the van to try and escape.

'My mum was raped when she was nine years old,' says Tamar. She took a deep breath. 'Ever since she has been terrified of the dark. She knew they were coming back for her, she was wondering what they were going to do with her, but she couldn't even think of walking the streets because, as a child, she was attacked when she was walking home from school. The man grabbed her off the street and, later in court, admitted that he'd planned to kill her and dispose of her body. Her whole life, you could never put your hand near her nose or mouth because it freaked her out. That's why she stayed in the van . . . she was more afraid of walking around outside so she waited for them to come back.'

The men who attacked her were arrested on the Thursday morning. One was eighteen years old and the other two were twenty-two. That morning, the children walked in on their mum as she was doing a live interview with the local news back in Yorkshire.

'I was listening carefully to what she was saying, but it wasn't sounding like Mum at all. Her jaw was still broken and she was so battered and bruised. I remember that it was the first time in my life I felt proper hatred in my heart. I was in a rage and it got even worse because, at the end of the interview, she told the TV station that she didn't bear any malice and she said, "If there are any Christians listening, can I ask them to pray that these men just didn't know my forgiveness, but God's forgiveness." I could have exploded. How could she say that when they'd tried to kill her and killed my dad? How dare she forgive them! I stormed out of the room and just stood on the balcony. I was angry with my mum, angry with God. The reality of my dad's death really kicked in and with that came all sorts of questions. I stood fuming on the balcony thinking, "Do I believe God is real?

Do I believe God is good? Is he kind?" I was wrestling with all this, but I knew the answer was "yes" to those questions. I had seen that from my own life. I was convinced that God was not just big and powerful but that he was interested in the small, tiny details.'

This was all racing through Tamar's brain during that thirty minutes on the hospital balcony. 'I was out there thinking, if this is all true, how am I meant to act? I knew I was meant to forgive because I had been forgiven but, at the time, it was just too big an ask. I was in the depths of despair. That is a lot to think about on a hospital balcony, but I firmly believe that God gave me the ability to forgive. As I prayed to him, I asked him to turn hatred to forgiveness, to turn anger to peace. I walked back into the room and told my mum that I could be with her in this. I have found that forgiveness is a daily choice. I am still working it through. It didn't reduce the grief. I was twenty and my dad had been murdered.'

Tamar's mum was in hospital for a week. The family needed to get back home for Andrew's A level results. The fact that Jo had forgiven Michael's murderers made the story even bigger. They arrived home the following Wednesday to a press conference at Leeds Bradford airport.

'I didn't know how I should look,' says Tamar. 'Did I need to look sad? Should I smile? What should I wear? People were staggered by the forgiveness thing. They couldn't get their heads around it. What Mum had done went against everything in human nature. She kept getting asked about revenge and she was asked why she wasn't angry after all the people they had helped, over so many years, across Eastern Europe. She was on the front pages of magazines. It was discussed on *Kilroy* and there were double-page spreads in the newspapers. She got a bravery award from the Queen and Tony Blair. Andrew got his A level results the next day.'

Jo Pollard seems like a remarkable woman. What she went through was truly tragic and the strength she showed in those first few days after the murder is hard to get your head around. Her ability to forgive baffled many of those who heard about it, but what she did next didn't make as many headlines but is arguably even more impressive.

Jo went back to Hungary in January 1998 with Rebecca for the trial. She wanted to look her husband's murderers in the eyes. The judge gave her the opportunity to say something at the end. She told them to their faces that she had forgiven them and gave them all a care package to help during their time in prison. It included toiletries, stationery, sweets, biscuits and a Bible. She asked to stay in contact with all of them and two out of the three said they would like that. For years they exchanged letters.

'I think about it a lot,' says Tamar, 'the way she treated those men after what they did to her. They nearly took her life away and she wanted them to have theirs back. The local mayor erected a memorial on the first anniversary of Dad's death. Mum kept going back too. She visited the two of them in prison, and one day she received a letter from the eighteen-year-old. His name was Istvan Dudas and he was the one who had beaten Dad to death with the iron bar. It said, "I caused death but I found life". He said in the letter that he just couldn't get over how she could forgive him. He said that whenever they met, Mum was always "banging on about God" but he had become convinced that he had to look into whether the Bible was true because Mum's faith was so real and there was no human explanation for it. The man who killed my dad had become a Christian.'

Jo Pollard got early Alzheimer's and died in 2008. In 2017, Tamar went back to Hungary on the twentieth anniversary of her father's death.

'Dad's killers were sentenced to six, seven and eleven years in jail so they are all out now,' says Tamar. 'I have tried to find them through Google and Facebook a few times, but the only photos I have are from 1997. I couldn't recognise any of their faces on social media as their names were quite common, so I didn't want to message the wrong stranger. I don't know what I would say to them if I met them . . . "Hi, you killed my dad!" I would love to know what they are doing. I would like to tell them that I forgive them too, just like my mum did. It is easy to say that when you are not in the room with them, but face to face it would be an incredible challenge. I would love to hear how their life is and, after being shown so much kindness by my mum, I want to know what they did with that.'

Tamar, just like Figen and Mina, is at peace with her decision to forgive and it has enabled her to continue to live her life. When you speak to her about what forgiveness looks like, she's honest and says sometimes you have to re-forgive and sometimes you have to remind yourself that it's ok to feel like that. She talks about the freedom that comes from letting go of your right to justice and fairness. We can all feel like we are entitled to get something first and, when we are wronged, we want people to know. Forgiveness means letting go of that sense of entitlement and, as Tamar told me time and time again, trusting God.

'What happened in 1997,' says Tamar, 'of course that shapes who I am, but it doesn't define me and, if I hadn't forgiven them, it would have defined me. I am shaped by what happened, but I am not defined by it.'

Tamar's brother and sister have been on their own journey. Rebecca found it hard for years and Andrew graduated in 2001 but then moved back home to become his mum's main carer when she was diagnosed with Alzheimer's.

'For a long time we didn't talk about it,' says Tamar. 'Forgiveness is one thing but tragedy and guilt leave deep scars. We don't do what normal families do and discuss memories from childhood and we all process it differently. I buried myself in work, I still do.'

I'll be honest with you. I've been sitting here and I haven't written a single word for about twenty-five minutes. I'm thinking about how I would react if I had a loved one stolen from me like Tamar, Figen and Mina. Would I be able to find a path to forgiveness? Having spent hours talking to these three incredible women, one thing that links them all together is that they would all say they are in a better place because they were able to forgive. They also all have something in their lives to keep them going. Figen has her passion for teaching the next generation about counterterrorism, Mina remains half-activist half-mum and Tamar has a passion for working with children and is about to move to Australia to start a new job. She takes huge inspiration from the way her parents cared for others.

'The more I think about it, the more I am staggered by what Mum and Dad did together. They were models of faith in action. They trusted in God's goodness and they taught me to be thankful for what I had and gave me a deep appreciation of other cultures, other ways of thinking, other ways of doing things. They spent their lives trying to understand others and they didn't see the boundaries that most of us see. They used all their time, all their money, all their holidays to help other people. I often think about them and, in the light of their actions, I ask myself what I'm doing. What am I investing in? How effectively am I spending my time? As I've got older, I think a lot about how we look after people who struggle. When Dad died, lots of people didn't know how to support me, and that has made me really aware of others who find themselves in that position and how I walk with them and care for them. I am much better equipped to help because of what my parents showed me, because of what they taught me. That is their legacy. I know it cost my dad his life and I know my mum's Alzheimer's was accelerated by her head trauma but, even though I wouldn't have chosen my life to go that way, I wouldn't change it. My mum and dad trusted in God above everything else and their love for Jesus shone out in their lives. She'll never know it but, when Mum forgave those men, just a couple of days after they killed Dad, she changed their lives and my life forever. I miss them both but my world is so much bigger because of what they showed me.'

ACKNOWLEDGEMENTS

I am never entirely sure what to put at the end of a book. I know I have to write a few thank yous and I'll get to those.

I really hope you have enjoyed reading about the people in this book. I have loved speaking to them and writing about them even though this all happened at the busiest time of my entire life.

I had just finished *Strictly Come Dancing* and then I started doing most of the interviews for *Standing on the Shoulders*, just at the time when I was having discussions about leaving *BBC Breakfast* to go to Channel 5. It was all happening at the same time!

What kept me going were the incredible people I was talking to. With each one of the chapters in this book, I have felt a deep responsibility to tell the stories with great care. Many of the people in here have either not spoken before or have trusted me with their deepest and most personal feelings.

So, the most important thing is to thank them all for their time and their trust.

Thank you to all those who were happy for me to pester them again after already appearing in *Remarkable People*. Paula

Hudgell, Lisa Ashton, Ilse Fieldsend, Terrence, Kia Tobin, John Sutherland and Tony Foulds . . . you are all amazing individuals, and my suggestion is we all get together for a cup of Tony's famous fiddy fiddy.

Thank you to the wonderful Rose Ayling-Ellis and her mum Donna. Rose mesmerised the nation during *Strictly* and learning more about her relationship with her mum and how she made such an impact on all of us, and Giovanni, was a real treat. I loved writing that chapter and I'm absolutely delighted that Rose agreed to write the foreword for this book too. She is officially the best!

A special thank you to my professional partner and two-time world champion, Nadiya Bychkova. Most of the people in this book have made me think about others in a different way; she changed the way I look at myself. With her mix of skill, style and serious hard work, she showed that I could enjoy something that I thought was completely beyond my capabilities. She also taught me how to eat a chocolate biscuit properly (chocolate side facing down). If you've never tried it, get involved. Believe me, it is a game changer.

My deepest appreciation also goes out to those who were willing to talk about loss. Figen Murray will never stop amazing me and Mina Smallman and Tamar Pollard were willing to tell their incredible stories of forgiveness in the face of such brutality. There is so much to take from their testimonies.

Tim, Mike and Andy – known collectively as the 3 Dads – continue to inspire millions of people out there, including Hollywood superstars like Nicole Kidman, who I still can't quite believe was happy to be part of this book. Thank you to Nicole, and to Kate Morley for helping to set that up.

The chapter about the 3 Dads was actually the first one that I wrote for this book. I don't mind telling you that, once I had finished it, I was in a bit of an emotional state for a while. I couldn't come back to the writing for another six weeks because I couldn't stop thinking about what they had been through and how heart-breaking it was. They have all been wonderful to deal with, as was Sandy, the man who found Sophie's body, and, to my mind, is a pretty incredible man. We could all do with a Sandy in our lives.

The chapter that took me the longest to complete was the one about the terrorist attack on Fishmongers' Hall. The interviews with Darryn Frost and Steve Gallant lasted for hours and I was so careful in trying to thread their stories into the chapter in a way that didn't glorify the violence. The event is still so raw for Darryn, for Dave and Anne Merritt and everyone touched and damaged by the actions of Usman Khan that day. I often think about the final words that Jack Merritt's mum uttered at the inquiry when she read out some of the tributes to her son: 'His death was a tragedy but his life was a triumph.'

One of my favourite chapters to write was the one about Jimi Olubunmi-Adewole. I was so struck by the love that his friends and family had for him. I learned so much about the life of someone who comes to the UK from talking to his old school friends David, Joseph, Marvellous, Adiatu and Yinka, and I thought that Bernard displayed a wonderful gift in being able to describe the beauty of real friendship and what it means to live in the light of that. My love goes out to Jimi's family, and thank you to his older brother, Ayodeji, for agreeing to be such an important part of that chapter.

The two people that made me laugh out loud on numerous occasions over the past few months are Paul and Nick Harvey. I've loved their relationship ever since I first met them on *BBC Breakfast* and it was a real delight to talk to them at length and to see the pure talent that Paul possesses in his fingers when he sits at a piano. It was lovely to hear from Nick, Alix and Dominic – his old students – Pete his former colleague, Grace from the dementia charity and Sir Tom Hunter who was one of those inspired by their appearance on the TV in the middle of lockdown.

Which brings us to the chapter 'Beyond the Pandemic'. I don't think any of us will ever forget those eighteen months from March 2020 onwards and coronavirus leaves a deep legacy, particularly for the people who feature in that chapter. The names of Maggie Keenan and May Parsons will always be associated with the way out of the hole the world was in, and Heather, Saleyha, Syira and Josh represent some of the thousands of families ripped apart by the loss of a loved one. I really appreciate the fact that they gave me the opportunity to tell their stories.

The final interview I did for the book was with the amazing Martin Hibbert. When I first spoke to him for this, we finished our chat by saying we would catch up after he'd climbed Kilimanjaro. Having done it myself for Comic Relief, I was aware of the scale of the challenge but there was no doubt in Martin's mind that he was going to get to the top just over five years after he was left without the use of his legs after the Manchester Arena bomb. I am part of a WhatsApp group that Martin used to update people on his climb and, in the video he posted on the day he reached the summit, he said, 'Don't write someone off just because they are in a wheelchair.' I get the feeling we will be hearing a lot more from Martin.

There are a few other people I need to mention. I want to thank my wonderful wife Sarah for being a constant support and encouragement. She remains a regular source of wisdom and I know how frustrating it must have been to see me come home from work and then disappear off to write this for the rest of the day. She is amazing, as are our three gorgeous children Susanna, Jessica and Joe. I hope they get to read this book one day and get an insight into some of the incredible people their dad gets to meet at work.

Many of these chapters came from conversations that started on the *BBC Breakfast* sofa. I loved my time on there, first with Louise Minchin and then Sally Nugent, and the team behind the camera remain some of the very best I have worked with. A significant thank you to my old boss Richard Frediani and, in particular, to Liam Blyth and Charlotte Simpson for their help and support – even though Liam ignored one of my texts for eight weeks.

I must also sprinkle a little love in the direction of the team at my publishers, Headline, led by Jonathan Taylor, who has once again been a delight to work with and a real encouragement along the way; and to my agent Jonny McWilliams for being a permanently present sounding board. Jonny was also the man who persuaded me that it was a great time to write another book.

I'm really glad he did, but this book has taken a long time to write and also a long time to think about. I have often found myself staring into the distance for vast amounts of time thinking about how I would respond to some of the situations in here. I have mentioned my faith in a few chapters and I kept coming back to the same thought: there is no way I could have dealt with some of the things detailed here without my faith in God.

When I was in the depths of writing one of the chapters, I could hear my kids playing a song downstairs. It's called 'Christ Is Mine Forevermore' by CityAlight and it includes lyrics I have kept coming back to:

> *Mine are tears in time of sorrow*
> *Darkness not yet understood*
> *Through the valley I must travel*
> *Where I see no earthly good*
> *But mine is peace that flows from heaven*
> *And the strength in times of need*
> *I know my pain will not be wasted*
> *Christ completes his work in me*
> *Come rejoice now, O my soul*
> *For His love is my reward*
> *Fear is gone and hope is sure*
> *Christ is mine forevermore*

Lyrics derived from 'Christ Is Mine Forevermore' written by Jonny Robinson and Rich Thompson. © 2016 CityAlight Music (APRA) (adm at Integrated-Rights.com) All right reserved. Used by permission.

My final thank you goes to all of you who, for the last few years, have asked me when the next book was coming out after enjoying the first one so much. I hope you have found the people in here just as inspiring and I look forward to talking to you about it all at either a book-signing, an event somewhere or wherever we happen to bump into each other.

I'll be happy to talk about anyone in here because I think they are all amazing. Many of them have come face to face with some of the most destructive waves that the sea of life can throw at us. 'Don't make it too sad,' said my wife when I started writing this and I hope it isn't. There is certainly sadness in here but there is also hope. I trust you can see that hope alongside the love, the encouragement, the determination, the struggle, the fight and the light at the end of the sometimes very long tunnel. What I wrote at the end of *Remarkable People* remains just as true a few years on . . . life can be a struggle and, as Joseph said in the chapter about Jimi, 'the struggle is real'. It arrives at our doorsteps in many different shapes and sizes. For some of us the battleground is grief, illness, persecution, stress, family breakdown, death, abuse, injury, but what I hope you've seen in these pages is that the people here are trying to find a way to cope with some of the horrors they have faced.

I don't know what trials you are currently facing in your own life, but I truly hope you have found something or someone in this book to inspire you. The people I have written about are those who, I think, help to give us a clearer picture. They are the people who enable us to think differently, to see further than we would on our own and sometimes change our perspectives. The people in here might not know it but, to me, they are 'giants' and I hope you've enjoyed spending some time on their shoulders. It has been an incredible honour to write about them all.

I am off to celebrate with a giant slice of cake.

INDEX